ARNOLD SCHOENBERG LETTERS

Also by Arnold Schoenberg
PRELIMINARY EXERCISES IN COUNTERPOINT

*

THE WORKS OF ARNOLD SCHOENBERG
A Catalogue of his Compositions, Writings and Paintings
by Josef Rufer

SCHOENBERG'S 'MOSES AND AARON'
by Karl H. Wörner

PORTRAIT OF SCHOENBERG BY KOKOSCHKA (1924)

ARNOLD SCHOENBERG LETTERS

Selected and Edited
by
ERWIN STEIN

Translated from the
original German by
EITHNE WILKINS
and
ERNST KAISER

FABER AND FABER
24 Russell Square
London

*First published in England in mcmlxiv
by Faber and Faber Limited
24 Russell Square London W.C.1
Printed in Great Britain by
Robert MacLehose and Company Limited
The University Press Glasgow
All rights reserved*

Originally published in Germany as
ARNOLD SCHOENBERG: AUSGEWÄHLTE BRIEFE
© 1958, B. Schott's Söhne, Mainz

English translation © *1964, Faber and Faber Limited*

CONTENTS

		page
	Editor's Introduction	7
	English Publishers' Note	11
	Translators' Preface	15
I	Biographical Notes: Vienna — Berlin — Vienna, 1910–1918	19
	Letters 1–32	23
II	Biographical Notes: Vienna (Mödling), 1919–1925	61
	Letters 33–86	63
III	Biographical Notes: Berlin — Barcelona, 1926–1933	115
	Letters 87–152	117
IV	Biographical Notes: France — America, 1933–1944	177
	Letters 153–199	181
V	Biographical Notes: Los Angeles, 1945–1951	229
	Letters 200–261	231
VI	Supplement: Vienna, 1909–1910	293
	Letters 262–265: Four Letters to Gustav Mahler	
	Index of Correspondents	299
	General Index	301

ILLUSTRATIONS

Portrait of Schoenberg by Kokoschka (1924) *frontispiece*
Reproduced by courtesy of Roman Norbert Ketterer, Campione d'Italia

Autograph of first page of Letter 29 *facing page* 54
Reproduced by courtesy of Mrs Gertrud Schoenberg and O. W. Neighbour Esq

Schoenberg in 1927 128
Photograph by Man Ray, Paris

EDITOR'S INTRODUCTION

The letters in this volume have been selected from those written by Schoenberg between 1910 and 1951, the year of his death. By 1910, when he was in his thirty-sixth year, he had already composed works of major importance. The first, or 'tonal', period concludes with his second string quartet (1908); several of the pieces of his second, or 'impressionist', period were then already written, among them the *Five Pieces for Orchestra* and the monodrama *Erwartung*. The year 1910 has been taken as a starting-point because it was from then onward that Schoenberg began keeping copies of his letters; those of the earlier years are carbon copies, mostly in letter-books, of letters written by hand, those of the later years carbon copies of typed letters. Had it not been for the fortunate existence of these copies it would scarcely have been possible to make this collection, for a great many, if not the majority, of the letters were destroyed or lost in the havoc of the last twenty or thirty years.

The selection was made from some 3,000 letters, the bulk of them copies. Those of musical and biographical interest were of course the first choice. The underlying principle has been that whatever Schoenberg says about art and about himself, his comments on works, persons, and events, is so vividly revealing that inevitably such a book must become a portrait. One watches the creative artist uncompromisingly forging ahead, regardless of failure and success, along the road he knows it is his destiny to take; the fighter seeing everything exclusively in terms of either-or, friend or foe, and scourging with merciless sarcasm whatever his standards cause him to condemn. His code of artistic honour is of the most stringent, and any artistic inadequacy is ruthlessly held up to scorn. Yet one also sees a man who can be good-humoured and kind, a loyal friend who is always ready to help. Schoenberg was no recluse, not the type of artist who is lost in self-absorbed brooding. He deeply felt the need to communicate, and he longed above all to meet with response from others. It was always his endeavour to contribute to the public world of music in whatever way he could. A great deal of his life was taken up with teaching, occasionally to the neglect of his own work—he described himself as an impassioned teacher—and many of his letters reveal this aspect of his personality. In some instances the subject-matter of a letter may seem trivial; such letters are included because they so intimately reveal some of the writer's essential traits. All contribute to the portrait as a whole. The collection may in fact be regarded as an experiment in presenting Schoenberg as portrayed by himself.

Since the bulk of the letters have their source in Schoenberg's copies, it cannot be definitely asserted that every one reached the person to whom it was addressed. In a few instances drafts have been included (always with an indication that they are such) because they are characteristic of the writer: among them are notes of congratulation or thanks, the drafts of which were evidently kept as a record of a letter's having been sent (see Letters 81, 97, and 103). Not only was it impossible to discover the fate of each letter; in the editor's view it was of but slight importance. What counts is what Schoenberg committed to paper. The situations and events of which the letters treat—interesting though they often are—, and indeed even the persons addressed, here have the function of supplying a background to the portrait of the man himself, or, as it were, the stage on which the Schoenberg drama is acted out.

In making this selection the editor has necessarily observed a certain restraint out of consideration for the living; yet this has never been allowed to go so far as to falsify the portrait of Schoenberg. In some controversial instances it was difficult to decide whether an event should be touched upon or a name allowed to stand. Occasionally names have been suppressed or passages in the letters shortened by excision. In defence of certain cases where this has not been done it should be pointed out that Schoenberg's polemics often ended in his making peace with his quondam opponent. It was his way to try to be on good terms with his opponent once he had made his own position clear. Those he attacked often became his friends—if, indeed, they were not already so.

Certain cuts have also been made in the letters in order to omit passages of minor interest, references to family affairs, and repetitions—although there is almost as little repetitiveness in Schoenberg's letters as in his compositions. Occasionally, isolated interesting passages from letters have been given. Names insufficiently well known to contribute anything to the context have sometimes been replaced by initials. All omissions have been indicated thus: [. . . . .].

The letters are arranged in five sections: I. the period from 1910 to the end of the first world war; II. the post-war years up to 1924, the period of Schoenberg's third creative phase, that of twelve-note composition; III. 1925–33, when Schoenberg was Professor at the Berlin Academy of Arts; IV. 1933–44, the period of his exile and emigration to America, including the years when he was Professor of Music at the University of California in Los Angeles; V. his retirement. Deviations from chronological order have been made only in exceptional instances in order to avoid separating letters that inherently belong together. Each of the five sections is preceded by a biographical note and a list of the works composed during that period.

The editor has retained such peculiarities of Schoenberg's style as a frequent use of the colon, exclamation-mark, and dash to convey shades of emphasis in a way that sometimes suggests 'instrumentation' of the sentence (see for instance Letter 138).

In Schoenberg's copies the letter-head is generally missing. It has nevertheless almost always been possible to identify the correspondent, even when not addressed by name. Most of the copies are dated; some erroneous datings could be established and corrected by the dates of the answers.

Letter-heads and forms of address are omitted wherever they contribute nothing to the interest of the letter. For the sake of avoiding cumbersome apparatus, no attempt has been made to achieve uniformity in this respect. Sometimes a letter-head has been included in order to avoid an elaborate footnote (see for instance Letter 200); sometimes the form of address is missing because the beginning of the letter has been omitted. Endings have been included only in instances where they are more than standard phrases and indicate Schoenberg's personal relationship to his correspondent.

Footnotes have been kept as brief as possible and are used only where explanation is really necessary. It is hoped that they will not distract the reader: the editor's wish is that the effect of the letters should not be interrupted and diminished by references. The information supplied is derived in part from Schoenberg's own writings, compositions, and correspondence, in part from the communications of those who knew him well, but in the main from the editor's personal knowledge as the master's pupil and friend. The same applies to the information given in the biographical notes preceding each section. It proved unnecessary to consult any other source.

Before 1933 the composer spelt his name 'Schönberg'. His justification of the later spelling occurs in a letter of the 25th June 1947: 'My name is to be spelt with "oe". I changed it when I came to America, because few printers have the "ö" type and I wanted to avoid the form "Schonberg".'

The following persons and institutions have kindly lent letters or supplied information:

Mrs. Gertrud Schoenberg; Dr. Joachim Birke, the late Hanns Eisler, Mr. Hans Keller, Dr. Josef Polnauer, Dr. Karl Rankl, Dr. Otto Reik, Prof. Josef Rufer, Herr Winfried Zillig; The Library of Congress, Washington, and, in particular, Mr. Harold Spivacke and Dr. Richard S. Hill, who supplied photographic copies of the letters in the Library; and the Staats- und Universitäts-Bibliothek Hamburg, which owns the letter to Richard Dehmel.

The editor wishes here to record his gratitude to all of the above.

ERWIN STEIN

London, 4th February 1958

ENGLISH PUBLISHERS' NOTE

This English edition of Schoenberg's Letters differs from the German edition in various ways. The letters which Schoenberg wrote in English (and which Erwin Stein, of course, translated for the German edition) appear here in their original texts, in most cases without any abbreviation (omissions, as throughout the book, are indicated), and we have added a number of letters in English* which were not included in the German edition. The English letters are, in each case, headed 'Written in English' and editorial work on them has been kept to a minimum. We have naturally been reluctant to tamper with texts which so signally bear the stamp of their author's personality. On the other hand, it would surely have been needlessly pedantic to leave, in the interests of 'authenticity', Schoenberg's spelling and punctuation uncorrected, or not to adjust the sense of a sentence when it was clear that his intention was defeated by an imperfect command of the language.

It should be remembered that when Schoenberg took up residence in America, he was already 59 years old, and the difficulties of facing up to the challenge of a new language would have taxed the resources of a much younger man. Schoenberg, with characteristic courage and vigour, did not hold back, and within a very short time he began to correspond, where necessary, in English. Part of the fascination of the book, indeed, rests in the insight it gives us into Schoenberg's gallant and often strikingly successful attempt to think and write in a new language.

The later and more fluent of the English letters pose the fewest editorial problems. We reproduce below part of an early English letter (No. 157, to Sir Adrian Boult), which is an *exact* transcription of Schoenberg's original text. If the reader cares to compare this with the edited version that appears in the body of the book, he will be able to assess for himself the extent and nature of the editing involved. We have, in every case, striven to retain the authenticity of Schoenberg's style, his inimitable tone of voice, while bearing in mind the need for readability and comprehensibility. There are few actual substitutions of words, and where we have felt that an alternative word or phrase was

* Letters 161, 174, 175, 186, 188, 189, 192, 201, 204, 217, 223, 245, 251, 253, 254.

necessary to clarify Schoenberg's thought, we have placed it in square brackets after his own text. In the very few cases where the sense of a passage has resisted analysis, we have preferred to let the obscurity remain rather than impose a meaning.

To distinguish Schoenberg's own footnotes (which he sometimes used in his letters), and those of the translators, from the footnotes of the editor of the German edition, the following signs are used: [Trans.] for Translators and [S.] for Schoenberg. Some of Erwin Stein's annotations have been slightly expanded in this edition.

We have not been able to trace the original French version of Letter 154 or the original English of Letter 199, both of which have been translated into English from the German. To clarify Letter 158, we have included the letter which prompted Schoenberg's answer.

Our thanks are due to Mr. Hans Keller, for his assistance with some points of translation; to Mr. O. W. Neighbour, who kindly lent us the MS. of Schoenberg's letter reproduced facing p. 54; to the composer's widow, Mrs. Gertrud Schoenberg, for her patient collaboration; and to the translators, Eithne Wilkins and Ernst Kaiser, who have generously involved themselves in every aspect of the enterprise.

At a late stage in the preparation of the book it was decided to add as a supplement four letters from Schoenberg to Mahler (Nos. 262–265). The texts of these remarkable documents first appeared in Mrs. Alma Mahler's reminiscences of her husband: *Gustav Mahler, Erinnerungen und Briefe*, Amsterdam, 1940.

The supervision of the book in this edition has been the responsibility of Donald Mitchell, who has also edited the texts of the English letters.

London, 1964.

---

157. To Sir Adrian Boult   New York, 14 April 1934

My dear Mr. Boult:

I was so occupied all this time, that I did not find the possibility to answer your kind letter of the 1st of November 33.

But now I have less to do: for: not only having been occupied, but also sick whilst this bad winter, I am now forced to rest, and rest will say: to write letters.

One of the first to you.

It was a great pity, that the planed concerts of November 1933 could not be done. I regret it very much, but if you will only consider the fact: that I had not the money to order the wanted orchestra-material and the parts for the Kolisch-Quartet etc..; and the other fact: that I waited in vain your contract, granting the fee, wanted to pay costs of the copies etc — this two facts will conceive you, that I was unable to act otherwise, than I did.

Now I learned, you plane anew to perform the concerts. But I have not been told, whether you have in view the Violoncell-Concert* or the String-Quartet-Concert with the Kolisch's. I should be very glad to conduct this particular performance, supposed, I can come to Europe, what till now is not quite sure. But if you have the intention to ask me for conducting, I would like tou know it at least in the end of May. As before mentioned, I was sick the whole winter and, my vacations beginning with 1st of June, I must fix in time the place for my recreation: the southern Europe or the southern America.

* with Feuermann [S.]

TRANSLATORS' PREFACE

German epistolary style is stiff and complicated by comparison with English, and has many formulae for which there is no English equivalent. One cannot translate such gradations in the mode of address as 'Honoured Mr. Dr. Professor', 'Dear, venerated Mr. Professor', and so on, nor the sometimes fulsome expressions of respect, esteem, and regard with which formal letters tend to be concluded even nowadays. One striking example in the present collection is Letter 81. Although it is plain that the writer felt the appropriate style for intercourse with princely grandeur must be somewhat eighteenth-century, the English reader need not take the obsequious tone too seriously; allowance must be made both for the formality of the German language and for the fact that even now, long after the disappearance of the Habsburg empire, Austrian society has remained very conscious of a social hierarchy, so that on both counts, even had Schoenberg felt so inclined, he would scarcely have been able to write 'Dear Prince Fürstenberg, Thank you very much' etc. A special difficulty arises when the translator is confronted with letters beginning 'Lieber Freund'. An English person who receives a letter addressing him as 'Dear friend' is likely to feel mildly exasperated at being claimed as a friend by someone who will not trouble to use his name. This is by no means felt so on the Continent (nor, apparently, in the United States, where usage is often of Continental origin). The convention adopted here has been to translate Schoenberg's mode of addressing Berg and Webern (generally 'Dearest friend') by a correspondingly affectionate phrase, but in most cases to supply the addressee's name. In Letter 248 the rendering had perforce to be literal. The principle has been to be guided by the tone of the letter and the nature of the relationship. The problem of the German 'thou', especially in Austrian usage, defies solution. Letter 190 refers to a sort of initiation ceremony that Germans often use in order to shift on to the 'thou' footing. Again, since Schoenberg was on 'thou' terms with Frau Mahler-Werfel, the natural English beginning would be 'Dear Alma'; but Schoenberg's baroque flourish (literally: 'Dear highly venerated female friend') seemed too characteristic of the

Viennese social tone to be sacrificed in the cause of English convention.

The basic principle throughout has been to preserve as strictly as possible, to the limits of what English will stand, the exceedingly personal quality of Schoenberg's style. This was strongly recommended by the late Erwin Stein, who from his long and intimate knowledge of Schoenberg was able to give invaluable guidance in this respect. Further, Schoenberg's letter to the translator of his essays (Letter 219) insists that any *bettering* only *worsens* his style. Pains have therefore been taken to observe the faithfulness to the original that he himself demanded. Wherever at all possible, his punctuation is reproduced, as are all such mannerisms as 'above all', 'I must say', 'I am convinced'. The same applies to certain touches of repetitiveness. This latter may be of the simple kind that befalls many a letter-writer (e.g., 'perhaps' three times at the end of Letter 228; 'in a position' twice running in Letter 236). Sometimes, however, it is ambiguous, as at the end of Letter 124, where 'hear', after referring for some time to broadcast concerts, is all at once used to mean, evidently, 'receive a letter'. Nor is the original always as clear as the writer may have thought. In Letter 112, for instance, it has been considered best to assume that Schoenberg did not wish to suggest repeating the unsatisfactory records as concerts, but to repeat the concerts in order to make ('repeat') the recordings all over again; the translation has accordingly been given an inappreciable slant.

To a certain extent, though for obvious reasons not at all costs, the translation reproduces a tendency of the original to change the grammatical construction in mid-sentence. But grammatical errors, dialect usage (few Viennese entirely avoid lapses into their native idiom, which does not quite correspond to literary German), and a very slightly wrong choice of a word are peculiarities that do not lend themselves to transposition from one language to another. Perhaps the chief example of a loss in this direction is in Letter 82, in which, among other oddities, the original says that the pleasure of devotion to a cause or a person is, 'to my knowledge, not compensated for by the gravest disappointments'. At the risk of flouting the writer's wishes and worsening by bettering, the translators have taken it on themselves to replace 'compensated for' by 'outweighed by'. All in all, however, it is hoped that the English reader will get most of the flavour of the idiosyncratic original.

E.W., E.K.

Rome, 1964

Section I
VIENNA — BERLIN — VIENNA
1910 – 1918

BIOGRAPHICAL NOTES

Arnold Schoenberg was born in Vienna on the 13th September 1874. He was self-taught. His earliest works include chamber music and songs.

Approximately 1900: Composed the *Gurrelieder*, instrumenting about two-thirds of the work.

1901: Married Mathilde von Zemlinsky. Moved to Berlin.

1903: Returned to Vienna. First performance of the sextet *Verklärte Nacht*. Taught music theory.

1904: Schoenberg and Alexander von Zemlinsky founded the *Society of Contemporary Musicians*, under the aegis of which Schoenberg conducted his symphonic poem *Pelleas und Melisande*. His first pupils included Alban Berg, Anton von Webern, Heinrich Jalowetz and Erwin Stein.

1907/08: First performance of Schoenberg's first two string quartets (by the Rosé Quartet) and of the (first) chamber symphony, occasions on which there were 'scenes' in the concert-hall.

1908: With the 'Fifteen Poems' from Stefan George's *Buch der hängenden Gärten* ('The Book of the Hanging Gardens') Schoenberg achieved a new style (erroneously called 'atonal') that excluded the traditional use of keys. About the same time he began to paint.

1909: Schoenberg's first publisher was the Dreililien Verlag (Three Lilies Press), Berlin. He changed to Universal Edition, Vienna.

I
1910–1918

At the time when the present correspondence begins Schoenberg's material situation had become extremely difficult. His works had aroused intense interest, attracting the attention of musical circles abroad. In Vienna, however, he was violently attacked both by word of mouth and in print. Two concerts at which compositions by his pupils

Biographical Notes

were performed (among them works by Webern and Berg) were turned to account to denigrate him as a teacher, which had very grave consequences for him, since his earnings came entirely from fees for lessons. It was while he was in this situation that he applied for permission to teach at the Academy of Music and the Fine Arts (see Letters 5 and 6).

1910/11: After an interval of about eight years Schoenberg completed the score of the *Gurrelieder*. From the autumn of 1910 until the summer of 1911 he taught at the Academy as a *Privatdozent*, i.e., not as a member of the permanent staff. But his wretched financial situation, lack of public recognition, and antisemitic attacks from political quarters (it having become known that he was to be offered a professorship at the Academy), combined to disgust him with Vienna. In the autumn of 1911 he moved to Berlin, where he had been given to understand there were better prospects for him. There, in fact, his circumstances improved (see Letter 8).

1912: Schoenberg declined an appointment at the Academy in Vienna (see Letter 9). He conducted *Pelleas und Melisande* in Amsterdam, St. Petersburg (Leningrad), and other cities. He composed *Pierrot lunaire* and conducted the work in many cities in Germany and Austria, the ensemble having been intensively rehearsed by himself. Many of the performances were the occasion of uproar and 'scenes'.

1913: The first performance of the *Gurrelieder* in Vienna, conducted by Franz Schreker, was Schoenberg's first great unqualified success (but see Letters 12 and 13).

1914: He conducted the *Gurrelieder* in Leipzig and the *Five Pieces for Orchestra* in Amsterdam and London. Numerous plans for the autumn were nullified by the outbreak of war.

1915: Schoenberg moved to Vienna. Towards the end of the year he was called up for military service.

1916: He completed training as an officer of the Reserve and in the autumn was given leave for an indefinite period.

1917: He began composing the oratorio *Die Jakobsleiter*. Late in the summer he was again called up and, being classified C3, was assigned to the 'Exhibition Orchestra', in which the Viennese musical élite did their military service. Towards the end of the year he was finally discharged from the army on grounds of physical unfitness.

WORKS

Before 1900: *Two Songs* for male voice, op. 1.
Four Songs, op. 2.
1899: String sextet, *Verklärte Nacht* (after Richard Dehmel's poem), op. 4.
1899/1903: *Six Songs*, op. 3.
1900/01: *Gurrelieder* ('Songs of Gurra', setting of German translation of Danish poems by J. P. Jacobsen), for 5 soloists, speaker, mixed chorus and large orchestra. No opus number.
1902/03: *Pelleas und Melisande*, symphonic poem for large orchestra (based on Maeterlinck's play), op. 5.
1903/05: *Six Songs* for voice and orchestra, op. 8.
1904: *Eight Songs*, op. 6.
1905: First string quartet, in D minor, op. 7.
1906: *Chamber Symphony* for 15 solo instruments, op. 9.
1907: *Two Ballads*, op. 12.
Friede auf Erden ('Peace on Earth'), for mixed chorus *a cappella*, op. 13.
1907/08: *Two Songs*, op. 14.
Second string quartet, in F sharp minor, op. 10.
1908/09: Fifteen Poems from Stefan George's *Buch der hängenden Gärten* ('The Book of the Hanging Gardens'), op. 15.
1909: *Three Pieces for Piano*, op. 11.
Five Pieces for Orchestra, op. 16.
Erwartung ('Expectation'), monodrama, op. 17.
1911: *Six Little Piano Pieces*, op. 19.
Herzgewächse ('Flowers of the Heart'), after Maeterlinck, for soprano, celesta, harmonium and harp, op. 20.
1912: *Pierrot lunaire*, three groups of seven poems (melodramas) by Albert Giraud, for *Sprechstimme*, piano, flute, clarinet, violin, and 'cello, op. 21.
1910/13: *Die glückliche Hand* ('The Lucky Hand'), drama with music, op. 18.
1913/16: *Four Songs* for voice and orchestra, op. 22.
1915/17: Text for the oratorio *Die Jakobsleiter* ('Jacob's Ladder').
1910/11: *Harmonielehre* ('Theory of Harmony'). (Revised version 1921/22.)

1. To EMIL HERTZKA[1]   *Vienna, 5 January* 1910

Dear Herr Direktor,

I think it would be a very good thing for me if the following were tried. Perhaps after all the two men in whose hands the Conservatoire's destiny lies, the President and the Director, can be brought to realise who I am, what a teacher the Conservatoire would deprive itself of, and how ungifted of them it would be to take on someone else when I am to be had for the asking. And alas I am to be had!!!

I think what I should do about it is the following. I should like some piano pieces by two of my present pupils, who constitute really extraordinary testimony to my teaching ability, to be performed at a Tk. Ver.[2] concert. If the two gentlemen responsible for the ruination of the Academy could be invited and thoroughly worked on to make them hear what more gifted and intelligent people notice for themselves — perhaps something can be done after all.

What I have achieved with these two in particular could so easily be convincing. One (Alban Berg) is an extraordinarily gifted composer. But the state he was in when he came to me was such that his imagination apparently could not work on anything but *Lieder*. Even the piano accompaniments to them were song-like in style. He was absolutely incapable of writing an instrumental movement or inventing an instrumental theme. You can hardly imagine the lengths I went to in order to remove this defect in his talent. As a rule teachers are absolutely incapable of doing this, because they do not even see where the problem lies, and the result is composers who can think only in terms of a single instrument. (Robert Schumann is a typical example.) I removed this defect and am convinced that in time Berg will actually become very good at instrumentation.

But there is something else one cannot fail to observe about these two men. The fact is, their things aren't at all like 'exercises' but have the maturity of 'works'. And these young men can, *with complete success*, tackle problems of whose existence other people have no notion or which — to say the least — they would not know how to deal with.

[1] Managing director of Universal Edition (music publishers), Vienna.
[2] *Wiener Tonkünstler-Verein* (Viennese Composers' Association).

To Emil Hertzka JANUARY 1910

Yet the second (Erwin Stein) in my opinion scarcely has the makings of a real composer, he is only an imaginative, gifted musician, a conductor or something of that sort. And that I could get him to write anything as good as the Rondo or the Andante that I should like to have performed is, I consider, brilliant testimony to my success as a teacher.

It doesn't take much doing to let smooth talents evolve smoothly. But when you are up against problems; to recognize them; to cope with them and — last not least — to do so successfully: that's the mark of the teacher.

ARNOLD SCHÖNBERG

2. TO HEINRICH JALOWETZ[1] *Vienna, 6 January* 1910

Dear Jalowetz,

I was very angry with you. Your not writing seemed grossly neglectful. For I consider I have a claim to be the first person my pupils inform of their artistic activities. Perhaps after all a teacher's sole reward for his efforts is liking to ascribe his pupils' successes in some degree to himself! But your not writing also has an obverse: not wanting to hear from the other person. This is very nearly insulting!

But I mean to give you the benefit of the doubt because I know you are a good chap. Still, you ought to get into the habit of giving a sign of life from time to time. Of course for you it may be a sufficient sign of life to feel yourself breathing — but do breathe a bit for others as well [. . . . .]

Finally, very many thanks for the Christmas present of Wagner's writings. I was very pleased. Particularly because you guessed what I would have asked for.

ARNOLD SCHÖNBERG

3. TO ARTUR BODANZKY[2] *Vienna, 14 February* 1910

My dear Bodanzky,

Well, if I've got to conduct, I must have my *piano-reduction*. And my score too, as soon as the parts have been copied. I'm sure I can rely on

---

[1] Dr. Heinrich Jalowetz, one of Schoenberg's oldest pupils, was at that time Second Conductor at the Stadttheater in Danzig.

[2] Artur Bodanzky was chief *Kapellmeister* at the National Theatre in Mannheim. The subject of this letter is the intended first performance of Schoenberg's monodrama *Erwartung* ('Expectation'), which did not, however, take place as planned. It was first performed only in 1924, in Prague.

AETAT 35 *To Emil Hertzka*

you to see to all this at once. For your offer to conduct preliminary rehearsals for me very many thanks indeed. But I don't think it a good idea — for me. First of all, I shall probably need the rehearsals to a certain extent in order *to be sure of myself*, and besides it's probably better if I know somewhat more about it than the orchestra does. And if they've rehearsed it already, they're ahead of me instead of vice versa. What I should be *very grateful* for is if you would try to get me copies without mistakes in them. If you don't think one can rely on your copyists, please send me the material so that I can correct it. This I do beg. It's very important to me [. . . . .]

ARNOLD SCHÖNBERG

4. TO EMIL HERTZKA   *Vienna, 7 March* 1910
Dear Herr Direktor Hertzka,

Schreker's[1] arrival prevented my discussing yet another matter with you.

The thing is, I should like to ask you if you could give me some work to do (proof-reading, piano-arrangements, or the like) for Universal Edition, since I am compelled to supplement my income somehow. You know I have few pupils this year. My income has shrunk, and my expenses have increased. So I must do something. It doesn't seem likely that being published will bring me in anything for a while. The long and the short of it is that I need money *now* very urgently. I'm sure you can find some sort of work for me (perhaps instrumentation?).

But there is also something else I wanted to talk to you about. You know that I paint. What you do not know is that my work is highly praised by experts. And I am to have an exhibition next year. What I have in mind is that you might be able to get one or the other well-known patron to buy some of my pictures or have his portrait done by me. I should be prepared to paint a sample portrait for you. I would do your portrait free of charge if you give me your assurance that you will then get me commissions. Only you must not tell people that they *will* like my pictures. You must make them realise that they cannot but like my pictures, because they have been praised by authorities on painting; and above all that it is much more interesting to have one's portrait done by or to own a painting by a musician of my reputation than to be painted by some mere practitioner of painting whose name will be

---

[1] Franz Schreker, composer of operas and conductor, later Director of the Academy of Music in Berlin, at that time choirmaster of the newly formed Philharmonic Choir in Vienna.

To Emil Hertzka　　　　　　　　　　　　　　　　　MARCH 1910

forgotten in 20 years, whereas even now my name belongs to the history of music. For a lifesize portrait I want from 2 to 6 sittings and 200 to 400 kronen. That is really very cheap, considering that in 20 years people will pay ten times as much and in 40 years a hundred times as much for these paintings. I am sure you quite realise this, and I hope you won't make any feeble jokes about a matter as serious as this, but will take it as seriously as it deserves.

As I have said, I am prepared to paint your portrait free of charge by way of a sample if you assure me that I shall get commissions on the strength of it. But there is just one thing: I cannot consider letting the purchase of a portrait depend on whether the sitter likes it or not. The sitter knows who is painting him: he must also realise that he understands nothing about such things, but that the portrait has artistic value, or, to say the least of it, historical value.

I should be very grateful to you if you would help me in this matter, and I think you would deserve well not only of me by getting down to it not in Viennese style but generously, as a citizen of the world.

　　　　　　　　　　　　　　　　　　　　ARNOLD SCHÖNBERG

Please order the Gurre music-paper[1] instantly. In spite of your maliciously interpreting my remark as a 'dangerous threat' I have already begun the preliminary work.

5. TO KARL WIENER[2]　　　　　　　　　　　*Vienna*, 19 *March* 1910
Dear Herr Präsident,

Since, as I learn, no definitive decision has yet been arrived at with regard to the appointment to the professorship of composition at the Academy of Music, may I be permitted to make a suggestion that may serve to postpone the solution of the problem until such time as the situation in general becomes clearer.

I intend applying to the Board of the Academy for permission to lecture on (teach) musical theory at the Academy, in the capacity of *Privatdozent* [lecturer by special appointment]. Since the Academy has university status, I imagine it must be possible to treat such an application in the same way as is customary at universities, where a

---

[1] The score for the huge orchestra of the *Gurrelieder* necessitated the printing of special music-paper. Schoenberg now intended finishing the orchestration of the work after a pause of about eight years. The first performance was conducted by Schreker two years later.

[2] President of the Academy of Music and Fine Arts, Vienna.

certain degree of scholarly (in my case, artistic) achievement makes one eligible for such an appointment.

[..........]

The advantage to the Academy would be as follows. The problem of establishing a department of advanced studies could be postponed, since a department of advanced studies would then in fact exist. I assume your only reason for hesitating to appoint me to the Academy staff is that you are, understandably, afraid of protests from that section of the public which keeps on forgetting, despite everything, *who* I am and what abilities I have, and this although I have proved it a hundred times. This although I have so often shown both what people can learn from me and what people do learn from me, namely how to develop one's own talent in the way most suited to it. I do not force anyone to compose in the modern manner if he does not feel in a modern way; but he will learn to understand classical music more throughly than he would if taught by the dyed-in-the-wool academicians. On the other hand: anyone who wants to study modern music will learn from me all that can be learnt: based on a solid classical foundation, right up to the latest achievements in our art. I take it for granted that you are aware of all this, since, having a position of such great responsibility in the world of art, you must be aware of it. I take it for granted that you know you cannot find a more suitable teacher for the Academy than myself and that the only reason why you could not risk engaging me is that you do not wish to expose yourself to the criticism of those who constantly forget what you yourself have already understood, and of those who do not understand anything at all.

It seems to me that if you were to grant my application you would, without in the least committing yourself, have the opportunity to see how public opinion reacts, and then, in due course, how many students come to my lectures and results I achieve. So you could wait and see whether you wanted to engage me or someone else, and engage the other man when you find him. And: you would have a modern teacher without there being any need for you and your committee to identify yourselves with him.

[..........]

All that might be brought up against me, I think, is that I write a kind of music that does not appeal to those who do not understand anything about it. On the other hand, it must be admitted that it does appeal to those who do understand it. (This is really what the whole thing comes to.) And also that my example leads young people to compose in a similar manner. This objection will not hold water at all. First

To Karl Wiener   MARCH 1910

of all, I do not in fact have this effect on my pupils and do not even wish to have it. In that objectionable sense I influence only those who are inclined that way from the start, whereas those who are constitutionally immune to my art (=untalented) remain so and develop the way they would have developed in any case. Only, they will know a bit more. Secondly, it will not be possible to prevent the young and gifted from emulating my style. *For in ten years every talented composer* will be writing this way, regardless of whether he has learnt it directly from me or only from my works. Any influence, whether to impede or to encourage such a development, therefore does not depend on whether it is I or someone else who teaches at the Academy. What might hasten it, however, would be continuing to exclude me from everything as has been done in the past. It has been found often enough how dangerous it is to make martyrs. *I* do *not* wish to become a martyr. I have no taste for striking attitudes. But I shall become one, not as a result of my further development, but owing to circumstances that do not arise out of my own nature.

I hope to hear from you soon and should be particularly grateful if you would give me an opportunity to put my case before you in person, which I could do much more clearly and with more evidence to support it.

                                                        ARNOLD SCHÖNBERG

6. TO THE BOARD OF THE IMPERIAL-ROYAL ACADEMY OF MUSIC AND THE FINE ARTS, VIENNA

                                       Vienna, [*no date* (*evidently Spring* 1910)]

I herewith apply to the Board of the Academy of Music for permission to give lectures on the various branches of musical theory and teach the principles of composition at the Imperial-Royal Academy in the capacity of a *Privatdozent*. I envisage my relationship to the Imperial-Royal Academy as being similar to that of *Privatdozenten* at the Universities, who are granted permission to lecture on the basis of certain achievements in their fields, this not constituting appointment to the permanent staff, since they do not receive a salary, but only lecture-fees, yet still constituting membership of the institution in a manner that is not binding on either side.

The following are my reasons for making this application.

It is demonstrable that it is the duty of a State Academy, being aware of the needs of the time, in every way to assist its students in their proper endeavour to become fully acquainted with what their contemporaries have achieved. There is no doubt — and it may be said frankly, without any implication of hostility — that those who teach composition at the Academy do not recognize these needs, considering themselves, on the contrary, in honour bound to oppose what they cannot prevent, what is actually on the way, has indeed already come to stay, and which is nevertheless not taught at the Academy.

I should like to be given the opportunity of filling this gap, should like to be able to contribute to the training of those talented individuals in whom Vienna is so rich but who find those doors closed that should be wide open to the spirit of the age. By virtue of the special nature of my artistic development, which, taking the classical masters as its point of departure, has led me — as I must suppose: logically — into the forefront of the modern movement in music, and also by virtue of my marked taste for theoretical research, I believe myself suited to communicate to the young what would otherwise not be communicated to them.

I should like however to stress yet another point. The public has repeatedly had the opportunity to form an opinion of my creative work, as also of my capacity as a teacher. Today I am known even in Vienna, and abroad my reputation is growing. Despite this, I have hitherto not been accorded that scope which would certainly not have been withheld from me in Germany had I had the same amount of success and recognition there. I am by nature inclined towards teaching, which is why I seek scope for this ability of mine. Now, an Academy of Music of which I am not a teaching member wrongs me doubly in that it withholds from me a sphere of activity that is my due and seeks to deprive me of that which I have already. This wrong passively done to me, striving as I do with undeniable ability towards the highest, is all the more hurtful since it is unjust.

I am prepared to admit that it is not easy for the Imperial-Royal Academy to engage an artist of my views without more ado as their teacher of composition, since it is difficult to convince our Viennese public of the value of an artistic movement by any means other than unchallenged great success (preferably abroad).

I am prepared to admit that I still lack this kind of success, and must lack it if what I have to give is as good as I believe it to be. But it cannot be gainsaid that the small group of very highly cultivated persons of taste who even now espouse my cause represent a beginning that deserves

To Academy of Music SPRING 1910

to be taken into account. And it has never been denied that in spite of many objections my achievements as a teacher are such that my qualifications for a teaching appointment are perfectly obvious.

Thus it seems to me that in making the application put forward in this letter I have found the way in which it would be possible for the Imperial-Royal Academy to make the experiment of having a modern teacher without finding itself in any way committed. The technical and material aspect of this matter I would leave entirely to the discretion of the Board, and wish only to add that I should prefer to receive lecture-fees, but that I am also prepared to deliver the lectures without payment if technical difficulties should arise. For what I most desire is a sphere of activity.[1]

Looking forward to receiving a favourable answer, I remain,
                yours etc.,
                        ARNOLD SCHÖNBERG

7. TO MAX MARSCHALK[2] *Vienna, 12 November* 1910
Dear Herr Marschalk,

A week ago I had an angry difference of opinion with Herr Direktor Hertzka (who has a taste for rather offensive jokes of a kind not justified by anything in our personal relationship), as a result of which I have broken with him. That is why I have not yet concluded an agreement for Pelleas[3] with him and therefore, on the strength of the (previous) written assent, which has not yet been revoked, consider myself at liberty to dispose of Pelleas as I think fit.

So I am prepared, without making any new demands regarding a fee, to let you have the work on the condition that the advances shall be regarded as cancelled, i.e., forfeited in my favour, and that a printed (lithographed or engraved) score shall be produced within two months at the latest and that the material (parts) shall be copied (either by hand or lithographed).

I can keep this offer open for eight or ten days at the most, for I am sure Hertzka will not be able to stand being on bad terms with me for longer (I could!). So I should have to have the contract by the 22nd November at the latest. In any case I should not like to wait longer than

---

[1] Schoenberg's application was granted (see Biographical Notes, p. 20).
[2] Director of the Dreililien Verlag, Berlin, the house that published Schoenberg's first works.
[3] Schoenberg's op. 5, *Pelleas und Melisande*, a symphonic poem for orchestra, after Maeterlinck's play.

AETAT 37   *To Emil Hertzka*

that, since I now feel it is high time for me to have a printed orchestral-score[1] of mine.

ARNOLD SCHÖNBERG

8. To EMIL HERTZKA   *Berlin-Zehlendorf, 31 October* 1911

Dear Herr Direktor Hertzka,

Before all else: I was very pleased indeed with the Pelleas score. [. . . . .] Please convey my best thanks to the printers.

[. . . . .]

You cannot imagine how famous I am here.[2] I am almost too embarrassed to mention it. I am known to everyone. I am recognised from my photographs. People know my 'biography', all about me, all about the 'scenes' I have occasioned, indeed know almost more than I, who forget such things very quickly. So if you would lend a bit of a hand, we should see some results soon. Everybody banks on you in this respect. You, personally, are very well spoken of here and are regarded as being different from the general run of Viennese. I too have sung your praises. Now please print my work!!! I am certain it's good!!!

[. . . . .]

Now another little matter. I was very pleased to find you getting publicity for me when I received the Liszt number of the All. D. Musikzeitung* (with my article in it). There is just one thing I'd like to ask of you; do take what I am about to say as a joke; but to some extent I mean it seriously.

What I mean is, in your announcements I am referred to as the 'courageous representative of the Viennese modern school of music'. Don't be cross with me, but: Richard Strauss is Generalmusikdirektor, Pfitzner has the title of Direktor, Reger is even a Hofrat. So couldn't you at least appoint me Representative-General of the V. mod. school of music? I should like to be a General too. But a 'courageous representative' — well, I don't know, it keeps reminding me of a commercial traveller who refuses to be thrown out. That's what 'courageous representative' means. And now seriously: Of whom does this modern school of music, which I represent, actually consist? Weigl? Stöhr? — Believe me, I don't represent anything whatsoever, I just write music as well as I can!! I don't even represent myself!!

You will see to it, won't you, that the gentleman in your office, who undoubtedly meant well when he wrote that, will not take offence at my

---

[1] The score was published by Universal Edition approximately a year later.
[2] Schoenberg had moved to Berlin (see Biographical Notes, p. 20).
* Presumably: *Allgemeine Deutsche Musikzeitung*. [TRANS.]

To Emil Hertzka OCTOBER 1911

jokes. It is by no means my intention to hurt his feelings! But that epithet is really not at all to my taste. Just think how ready musicians are to make fun of such things and how bad it is if they are actually given cause to do so. Well, you know what we musicians are like. And nobody more so than I.

ARNOLD SCHÖNBERG

9. TO KARL WIENER[1] *Zehlendorf, 29 June* 1912

Dear Herr Präsident,

I have long put off this letter, for the last thing I want is to appear unreliable. But my growing disinclination to take up the Viennese position is stronger than all qualms, and so I must, with all regret, inform you that I cannot accept the appointment at the Academy, and must ask you to regard all that was agreed between us in this matter as null and void.

I feel obliged to state my reasons, all the more since I hope they will earn me your understanding and forgiveness.

First and foremost: it is not primarily the salary question, although this is also not the least consideration. I had realised all along that I could not live on the salary, and likewise that I have hardly any prospect of earning as much as I need in Vienna. I should not have been happy about taking it on, but I should nonetheless have done so had there been no other considerations. I write about this so cautiously and at such length because I wish at all costs to avoid giving the impression of trying to extort a higher salary. I therefore wish to say explicitly that I would not come to Vienna even if you were to double the salary.

My main reason is: for the present, I could not live in Vienna. I have not yet got over the things done to me there, I am not yet reconciled. And I know I should not be able to stand it even for two years. I know that in a very short time I should have to start fighting the very same battles I have been trying to escape from. Not because I am afraid of fighting. But because I *hope for* the very outcome that is the end of every movement in Vienna, a draining away into shallowness.

There are other reasons besides: the position you offered me is not the one I wished for. It would mean spending my whole life, up to my 64th year, droning over harmony and counterpoint. And that I cannot do. Since I am incapable of repeating myself without blushing for shame

---

[1] At the head of this letter, which is written in indelible pencil, are the following words in Schoenberg's hand: 'Copy of letter: refusal to Academy.' While Schoenberg was still in Vienna, teaching at the Academy in the capacity of *Privatdozent*, Wiener had promised him a professorship at the Academy (see Biographical Notes, p. 20).

AETAT 37 　　　　　　　　　　　　　　　　　*To Ferruccio Busoni*

and since teaching year in year out makes it impossible to produce something entirely new each year, I could scarcely escape the petrification inherent in the situation. And this is a danger I must avoid; again, not because I am afraid of it, but because I consider it beneath the dignity of my rank. It is the sort of danger to which common mercenary soldiers may expose themselves, but not officers. What I had in mind was that I would organise the harm. and cpt. teaching according to my own ideas and then hand it over to one of my pupils, so I should be free to devote myself exclusively to teaching composition. But your intention is to engage two other teachers of composition besides myself, as a result of which all three would have to teach harmony and counterpoint. To all eternity, until the arteries are quite hardened.

Perhaps you will be annoyed with me, but I am not the only one to blame. You will recall: I asked for time to think it over; you insisted on an immediate acceptance. Only two days later I regretted having accepted! And had I not wished to avoid having to refuse, I should at once have written to tell you I cannot come. Had I had time to think it over, you would have been spared these vexations!

I must ask you, my dear Herr Präsident, to regard this decision as irrevocable. I shall not come, would not even if all these qualms about the appointment were removed. The main cause is something that you cannot do anything about; my dislike of Vienna! At least not for the present!

Perhaps, even if you should now be as irate with me as I now am with Vienna, perhaps after a while you will think of me less harshly, and perhaps after some time I shall feel a greater affection for my native city than I do now; perhaps you will then think of me and I shall then certainly wish to return.

But now I cannot.

Please do not hold this against me more than you must.

With my compliments to you, Herr Präsident, and to the Herr Direktor, with deep gratitude for your interest, I remain,

　　　　　　　　　　　yours etc.,
　　　　　　　　　　　　　　Arnold Schönberg

10. To Ferruccio Busoni[1]

　　　　　　　　　　Carlshagen, Island of Usedom, 28 *July* 1912

Dear Herr Busoni,

You wrong me and my imagination. I do not deny that it has sometimes been kindled by something the real value of which was solely of its

[1] Answer to a letter of 27th July 1912 from Ferruccio Busoni, saying: 'In conversation — with Clark [Edward Clark, at that time a pupil of Schoenberg's] — I threw off an

To Ferruccio Busoni   JULY 1912

own making. Perhaps this is a habit it has developed from my allowing it to collaborate in works of art; perhaps, having thus acquired the habit, it has always done the same: actually creating the things, their value, and the fire of enthusiasm. But in this case it is all rather more prosaic.

The fact is: what I wrote to you is what Clark reported to me as your intention. Nothing else. I added nothing! Really nothing! For the things I do something about (or even add something to, which means that something must have been there to begin with) start out by being altogether on a larger scale! You must pardon me: but I cannot permit my imagination to be wronged. For my imagination is myself, for I myself am but a creature of this imagination. And no one will let his parents be insulted.

Do you, my dear Herr Busoni, really assume my imagination to be incapable of picturing a relationship to you at some school of music where you give advanced courses and where I am in charge of studies in any way other than that one of us would have to be the other's chief? Is not someone who takes advanced courses automatically outside any supervision by whoever is in charge of studies? But then again, is not someone who spends ten months in Berlin much better suited to take over the supervision of studies than someone who 'is away from Berlin for 8 months of the year and who, besides, holds a part-time appointment?'

I do not want to argue the point any further. Perhaps all that happened is that you made some non-committal remarks that were then passed on to me as indicating something more in the nature of an obligation. You do indeed say a number of obliging things in your letter, thus carefully wrapping up the incivility that you actually wish to convey to me. But you must allow me to regard that too as not constituting any obligation. I always want things to be clear, so such wrappings are a bother to me. With your permission I shall store the packing-material of obligingness, in which you wrapped your incivility, in the place where I (and I am, as those who know me can confirm, a passion[ate collector of parcel-wrappings])[1] generally store packing-material, and the real content, the enclosed incivility, in the place where I keep a

---

idea that had occurred only that moment and in my own head. With your usual impulsiveness you at once caught hold of this idea and, your imagination being as active as always, embroidered on it, unless it be that the remark was reported to you in a distorted form.' The idea was to create a position of responsibility for Schoenberg at a German school of music. Busoni's letter, incidentally, is markedly amiable throughout. The two men subsequently became good friends.

[1] Here a line is missing from the carbon copy; the original was doubtless more or less as rendered in square brackets. Schoenberg was in fact a passionate collector of packing-paper and string.

AETAT 38   *To Richard Dehmel*

record of that sort of thing. And permit me to sum up the contents of your letter as follows: a reprimand for my presumption in wishing to be in a position of superior authority to you, this being a product of my vivid imagination!

I remain, with sincere respect,

yours etc.,

ARNOLD SCHÖNBERG

11. TO RICHARD DEHMEL[1]   *Berlin-Zehlendorf, 13 December* 1912

Dear Herr Dehmel,

I cannot tell you how glad I am to be directly in touch with you at last. For your poems have had a decisive influence on my development as a composer. They were what first made me try to find a new tone in the lyrical mood. Or rather, I found it even without looking, simply by reflecting in music what your poems stirred up in me. People who know my music can bear witness to the fact that my first attempts to compose settings for your poems contain more of what has subsequently developed in my work than there is in many a much later composition. So you will understand that the regard in which I hold you is therefore both cordial and — above all — *grateful.* And now I have had the pleasure of meeting you in Hamburg, where your great kindness at once made me feel at home though I was a stranger in that city. And here now is your very kind letter, which at last gives me courage to ask you a question that has long been in my mind. It is this. For a long time I have been wanting to write an oratorio on the following subject: modern man, having passed through materialism, socialism, and anarchy and, despite having been an atheist, still having in him some residue of ancient faith (in the form of superstition), wrestles with God (see also Strindberg's 'Jacob Wrestling') and finally succeeds in finding God and becoming religious. Learning to pray! It is *not* through any action, any blows of fate, least of all through any love of woman, that this change of heart is to come about. Or at least these should be no more than hints in the background, giving the initial impulse. And above all: the mode of speech, the mode of thought, the mode of expression, should be that of modern man; the problems treated should be those that harass us. For those who wrestle with God in the Bible also express themselves as men of their own time, speaking of their own affairs, remaining within their

[1] Answer to a letter of 12th December 1912 from the poet Richard Dehmel, beginning: 'Last night I heard "Verklärte Nacht", and I should feel it to be a sin of omission if I did not send you a word of thanks for your wonderful sextet.' Schoenberg's sextet, *Verklärte Nacht*, is based on Dehmel's poem of that title. Several of Schoenberg's early songs were also settings of poems by Dehmel.

To Richard Dehmel DECEMBER 1912

own social and intellectual limits. That is why, though they are artistically impressive, they do not offer a subject for a modern composer who fulfils his obligations.

Originally I intended to write the words myself. But I no longer think myself equal to it. Then I thought of adapting Strindberg's 'Jacob Wrestling'. Finally I came to the idea of beginning with positive religious belief and intended adapting the final chapter, 'The Ascent into Heaven', from Balzac's 'Seraphita'. But I could never shake off the thought of 'Modern Man's Prayer', and I often thought: If only Dehmel . . . !

Is there any chance of your taking an interest in something of this kind? Let me say at once: if you should think it possible, it would be not merely superfluous but actually a mistake to write the text with any thought of the music in mind. It should be as free as if there had never been any question of its being set to music. For a work by Dehmel is something that I — being in such profound sympathy with every word — can set to music just as it stands. There would have to be only one limitation: considering the average speed of my music I do not think that the words for a full-length work should much exceed the equivalent of 50 or, at the most, 60 printed pages. On the contrary, that would almost be too much. I dare say that is a great difficulty. But is it an insuperable one?

I should be very grateful if you would write and tell me what you think. I really do not know whether I am not asking too much. But my excuse is: I must write this music! For this is something I have to say.[1]

Now let me once more thank you most warmly for your very kind letter and above all for the wonderful poem that you appended to it. May I add one more request? Can I have a photograph of you?

I remain, with most cordial esteem and regard,
        yours very sincerely,
                ARNOLD SCHÖNBERG

---

[1] Dehmel's reply to Schoenberg's letter was very amiable but contained a refusal. The correspondence proceeded in a very cordial tone. On the 28th December of the same year Schoenberg wrote: '. . . I sensed what your answer would be, for I too can only write when a subject provides the urge. Yet I felt I ought to try. . . .' He himself then wrote the words for the oratorio that he planned, giving it the title *Jacob's Ladder*, but had to put the composition aside in 1917 when he was called up for military service (see Letter 42).

AETAT 38   *To Emil Hertzka*

12. TO EMIL HERTZKA   *Berlin, 6 February* 1913

Dear Herr Direktor,

Berg's letter has not yet come. Should it cause me to change my opinion, I shall gladly withdraw all I must now say.

First of all: in reply to the telegram from you and the Philharmonic Choir[1] I have just wired to you as follows:

> 'If Schreker has no time, shall gladly come to conduct, but not to correct mistakes. Bad material not my fault. Please do not hesitate to cancel.'

The purpose of this letter is to elucidate that telegram, to show you why you were wrong, and to prove to you that it can all be settled perfectly well without my coming.

I. Above all, the expression 'Schreker urgently *requires* (!!) your immediate presence' strikes me as pretty steep. I should expect somewhat more civility even if I had committed a crime.

II. I am expected to lay out something like 150–200 Marks for travelling expenses, while no one at your end is prepared to spend 10 Kronen in order to specify the reasons why I should incur such expenses.

For I shall demonstrate to you that those given in the telegram are no reasons at all.

III. I am expected to incur such expenses, but nobody asks *whether I am in a position to do so*!!

IV. Those who made such demands on me should first of all have undertaken to pay all my expenses.

V. But now the main point: I, the creator of the work, am required to do donkey-work for the conductor because he, forsooth, has no time to concern himself with the matter, as would be his duty as an artist: his duty to me and to himself!!

For: if Schreker had studied the score properly, *as is his duty*, it would be quite impossible for him only now, all of a sudden, to discover that it is as faulty as he says. (Incidentally: if it is faulty, I am not to blame! One simply has to see to it that the stuff is corrected in good time!!) He ought to have noticed it long ago! But that he does not know the score is something I gathered some time ago from Berg's ingenuous remark that it 'is so difficult to detect (!!) the mistakes in

---

[1] Franz Schreker, the conductor of the Vienna Philharmonic Choir, was rehearsing for the first performance of the *Gurrelieder*, which was given on the 23rd February. The contents of the telegram in which Schoenberg was peremptorily summoned to Vienna can be gathered from this letter. Evidently rehearsals had been delayed because of faulty copying of the parts. The performance was very successful, and Schoenberg and Schreker became friends.

To Emil Hertzka   FEBRUARY 1913

the brass and woodwind parts'. Of course only if one does not know the score!

I realise that Schreker has not enough time to study the work. I can even understand and condone that. What I cannot understand and cannot condone is that he nevertheless insists on conducting the work himself. It would not only be humanly more generous of him to invite me to do so, it would also show more artistic decency!

VI. And now, pray: what shall I come to Vienna for? It is a complete mystery to me. You all seem to have lost your heads, and now you want me to come and save the situation. Very well, but only as far as is necessary. And above all only for work that needs the composer (to conduct), but certainly not to do a copyist's job! Nobody makes a journey like that for *that* sort of thing!!

You telegraph about 'disentangling' the score. What is that supposed to mean? Surely the score is not in a tangle, the pages not in confusion? There are mistakes in it; but surely two musicians are capable of correcting those themselves [..........]

The importance of this performance to me is being grossly overestimated. It may be very useful to me. But even so I will not be bullied by anyone. And above all I will not put up with threats like: 'otherwise must cancel performance'. I am not *so* very eager for success. In particular: what I am interested in is not *a* performance, only a good performance. And this one is obviously not going to be a good performance anyway. Only ten rehearsals with that miserable *Tonkünstler* Orchestra!! I shall have 9–11 rehearsals with the Berlin Philharmonic, which is an excellent orchestra!!

Finally, then: I am quite prepared to give you any advice that occurs to me. I am quite prepared to conduct the performance myself if my expenses are paid. I am quite prepared to come to Vienna on the 18th February to put the finishing touches to the last rehearsals. But if anyone thinks I can be intimidated by threats, he underestimates me. To threats I have only one answer: Please do not hesitate to cancel the performance.

It would certainly be very deplorable for you, if you had to cancel the performance. As for me, I shall manage on my own.

You will probably find this letter rather irritable. I cannot help that. I am sick and tired of the everlasting patting on the back I get from Vienna. I really do not know why else I should have turned my back on Vienna. Wherever else I may go to have my works performed, it is regarded and treated as what it is: people thank me for the chance to perform my work. In Vienna everyone tries to trap me into risking my neck for the furtherance of his interests, claiming that it is to further mine. But I will not lend my neck to such machinations, nor my shoulders to such patronage. I maintain the attitude to Vienna that I assumed when I left.

[..........]

No offence, I hope.

ARNOLD SCHÖNBERG

13. TO HERR DR. K.[1]   *Berlin-Zehlendorf, 28 April* 1913

Dear Herr Dr. K.,

You are no doubt aware that while I was in Vienna at my publisher's expense, attending the performance of the 'Gurre-Lieder', the day before the final rehearsal (!!) your father caused my personal effects to be seized in the boarding-house where I was staying, the two clamorous bailiffs depriving me of more than half the money for my journey. Had I not been helped by friends, I do not know how I should have settled my bill and paid my return fare.

I fail to understand your father's proceeding thus against a man who has done him no harm. But that you could permit such a thing to happen, when you could not but know that you, after all, *yourself owe me* part of the money and had undertaken to pay the whole of that debt as a way of proving your gratitude to me — that is incomprehensible, and I must leave it to you to come to terms with your conscience, which will tell you: by not fulfilling your promise you have not only caused me indescribable agitation but, above all, have caused me to incur new and onerous expenses (lawyers' and court fees!), once again with interest, and furthermore deprived me of any chance to pay off this debt slowly in small instalments. I should have settled it by now, but because of you I am once more in difficulties.

Still, I do not want to remonstrate with you. As I have said, I leave it to your conscience to work it out for itself, and to reflect how you can answer for what your father and you have done to me. And believe me: some day you will be asked that question!!

Instead I want to ask you: Do you not want to pay at least that part of the debt that you owe to me and the costs that I have incurred as a result of your failure to pay?

[..........]

Let me know soon what you decide.

Meanwhile: kind regards,

ARNOLD SCHÖNBERG

[1] Dr. K. was one of Schoenberg's early pupils.

To Marie Gutheil-Schoder AUGUST 1913

14. To MARIE GUTHEIL-SCHODER[1] *Berlin, 22 August* 1913

Dear Madame Gutheil,

You may well be surprised to receive a letter from me after so long. I have to write so many letters that I do not enjoy writing that I never find time for those I would enjoy writing. I had often intended reminding you of my existence, but as a result of the tremendous amount of forced labour that I have to accomplish in letter-writing I scarcely find time to write any letters other than those that give me no pleasure, and the sordid result is that it is only when I want to ask them for something that I write to those people of whom I think much and often. That's the way everything in life grows sordid!

You will remember that I have repeatedly spoken to you of a dramatic work in which there is a part for you. It is a monodrama,[2] with only one part, a real part, conceived as a Gutheil-part. Now, Bodanzky wants to conduct a performance of this piece in Mannheim if you would agree to sing the part, and he urges me to ask you. Please be so kind as to read the enclosed libretto (I have not got the piano reduction with me at the moment) and to answer the following questions:

    I. Do you like it and does it interest you?

    II. Would you care to sing it in Mannheim?

    III. Do you think you might get leave of absence for this purpose?

There remains question IV, whether it suits your voice. But that you can answer only when I can send you the reduction.

The thing is musically very difficult. But then, after all, you did manage my 2nd Quartet!!!

I should be very grateful if you would answer my questions soon and if you would at the same time tell me how you are! With very cordial regards,

        I am, yours very sincerely,

                ARNOLD SCHÖNBERG

15. To FRITZ SOOT *Berlin,* 18 *November* 1913

My dear Herr Soot,

I have already written to Walter[3] on your behalf. He is thinking of engaging you for the Gurre-Lieder. I have now suggested that he should

---

[1] Marie Gutheil-Schoder had sung the voice part at the first performance of Schoenberg's second string quartet, played by the Rosé Quartet.

[2] *Erwartung* ('Expectation') (see Letter 3). Gutheil-Schoder sang the part at the first performance in Prague eleven years later.

[3] Bruno Walter. It was hoped to perform the *Gurrelieder* in Munich, but this plan could not be realized until after the war. Kammersänger Fritz Soot was being considered for the part of Waldemar.

invite you as a guest-singer so as to get to know you better. The fact is, the third part of the Gurre-Lieder demands such a very powerful voice that it would be unfair to expose you to any chance of failure. Having such a splendid reputation, you do not need to take such risks. I cannot really judge, though I do believe that your voice has extraordinary volume. But there is a gigantic orchestra (150 players), and the third part in particular is very exacting. I hope however that (and I shall be delighted if) Walter seizes the chance!!!

Now, as for *Nikisch*, I should really rather not get in touch with him directly. After all, he has not given me the slightest reason to think that he wants to perform anything of mine, and I do not yet believe it myself!! Perhaps it is merely a matter of form!

But I have nothing against your writing to him yourself, if you wish. On the *contrary*, I should, as I have said, be very, very much obliged. For many reasons. Above all because I am firmly convinced that Nikisch has not yet looked at my chamber symphony and that he is too little given to exerting himself to be likely to study the score. So it is almost certain he will not perform it, and that is why I think there is a good chance of his doing the songs for orchestra instead, which he can study much more easily and which are not so difficult anyway.

In any case, however, I beg you (for my sake) to enquire *cautiously*. For perhaps I am wronging Nikisch! Perhaps he has already studied my chamber symphony heaven knows how carefully and is dead set on doing it. In that case I shouldn't want to vex him. For if he likes it he will certainly do it well. And that would be very useful to me because Nikisch sets the standard for other German orchestras programmes.[1]

As I have said, I don't want to do anything myself because of my personal relations with Nikisch. But I shall be *delighted* if you succeed in persuading him to do the songs for orchestra.

The 'Glückliche Hand' ['The Lucky Hand'] is at long last finished. The piano reduction should be ready in about a week's time and then we could come to Dresden. I should like to arrange the *Man's* part for *you*! It would turn out very well!! For it is primarily acting ability that matters here, so that it should be sung by the singer best suited from this point of view, regardless of whether he is a tenor, baritone, or bass. It can certainly be done.

[..........]

ARNOLD SCHÖNBERG

[1] Nikisch did conduct a performance of the chamber symphony (see Letter 19).

To Artur Bodanzky   NOVEMBER 1913

16. TO ARTUR BODANZKY[1]   *Berlin*, 21 *November* 1913

Dear Bodanzky,

Don't be annoyed with me, but I didn't know your people couldn't find room for an orchestra any larger than you describe. But that really won't do, you know! Six violas! That cannot possibly sound well. And I must point out: for the first performance I should have to have a full orchestra. If my music is to assert itself against the prevailing scepticism, it is absolutely essential that it should be performed the way it is meant to be. I am quite convinced (and have indeed often been told) that your orchestra is very highly disciplined, but it simply isn't big enough. And so I think we had better drop the whole thing.

[..........]

And now let me thank you once more for your interest. What a pity that nothing is to come of it![2]

                                                   ARNOLD SCHÖNBERG

17. TO FRITZ SOOT   *Berlin*, 28 *November* 1913

My dear Herr Soot,

I have the feeling you are cross with me about Munich.[3] But you wrong me. I couldn't do otherwise. On my own impression I could not judge whether you are a *Heldentenor* or not and whether the part of Waldemar would suit you. But it would have been criminal of me to pass it over in silence and simply recommend you to Walter. It would have been a crime against my work and against you. For if this part should not suit you and you were nevertheless to sing it, your failure would, to say the least of it, be as certain as mine. I can easily get over that sort of thing. But to you it would be very damaging. I do beg you to see that. And you see from this how very sincere and warm my praise has been and how you can rely on me in this respect. Surely that is something! If my praise is to be of any value, I must have the courage to speak up whenever I don't approve. It is of course possible that I was mistaken. But that is why I suggested that Walter should ask you to come as a guest-singer. I myself have not enough experience to decide in such a matter.

Just one more thing: as agreed, I have let Schuch[4] know that the 'Glückliche Hand' is now ready, both score and piano-reduction, and

    [1] See Letter 3.
    [2] Referring to the plan for the first performance of the monodrama *Erwartung*.
    [3] See note 3 to Letter 15.
    [4] Geheimrat Ernst von Schuch, conductor of the Dresden Court Opera.

AETAT 39   *To Emil Hertzka*

that we are prepared to come. Are you still interested, or have you really done with me? I should be *awfully sorry*, for I have a *very particular affection for you and the highest esteem for you and your achievements*! So I hope not. With kindest regards and best wishes,

                              yours sincerely,
                                         ARNOLD SCHÖNBERG

18. TO EMIL HERTZKA

         [*No date or address. Presumably Berlin, autumn* 1913]
Dear Herr Direktor,
    You ask what are the artistic terms on which my 'Glückliche Hand' might be reproduced cinematographically.[1] There is little I can say at the moment about details, which will arise only during the work of adaptation. But in general I can say as follows:
    I. *No change is to be made in the music!*
    II. If *I* find it necessary to make improvements in the text, I shall make them myself and nobody else, whoever it may be, shall have the right to require them of me.
    III. As many rehearsals as I think necessary! This cannot be estimated in advance. Rehearsals must go on until it goes as well as 'Pierrot lunaire'.
    IV. Performances may be given only with performers approved by me, and if possible with the original ensemble. But I am prepared to consider rehearsing with several sets of performers, or, alternatively, to let friends of mine rehearse them under my supervision.
    V. Performances may be given only with a (full) orchestra rehearsed and directed by me or my trusted deputies, or (if these mechanical organs turn out to be as good as I hope) with an organ (e.g., Aeolian organ). Further, in large cities it must always be an orchestra. When and under what conditions an organ may be used cannot be said at this stage. For that, after all, depends to a great extent on what these organs are like. If they satisfy me, I shall make no difficulties. On the contrary, I expect great things of these instruments with their magnificent bass stops and the innumerable precisely defined timbres.
    VI. What I think about the sets is this: the basic unreality of the events, which is inherent in the words, is something that they should be able to bring out even better in the filming (nasty idea that it is!). For

[1] It must be borne in mind that this letter was written in the era of the silent film. Nothing came of the proposal to film the work.

To Emil Hertzka   AUTUMN 1913

me this is one of the main reasons for considering it. For instance, in the film, if the goblet suddenly vanishes as if it had never been there, just as if it had simply been forgotten, that is quite different from the way it is on the stage, where it has to be removed by some device. And there are a thousand things besides that be easily done in this medium, whereas the stage's resources are very limited.

My foremost wish is therefore for something the opposite of what the cinema generally aspires to. I want:

The utmost unreality!

The whole thing should have the effect (not of a dream) but of chords. Of music. It must never suggest symbols, or meaning, or thoughts, but simply the play of colours and forms. Just as music never drags a meaning around with it, at least not in the form in which it [music] manifests itself, even though meaning is inherent in its nature, so too this should simply be like sounds for the eye, and so far as I am concerned everyone is free to think or feel something similar to what he thinks or feels while hearing music.

What I have in mind is therefore the following:

A painter (say: I, Kokoschka, or II, Kandinsky, or III, Roller) will design all the main scenes. Then the sets will be made according to these designs, and the play rehearsed. Then, when the scenes are all rehearsed to the exact tempo of the music, the whole thing will be filmed, after which the film shall be coloured by the painter (or possibly only under his supervision) according to my stage-directions. I think however that mere colouring [will] not suffice for the 'Colour Scene'* and other passages where strong colour effects are required. In such passages there would also have to be coloured reflectors casting light on the scene.

Another problem, it seems to me, is that of the opening and concluding scenes, which are to be *'almost entirely in darkness'*. I do not know whether the cinematograph can do this, since there is no such thing as 'dark light'. But I dare say there are solutions even for such problems.

Regarding the music:

The 6 men and the 6 women would of course have to be there, just like the Man. I mean: they would have really to sing and speak. Naturally behind the stage or the orchestra, beside the organ, or in some such place. That can be worked out.

They would naturally have to be outstandingly good singers. Still, that is a comparatively small expense. What I mean is: e.g., one of the

* See full score of work. [TRANS.]

AETAT 39 *To Arthur Nikisch*

6 men (the first) has to be a good soloist, the others capable choral singers. The same applies to the women!

For the film the part of the Man can be played by somebody who does not need to sing. The actor chosen should therefore be an outstandingly good one.

For the time being I can't think of any other details. Everything else will transpire in rehearsal.

One very important thing: try to interest a Berlin company. If for no other reason than that I can then take all rehearsals myself.

[..........]

ARNOLD SCHÖNBERG

19. TO ARTHUR NIKISCH *Berlin, 31 January* 1914

Dear Herr Professor,

Having meanwhile been in London and Prague, I have only today found time to tell you how much pleasure your Leipzig performance of my chamber symphony gave me.[1] Above all because it constituted a *démenti* of the remark about myself attributed to you and circulated by loutish newspaper-scribblers in order to damage me.[2] In calmer moments I myself always knew that there could not have been anything more behind it than, at the most, one of those momentary outbursts so frequent with all those of us who have a temperament and which none of us would care to be called to account for in their totality. As I have said, I am very glad that such wretched mischief-makers can no longer take your name in vain.

But then too I was particularly delighted when at the final rehearsal I realised that you had applied yourself to my music with great devotion and warm interest. I gathered this with pleasure from the fact that in this complicated contrapuntal texture, which reveals its meaning only to people of insight, all the important main parts and also the secondary parts were clearly and meaningfully brought out. I have furthermore to thank you for the fact that despite all the demands upon your time you undertook a task that is often hard for much younger musicians, even those who are close to me: I mean taking the trouble to get to know this score.

There is only one thing I regret (and I cannot be so lacking in can-

---

[1] Nikisch had conducted Schoenberg's chamber symphony in the Gewandhaus concerts at Leipzig.
[2] The press had reported a derogatory remark about Schoenberg's music, alleged to have been made by Nikisch.

To Arthur Nikisch JANUARY 1914

dour as to leave it unmentioned, the less since it accounts for my not coming to the performance): the fact that you did not let me know either about the rehearsals or the date of the performance. For I would have put at your disposal my parts and score, which not only contain corrections of mistakes* but, above all, a number of polishings and improvements that contribute a good deal towards improving the sound and making for clarity.

(I should like to take this opportunity of saying that I shall carry this polishing still further and shall make a special edition for orchestral performances.)

But be that as it may: first and foremost I want to thank you, for the Leipzig performance will be of great importance in making my work better known.

Please accept my cordial thanks and kind regards.

ARNOLD SCHÖNBERG

20. To EMIL HERTZKA *Berlin, 31 January* 1914

Dear Herr Direktor,

The songs for orchestra in Prague were very fine. It's true, Winkelmann was not particularly adequate. But Zemlinsky[1] did them magnificently. In fact, Zemlinsky is certainly the best conductor alive. I once heard a wonderful 'Parsifal' from his baton and watched him rehearsing Tchaikovsky and 'Tod und Verklärung'. It's incredible what he can wring out of such by no means first-class stuff. It's very sad that one can't hear that sort of thing in the artistic capital!

I am delighted to hear you are going to publish a small cheap score of 'Pierrot'. It's the only way the work can become better known.

[..........]

Please answer the following question by return:

Have I the right to forbid a performance of my 2nd Quartet if the singer isn't adequate or if rehearsals show that the quartet won't do? Must I put up with a failure due to an inferior performance? Is there nothing at all I can do to prevent it?

I am sending you the title-page of 'Pierrot' today.

Now I must study the Gurre-Lieder score.[2]

ARNOLD SCHÖNBERG

---

* This is presumably the meaning. Schoenberg actually wrote *Fehlkorrekturen*, 'erroneous corrections'. [TRANS].

[1] Zemlinsky was the musical director of the German Theatre in Prague.

[2] Schoenberg conducted the *Gurrelieder* in Leipzig in March 1914; the rehearsals began at the beginning of February.

AETAT 39   *To Hermann Scherchen*

21. To Hermann Scherchen[1]   *Berlin*, 1 *February* 1914

Dear Scherchen,

There are several very important things I must tell you about yesterday's rehearsal of the chamber symphony.

First the good points: the thing as a whole seems to have been worked out pretty well. Except for some casual and some wrong rhythms and some passages that don't come out at all, almost everything else would make an excellent impression if it were not that

(and now come the bad points, which I must state most emphatically and which I wish you to pay the utmost attention to) *your tempi were much too fast throughout.*

You seem to labour under the delusion that temperament means speed!! But temperament in itself doesn't mean anything and so far as I'm concerned, if it means 'fiery temperament' or the like, it strikes me as worthless, because the most it can do is to impress the womenfolk. Cast off this error and make music with a muted, with a restrained temperament!!

Now for the details: in general, then, this rushing of tempi means losing all the clarity gained by careful study of the score. All the lines become blurred and one can't understand a thing!

For instance, the first part of the Scherzo is too fast by more than half. The same for the Trio:

That simply won't do. It must go much slower.

But the main thing is the *Adagio*: you take it almost allegro!!! Of course it mustn't be treacly slow, but must have an inward emotion, only adagio, (about 50)!!! Then the B major part of the *Adagio* much too fast!! This begins quietly and contemplatively, and its intensification must *not* be *passionate*, but 'inwardness intensified'. It's a remarkable thing: passion's something everyone can do! But inwardness, the chaste, higher form of emotion, seems to be out of most people's reach. On the whole it's understandable: for the underlying emotion must be felt and not merely demonstrated! This too is why all actors have passion and only a very few have inwardness.

---

[1] Hermann Scherchen, who was then 21 years old, was just beginning his career as a conductor. See also the later letters to Scherchen, 68, 84, etc.

To Hermann Scherchen FEBRUARY 1914

I can't regard it with tolerance!

To go on: the whole recapitulation section is rushed. It's all fluffed, no note is left clear. Do use only as much expression as is in the piece, and don't always try to give more!

I beg you to observe these criticisms exactly, if you want to remain on good terms with me!!!

One more request: please send me some tickets for the concert as soon as possible.

I hope you won't be foolish enough to be cross with me for these strong words. But I have come to realise that bad performances do me so much harm that I can't go on allowing them. I always used to console myself with thoughts of the future. But recently I have been feeling more and more that every inadequate performance of a work of art is a grave crime, simply immoral.

Yrs. ever,

SCHÖNBERG

Ring me up and tell me when the next rehearsal is. Or call if you possibly can: I have some more points of detail for you.

22. TO THE CHAIRMAN AND COMMITTEE OF THE GERMAN STUDENTS' COMMONROOM, PRAGUE

[*No date: presumably Berlin 12 February* 1914]

You are mistaken in considering my silence an oversight. It was my answer to your question. But since you insist, I will translate that answer for you:

There is nothing, nothing at all, that I have to say to you all as Germans in Austria.

Above all nothing political.

At most to some individuals, and that you can, if you like, generalise.

Well then:

Let every individual try to be as decent as he is gifted, as modest as he is efficient, and as inconspicuous as he is ungifted. For nothing can be done for the Germans in Bohemia, any more than for the Germans in Germany and the French in France, unless there is a sufficiently large number of people with ideas and a still larger number who have been

AETAT 39   *To Emil Hertzka*

brought up not to stand in the way of ideas any more than is absolutely necessary.

Yours faithfully,
ARNOLD SCHÖNBERG

23. TO EMIL HERTZKA   *Berlin*, 21 *April* 1914

Dear Herr Direktor,

    I sent the *Gurre-Lieder score* to you yesterday and am today posting *the score of the monodrama*, both ready for the lithographer. Please acknowledge receipt.

    I beg you, dear Herr Direktor, to have *both the Gurre-Lieder and the monodrama lithographed* without fail!!

    You can scarcely complain of the sales of *my* music. But to make me suffer because others' work isn't yet selling would be downright *unjust*!! After all, for the last fifteen years I've been the whipping-boy for all these people who are nowadays making names for themselves with feeble imitations of my achievements, and I am still taking punishment. Surely then I am entitled to be given preference over them for once!

    But apart from that

    I. it would mean limiting my chance of getting my work better known,

    II. my income would be reduced,

    III. it would infallibly damage my reputation and that of Universal Edition if *no lithographed large* and *well-made miniature score* were to appear. (For everyone would say that there was no market for the work!!)

    I devoutly hope you will accept these arguments and have the works published with all speed. Since my music sells instantly (think of the chamber symphony), as it comes from the press, any economising here would be quite out of place. On the contrary: the sooner the things are available in a good edition, the sooner you will make your profit!

In any case:

    The Gurre-Lieder must (I beg you) on no account be *duplicated* [*autographiert*], for then there would be no hope of selling miniature scores for years to come.

    Please return the enclosed letter. I enclose a copy of my answer. What I expect of you is above all *that you should prevent the founding*

To Emil Hertzka APRIL 1914

of a 'mixed' society. Such a society would do me more harm than good.

I should also like to have your views on (1) whether by now I really need such a thing at all, (2) whether, on the contrary, it isn't still too early for it; for I have written too little, so that such a society would not last for more than 3–4 years.

ARNOLD SCHÖNBERG

24. TO AN UNKNOWN CORRESPONDENT *Berlin, 21 April* 1914

Dear Sir,[1]

The founding of a 'Schönberg Society'[2] is something from which I personally should have to hold entirely aloof.

But once such a society exists and [provided] the persons in charge [are] acceptable and the society's policy of such a lofty nature as to be in harmony with my principles, it is thinkable that I might take an active part in concerts.

However, I must warn you that I am extremely fastidious in this respect, and I therefore suggest that you should get in touch with someone who knows me well enough.

One such person is, for instance, the Director of Universal Edition, Herr Emil Hertzka, Reichsratsstrasse 9, Vienna I. Perhaps you will discuss the matter with him.

ARNOLD SCHÖNBERG

25. TO AN UNKNOWN CORRESPONDENT *Berlin, 22 April* 1914

Dear Sir,

I regret that I am unable to accept your invitation to write something for Richard Strauss's 50th birthday.

In a letter to Frau Mahler (in connection with the Mahler Memorial Fund)[3] Herr Strauss wrote about me as follows:

> 'The only person who can help poor Schönberg now is a psychiatrist....'.
>
> 'I think he'd do better to shovel snow instead of scribbling on music-paper...'.

---

[1] See previous letter to Hertzka.
[2] The Society was not founded.
[3] After Mahler's death a Memorial Fund was instituted, the interest on which was annually awarded to a distinguished composer in recognition of his achievements.

It seems to me that the opinion I myself and indeed everyone else who knows these remarks is bound to have of Herr Strauss as a man (for here is envy of a 'competitor') and as an artist (for the expressions he uses are as banal as a cheap song) is not suitable for general publication in honour of his 50th birthday.

I have no intention of damaging Herr Strauss 'morally'; [..........] He is no longer of the slightest artistic interest to me, and whatever I may once have learnt from him, I am thankful to say I misunderstood.

I cannot deny that in my urge to venerate an elder composer I quite often had to give this misunderstanding a helping hand. I had to make an effort not to see, in the themes of *Ein Heldenleben* and *Zarathustra*, what becomes all too obvious in the song themes and the Mahler Memorial Foundation letters. I will not deny that in other circumstances I might have preferred to remain a prey to that misunderstanding and — unconsciously, instinctively doing my duty — would have declined to write about Strauss for another reason. I cannot refrain, however, from mentioning that since I have understood Mahler (and I cannot grasp how anyone can do otherwise) I have inwardly rejected Strauss. That I, as one whose conduct will never be guided by envy of 'competitors', have no cause to take a public stand against Strauss, you will understand. That I am not afraid of doing so, you will necessarily believe since for this purpose I empower you to publish this letter at any time you may think fit and at your discretion; but if you do so, then in its entirety; not excerpted.

Yours faithfully,

ARNOLD SCHÖNBERG

26. To ALEXANDER SILOTI[1] *Berlin*, 15 *June* 1914

Dear Herr Siloti,

I am very pleased about your decision and hope I can make a good job of the chamber symphony in the allotted time of four rehearsals. I should be very glad if you would let me know the rehearsal dates soon. But, you do agree, don't you: I must have four *full* rehearsals. The work is really *very difficult* and I should not like to have a success on account of unclarity, but would prefer a failure on account of clarity. No, but seriously: people must be shown what I mean!!

Now I have another request. Could you not postpone the performance

[1] Alexander Siloti, the Russian pianist and conductor, had the previous season engaged Schoenberg to conduct *Pelleas und Melisande* in St. Petersburg (Leningrad). The concert planned for the coming season, at which Schoenberg was to have conducted his chamber symphony, was never held, owing to the outbreak of war.

To Alexander Siloti JUNE 1914

of my 'Pierrot' till next year or the year after? I should prefer not to set out my reasons in a letter unless you absolutely insist. I should rather explain when I get to Petersburg. Meanwhile just this: it is at least as much in your interest as in mine that you should not do it this year. You can, after all, write and tell Frau Zehme that it's unfortunately impossible this year.

'Pierrot' would be a failure this year, which would do the chamber symphony no good. And I should like the chamber symphony to be a success. It is my ewe lamb, one of my very best works, and yet up to now (owing to bad performances!!) it has hardly been understood by anyone. I am convinced that it would make a great impact if well performed.

I look forward to having your decision soon and remain, with best wishes to yourself and your family, yours sincerely,

ARNOLD SCHÖNBERG

27. TO ALEXANDER VON ZEMLINSKY[1]   *Vienna, 9 October* 1915
Dear Alex,

Much as I rejoice at your intention to perform my chamber symphony and however fervently I look forward to hearing this work at long last (for it has never yet been sufficiently rehearsed and brought out in all its clarity), I do beg you to give up the idea until the war is over.

This request will surprise you, so I must give you my reasons in full.

You know that I have scarcely ever taken any account of whether my works were liked or not. I have become indifferent to public abuse and I have never had any inclination to do anything that wasn't dictated by the purely musical demands of my works. I can say this with a good conscience, and so I can also risk asking you to do something that people of ill will might interpret as making concessions: do, instead, perform one of my older works, either 'Pelleas' or perhaps part of the 'Gurre-Lieder', in a word, something that can by now count on being fairly well received by the public.

When I think of how badly my 'Pelleas' was treated here and of the opposition with which even the Songs for Orchestra were received, but above all when I remember the uproar about 'Pierrot lunaire', after which my name was dragged through the mud of all the newspapers at home and abroad under the headline 'Schönberg Scenes in Prague', surely it isn't cowardly if I now try to avoid that sort of thing. In peace-time — which means war-time for me — I am quite prepared to go back to being

[1] See note 1 to Letter 20.

everyone's whipping-boy, and everyone who is accounted indispensable today will be welcome to lash out at whatever bit of me he thinks most vulnerable. But for the present — more than ever — I should like to keep out of the limelight. I have never been able to keep right out of it. The reason for this was always what I have to say, and that had to be said. But I didn't need to bother about it. For, even though the fact was painstakingly hushed up in Germany and Austria, I had plenty of success abroad and gained a large following.

I can't deny that that success was a moral support to me. But nowadays, when I am deprived of that support, I am really a little discouraged, at least for the moment, and think with horror of what is in store for me. There is no longer any hope that the recognition I was gaining abroad will in the long run mean I'll at least be left in peace. I know I have to face the future without any such hope. Is it any wonder I want to put it off just a shade longer? Is it any wonder I should like to be left in peace just a little while longer (the only good thing the war has done for me is that I'm not being attacked by anyone), that I should like to enjoy this peace of mine just a little while longer, as long as the war lasts?

So don't be angry with me for asking something so odd and do, if you can, do as I ask.

ARNOLD SCHÖNBERG

28. To ALBERTINE ZEHME[1] *Vienna, 5 May* 1917

My very dear Frau Zehme,

It is a long time since I wrote, because I have been working pretty hard and have, besides, had Zemlinsky staying with me (his 'Florentine Tragedy', a magnificent work, had its first night here). First, the answers to your questions: so far, touch wood, I haven't been called up. — I am engaged on a number of theoretical works, and also still busy with the libretto for a large work for choir, solo, and orchestra.[2] Apart from this I give lectures, which are not at all badly attended. — As for my two operas, I would let a theatre have them only for inclusion in the repertory, not for one performance only.... — That nothing came of the American plan is a very sad blow to me! It was my last hope! All in

---

[1] A former actress, wife of an eminent Leipzig lawyer. In 1912 she had asked Schoenberg to compose something for her for an evening's recital (melodramas). This was the origin of *Pierrot lunaire*, which was first interpreted by Frau Zehme.

[2] *Jacob's Ladder*. The composition of this work was interrupted when Schoenberg was called up for military service. It was never completed.

To Albertine Zehme   MAY 1917

all, we aren't too badly off. The only difficulty is with food and coal! A difficulty steadily increasing. My wife (who sends her kindest regards) is often, indeed most of the time, far from well: inadequate diet, etc.

[..........]

                                                                      ARNOLD SCHÖNBERG

29. To ALEXANDER VON ZEMLINSKY   *Vienna*, 20 *March* 1918

Dear Alex,

I need a large sheet of paper in order to reply to the 'cutting conspiracy' and have to write in pencil because it is cold in my room.

First and foremost: my attitude to cuts is the same as ever. I am against removing tonsils although I know one can somehow manage to go on living even without arms, legs, nose, eyes, tongue, ears, etc. In my view that sort of bare survival isn't always important enough to warrant changing something in the programme of the Creator who, on the great rationing day, allotted us so and so many arms, legs, ears and other organs. And so I also hold the view that a work doesn't have to live, i.e., be performed, at all costs either, not if it means losing parts of it that may even be ugly or faulty but which it was born with.

The second preliminary question is that of consideration for the listener. I have exactly as little of this as he has for me. All I know is that he exists, and in so far as he isn't 'indispensable' for acoustic reasons (since music doesn't sound well in an empty hall), he's only a nuisance. In any case, a listener who can dispense with my work or with part of it is free to make use of his more fortunate situation and treat *me* as something he can dispense with *entirely*.

However, regarding the cut you have suggested,[1] here is what I have to say:

I have always told everyone who pays any attention to me that I consider the last part, precisely that from $\boxed{50}$ on, the best in the whole work, indeed the only thing in the work, with a few exceptions from what goes before, that is still of any interest to me now. Particularly the passage (50) – (55). I very clearly remember it was here for the first time (while I was composing it) that I realised the many sequences of the preceding parts were only of moderate artistic value and it was here (and I am amazed at your remark about 'the peculiar structure of two-bar periods that was at that time still one of your characteristics',

[1] Zemlinsky had proposed making a cut in *Pelleas und Melisande* for the performance about to be given in Prague.

AUTOGRAPH OF FIRST PAGE OF LETTER 29

which applies to much of the rest of the work, but not at all to this part) for the first time that intuitively and consciously I tried to achieve a more irregular and, indeed, more involved form and, as I can now see, did achieve it.

[..........]

Your other suggestion, that in this passage there is 'nothing that's any longer so strikingly new', is also, I think, incorrect. In the first place the motif occurs for the first time in the 2nd bar after $\boxed{50}$ (cor anglais). But then (quite apart from an amount of melodically, formally, and, in particular, harmonically interesting detail — you must forgive me for praising it, but I am at such a remove from the work now that I think myself entitled to praise it as objectively as I find fault with it), in particular, this repetition is here more than a recapitulation with variations. Apart from the fact that it follows the line of the drama (which would no longer strike me as the most essential thing), it seems to me justified (and this is more important to me than justification in the light of a formal scheme) by the sense of form and space that has always been the sole factor guiding me in composition, and which was the reason why I felt this group to be necessary. This must be taken on trust, blindly, and it can be taken on trust only by someone who has learnt to have confidence in the rest: I didn't put this part in merely because of the recapitulation section, but because I felt it to be *formally necessary*.

Furthermore, though I think you're right in holding that it isn't formal perfection that constitutes the merit of this work, the deficiency appears much more obviously in other passages, whereas here it doesn't strike me as being particularly apparent. (Frankly, in this respect too I think the passage better than what precedes it.)

You asked for my candid opinion. Here you have it. The fact that I give you my views so explicitly in spite of being dead set against cuts (and you will remember that in your own works I have always and increasingly urged you not to cut, since one's first inspiration is almost always the right one!) will, I hope, show you that I haven't treated your suggestion lightly. I hope you won't be annoyed and won't think I believe in 'infallibility'. On the contrary, if I had written more, I shouldn't much mind if this work didn't exist at all. True, I can't really think it bad, and even find plenty of very good stuff in it, and above all it has a number of features that indicate my subsequent development, perhaps even more than my first quartet. But I know exactly how far removed it is from perfection and that I have managed to do much better things. But I also definitely know that cutting isn't the way to improve

To Alexander von Zemlinsky MARCH 1918

a work. Brevity and succinctness are a matter of *exposition*. In this case the details are not conceived compactly; it is all long-winded. If I cut some such details, the other long-winded ones remain, and it remains a work of long-winded exposition. It will not take so long to play, but it *will not really be shorter*! A work that has been shortened by cutting may very well give the impression of being an excessively long work (because of the exposition) that is too short in various places (where it has been cut).

Anyway I am sure that while conducting you won't have the feeling it is too long. This is a fact I have noticed repeatedly and commented on: whenever I conducted it, the work never struck me as too long. I rely on your delight in music-making to win me a victory over the anxious, because responsible, concert-promoter and believe firmly that that faculty of yours will, in the end, find this music not too long.

In any case I am very grateful to you for the intention that led you to make this suggestion. I know you want to do the best for me. That is, after all, what counts most, and over against that it would be petty of me to take your suggestion amiss.

[..........]

ARNOLD SCHÖNBERG

30. To FRANZ SCHALK[1] *Mödling, 6 April* 1918
Dear Herr Hofkapellmeister Schalk,

Many thanks for your answer and your kind efforts. But I cannot be expected to attend the final rehearsal of Mahler's Eighth under *false pretences*,[2] when I consider myself entitled to believe that my attainments give me the *right* of entry, indeed to be such that not only am I entitled to attend but, rather, the organisers would be justified in inviting me. But it seems I am mistaken on this point so long as and as often as I am in Vienna.

[..........]

ARNOLD SCHÖNBERG

31. To FRITZ REDLICH[3] *Mödling, 19 May* 1918
Dear Herr Redlich,

Thank you very much for the extremely pleasant news, which you have conveyed to me, on behalf of the Board of Trustees, that I have

---

[1] Director of the Vienna Opera.
[2] Schalk had evidently sent Schoenberg a press ticket.
[3] A member of the board of trustees of the Mahler Memorial Fund, which consisted of musicians, music-lovers, and patrons of the arts.

been awarded the Mahler Memorial Prize for this year. I wish to thank you personally for the kind words in which you express the intentions prompting those who have thus shown their good will towards me, and I wish to record my deepest gratitude for it to all those concerned.

I herewith also confirm having received the cheque for 2,520 crowns, which arrived by the same mail and which together with the beautiful weather makes this Whit Sunday a particularly delightful day for me.

ARNOLD SCHÖNBERG

32. TO AN UNKNOWN CORRESPONDENT *Mödling*, 1 *November* 1918

My very dear fellow, your letter shows that you are well on the way towards getting a picture of the real issue and, what matters to me more, that you have regained your trust in my friendship for you, in other words, you once more realise that despite any wounded feelings you could always have trusted blindly in that friendship. I haven't many friends, it's true, but the few I have can rely on me entirely. If after all this I tell you that we still have to have a thorough talk to clear up some points that I think you still don't see in the right light, now at any rate you again have enough trust in me to know that it isn't that I'm trying to make use of you but that my aim is to make a clean sweep so that we can make an entirely fresh start.

So do come and see me as soon as you possibly can. Today if you like — but anyway for the next few days I shall always be at home here in Mödling. Come soon. Very best wishes,

Yours ever,

ARNOLD SCHÖNBERG

Section II
VIENNA (MÖDLING)
1919 – 1925

BIOGRAPHICAL NOTES

In the years immediately after the war Schoenberg spent more time being an executant musician and a teacher than composing. As early as the autumn of 1918 he founded the *Verein für musikalische Privataufführungen* (Society for Private Concerts), the aim being to accustom the public to the sound of modern music. A concert was given every week, the programme consisting entirely of modern works. Only members of the Association were admitted. The players were all young and outstandingly gifted musicians. Each work was rehearsed either by Schoenberg himself or by a 'director' (*Vortragsmeister*) appointed by him, in order to achieve the utmost clarity of musical presentation. The scope of works included was very wide, the composers being such as had, in Schoenberg's words, a real face or name. During the first two years Schoenberg did not allow any of his own works to be performed, but the programmes included works by Stravinsky, Bartók, Debussy, Ravel, Webern, Berg, and many others (see Letters 38, 54, and 57). After several years the Society had to abandon its activities owing to the rapid and steady depreciation of Austrian currency.

1920: Schoenberg conducted the *Gurrelieder* at the Vienna Opera. In the autumn he was invited to lecture and conduct in Holland.

1921: After the performance of the *Gurrelieder* in Amsterdam, Schoenberg returned to Austria in the spring. Rehearsals of *Pierrot lunaire* for the Society for Private Concerts. In the following years the Vienna *Pierrot*-Ensemble made numerous foreign tours.

1923: The year in which Schoenberg's method of 'twelve-note composition' matured (see Letter 78). On the occasion of a concert in Copenhagen (see Letter 55) he established relations with the publishing house of Wilhelm Hansen, which then published the *Five Pieces for Piano*, op. 23, and the *Serenade*, op. 24 (see note 2 to Letter 58), two works that represent the final stage leading up to his new method of composition.

Biographical Notes

- 1923: Autumn: death of Schoenberg's first wife, Mathilde.
- 1924: Schoenberg conducted the *Serenade*, op. 24, at the Donaueschingen Music Festival (see Letter 81). His fiftieth birthday was celebrated in Vienna and other cities (see Letter 84) by performances of his works. First performance of his operas *Erwartung* ('Expectation') in Prague, and *Die glückliche Hand* ('The Lucky Hand') in Vienna.
- 1925: Schoenberg was appointed director of an advanced class in composition at the Prussian Academy of Arts in Berlin (see Letter 87). Owing to an operation for appendicitis, his removal to Berlin was delayed until the beginning of 1926.

WORKS

- 1920/23: *Five Pieces for Piano*, op. 23.
- 1921/23: *Suite for Piano*, op. 25.
- 1923: *Serenade* for baritone, clarinet, bass clarinet, mandoline, guitar, violin, viola, and violoncello, op. 24.
- 1923/34: *Quintet* for Wind Instruments, op. 26.
- 1925: *Suite* for piano, three clarinets, and strings, op. 29.
- 1922: Two chorale preludes by J. S. Bach, arranged for large orchestra.

33. To Hugo Botstiber[1]   *Mödling*, 13 *March* 1919
Dear Dr. Botstiber,

What happened at yesterday's rehearsal was yet another painful lesson proving that business cannot be treated merely as a matter between friends; it becomes all the less possible the more one attaches importance to maintaining friendly relations.

I therefore consider it my duty to tell you now, clearly and without beating about the bush, the conditions under which I *consider possible* the concerts you proposed to me — *the sole conditions under which they are acceptable to me.*

I do beg of you (and, being convinced that you have my interests at heart, I feel I may do so) to take every word I am about to say quite seriously and literally.

You know I am not a careerist, but you also know that not only *am* I inexorable in artistic matters, I am constitutionally incapable of letting the slightest thing pass.

To get down to brass tacks: we agreed that this concert should be held next year and that apart from this the Gurre-Lieder should be done this year. The first thing I insist on is therefore:

I: A legally binding agreement, setting out in writing all the points verbally agreed on, within one *week*. [..........]

II: *For the concert on the 26th March:*

Since the players provided by Brunner[2] have no time to rehearse and some of them, besides, are not up to standard, and since the orchestra I asked for (8 first violins, 6 second violins, 6 violas, 6 'cellos)[3] is not forthcoming, I see only the following possibilities:

1. This concert must either be cancelled or
2. postponed for *at most* a week (a longer postponement would interfere with the Gurre-Lieder rehearsals), or
3. you must instantly engage the Philharmonic for this concert, so

---
[1] Secretary general of the *Konzerthaus-Gesellschaft* in Vienna.
[2] The agent.
[3] The unusual number of violas and 'cellos in relation to the number of violins indicates the programme of the concert, which took place after a postponement. Schoenberg's 2nd Quartet and his sextet *Verklärte Nacht* were performed by a string orchestra.

To Hugo Botstiber MARCH 1919

that I can get in a rehearsal with them this same week (*perhaps* I can then manage with one rehearsal less: *perhaps*!!).

4. A cancellation would have to be announced *instantly*, for later everyone would say it was because no tickets were sold.

5. If the concert is to take place I must make the following conditions for rehearsals:

(a) before and during rehearsals some *responsible* person must be there to see that everything is properly organized: music-stands, instruments, players, punctuality, etc. At this rehearsal nothing was seen to. Webern (!!!) himself brought down two 'cellos after we had been waiting an hour and after he had taken it upon himself, in spite of all warnings, to enter General Secretary Kaudela's lair[1] in order to get permission to fetch them!

(b) I must be able to have at least the last 4–5 rehearsals in the concert hall.

(c) It must immediately be ascertained whether the platform in the second-largest Konzerthaus is large enough for 28 instruments, the conductor (a small platform might be added if necessary), the singer *and* the piano.

[. . . . .]

I trust you will let me have your decision without delay, hope you will see my point of view, and remain, with kind regards,

Yours ever,

ARNOLD SCHÖNBERG

34. TO UNIVERSAL EDITION *Mödling, 30 April* 1919

The management of the Konzerthaus informs me that Schalk[2] wishes to perform the Gurre-Lieder in February and that he and Dr. Botstiber have agreed that the Konzerthaus-Gesellschaft shall perform them under my direction in the autumn and, independently of that, that the Singverein[3] shall do them in February.

Since however I do not believe:

I. that a performance can really be given in September, because up to now no performers have been engaged, nor has anything else been arranged;

---

[1] The secretary of the *Konzertverein* orchestra.

[2] Franz Schalk was the conductor of the *Gesellschaftskonzerte*, organised by the *Gesellschaft der Musikfreunde* (usually known as the 'Society of the Friends of Music').

[3] The *Singverein* (Chorus) of the Society of the Friends of Music.

II. that Schalk can possibly be interested in doing the G.L. again in February, when they will have *had* to be done at least *three times* (because of expense!) in September, —

since on the contrary I am convinced that Schalk will not agree to the *number of rehearsals* on which I *insist*,

I herewith declare that I shall permit a performance conducted by Schalk only if one has previously been conducted by me, and I therefore ask you to grant him the performing right *solely on the following conditions*:

I. He shall be entitled to perform the Gurre-Lieder only *after a performance in Vienna* conducted by me.

II. If he does not use the orchestra rehearsed by me and the same singers, he must agree to the number of rehearsals on which I insist.

I shall use all means at my disposal to prevent any performance, in any circumstances, that violates these terms.

In conclusion, to be on the safe side I wish to make clear the nature of the perhaps foreseen, but in any case foreseeable, eventuality against which I wish to be protected. It is this:

that for some (easily foreseeable) reason the performance in the autumn will probably not take place, so that Schalk will circumvent my conditions about rehearsals and fling the work at the public after no more than 5–6 rehearsals!

I won't let him get away with that!

Kindly acknowledge and reply.

ARNOLD SCHÖNBERG

35. TO UNIVERSAL EDITION *Mödling, 5 May* 1919

Your letter of the 2.v. is no answer to mine of the 30.iv. The protection I demand *cannot be provided by Dr. Botstiber*, but *only* by means of a *contract with Schalk* such as I demand. Although I would, admittedly, be interested in a performance within the framework of the Society's concerts, I am not short-sighted enough to delude myself into thinking that an insufficiently rehearsed performance (Schalk never rehearses more than 6 times, whereas 12 is the minimum necessary) could do anything but harm to the work, its chances of becoming better known, and thus also to me and to you, the publishers. All my enemies are just waiting for the chance to decide that the Gurre-Lieder are bad too, and no one can wish me worse than a bad performance.

For this reason, in the event that you do not undertake to protect me by concluding a suitable agreement with Schalk, I shall first endeavour

To Universal Edition MAY 1919

to settle the matter amicably with Schalk and shall then approach members of the Society's committee who are well disposed towards me and shall ask them to renounce their intention. Should even that — contrary to my expectations — fail, since I do not mean to knuckle under I shall be compelled to enter upon a course of action that is repugnant to me. But in that case the responsibility will not be mine. — I still hope, however, that you will re-read the clear exposition in my last letter and protect my interests accordingly. There is nothing I should like better than an amicable agreement with all concerned. For I wish for peace and quiet![1]

ARNOLD SCHÖNBERG

36. TO E. FROMAIGEAT   *Mödling, 22 July* 1919

Herr E. Fromaigeat,
Winterthur

It is very encouraging to hear that Paris is setting about revising the Internationale of the Things of the Mind. And it is indeed very necessary that this movement should originate in Paris, when one considers that it was precisely there, from the beginning of the war to the end of the war and indeed even subsequently, that there originated the most aggressive campaigns to destroy this Internationale in so far as Germany is concerned.

I must say: no one can feel more deeply than I do the need to see equality once more prevailing in the republic of the mind. For no one can have felt it a *greater* consolation than I have done to know that there are people here and there from whom I differ only in the mode of expression with which I offer up sacrifice to the things that are as sacred to them as to me.

Nevertheless I tell you (personally, for there is no one to back me up): it isn't as easy as all that.

I do not mean obdurately to insist that it would perhaps be well to stimulate a conciliatory mood in us by more effective means than — as if nothing had happened — a mere invitation that looks almost the same as the notorious 'admittance' to the League of Nations. After all, something *did* happen! It happened that for instance a man like Maeterlinck, someone to whom one would have liked to put the anxious question as to 'what he had to say about it all' — precisely this Maeterlinck took an attitude such as one could never have expected of the author of

---

[1] The problem was solved by giving up the performances planned by the *Konzerthausgesellschaft* and the Society of the Friends of Music and, instead, giving two performances at the Vienna Opera, under Schoenberg's direction, in the spring of 1920.

AETAT 44   *To E. Fromaigeat*

'The Treasure of the Humble'. It happened that Saint-Saëns and Lalo spoke of German music in outrageous terms, and that even after the armistice a man like Claudel goes on talking about 'Boches'.

There were sins on our side too, and here too in part committed by people who should have known better. But never and nowhere did anyone go to anything like the lengths that they did there. Here and in Germany French music was performed all during the war, and I know of no case of anyone speaking e.g., about Manet or Verlaine as Saint-Saëns did about Wagner.

I will not go so far as to say that I consider such things beyond forgiveness: I don't think atonement ought even to be demanded. For I can perfectly well understand what has been called war-psychosis; for those in power in all countries needed a 'war-cry' for mobilisation, and the blow on the head stunned the mind, concussed the brain.

But I think that those whose conscience urges them to revive the Internationale of the Mind ought, in so far as they are themselves beyond reproach, to dissociate themselves clearly from such things by making the sharpest possible protest against war-time excesses on the part of intellectuals.

They should publicly announce that at least now they consider such an attitude reprehensible and that they consider only those may be exculpated whose silence at least in recent days has indicated a return to better understanding. But those who have not made amends should be excluded from a community in which there can be only one kind of war: I mean war against all that is low and beastly, and only one mode of warfare: holding aloof from such things.

I do not wish to have any dealings with anyone who does not act in this way!

That I myself wish to resume such relations, and why, I wish to emphasise here at the end of this letter by repeating what I said at the beginning: No one can feel a greater need than I to see equality once more prevailing in the republic of the mind.

In conclusion I should like to ask you to use this letter in any way you see fit and to say that I am by no means averse to the possibility that those concerned in Paris may gather from its contents what I think on the subject. I should also mention that I am sending you under separate cover the printed material concerning a Society founded by me in October 1918,[1] which, without international agreements or any other ado, took up the very attitude that befits people like ourselves.

                                                   ARNOLD SCHÖNBERG

[1] The Society for Private Concerts (See Biographical Notes, p. 61).

To the Deutsche Zeitung Bohemia　　　　　　　　NOVEMBER 1921

37. TO THE EDITOR OF THE BOOK PAGE, *Deutsche Zeitung Bohemia*
　　　　　　　　　　　　　　　　　　　　　　19 *November* 1921

　　　Herr Arnold Schoenberg,
　　　We should be extremely obliged if you would have the kindness to answer the following question, which we are submitting to the most distinguished personalities in Europe:
　　　Which five people would you save if you were a present-day Noah and had to carry out his function on the eve of another flood?
　　　Your answer will be published under the heading 'The Choosing of the Five' in the Christmas number of 'Bohemia'. We shall be particularly grateful if you will let us have your answer by the 15th December.
　　　With most cordial thanks,
　　　　　　　I remain, yours very truly,
　　　　　　　　　　　　　EDITOR OF THE BOOK PAGE,
　　　　　　　　　　　　　　　Deutsche Zeitung Bohemia

'Deutsche Zeitung Bohemia',
Prague.
　　　Please, can't there be just a few more than five? The fact is, even I and my nearest and dearest come to more than that. And I should really like — to say nothing of the many other people I am fond of and all those I should feel sorry for — I should really like to be able to take at least my best friends with me. But it is to be hoped, surely, that the catastrophe is not imminent? What I should be very grateful for is if you would use the enclosed postcard to let me know of anyone who decides to rescue *me*, so that I can remain in his vicinity.
　　　　　　　　　　　　　　　　　　ARNOLD SCHÖNBERG

38. TO ALEXANDER ZEMLINSKY[1]　　　　*Mödling, 3 May* 1922
Dear Alex,
　　[. . . . .]
　　I shall most certainly come to the performance of *Pierrot* and to the *Society's* concerts.[2] True, the fee is very very small and in present conditions (rise in the cost of living, etc.) scarcely to be considered a fee at all. But after all I'm not coming to Prague for the fee. — I am very pleased about the founding of your Society. I hope it will be possible to make something really good of it. Let's hope the material side works out more or less well enough to see it through. — But now for something

---
　　[1] See Letters 27 and 29. The prefix 'von' was abolished after the war.
　　[2] A Society for Private Concerts on the Vienna pattern. Programmes were organised and players provided by the Vienna Society.

very important. I'm told that at *your* wish I have been elected honorary president. That's quite out of the question. I can't be honorary president of a society in which you're the chairman!!! I have suggested that we should *both* be honorary presidents, *you* and *I*.

ARNOLD SCHÖNBERG

39. TO ALMA MAHLER-WERFEL[1]   *Traunkirchen, 5 July* 1922
Dear lady, dear friend,
I have surely given proof of being no formalist in matters of 'casting' and that I consider ideas transposable. But to perform 'Pierrot' without recitation but with dancing does strike me as going too far. I don't think I'm being pedantic about it, even if I haven't much more to say against this transcription than against any other. Anyway: I should have to do such a symphonic version myself, in order to conduct it myself. In such a case one has to take the entire responsibility! But it isn't a job I feel any enthusiasm for. I'd rather write Massine something new — even though not immediately.[2] — If Milhaud wants me in Paris, either 'Erwartung' or 'Die glückliche Hand' can provide the occasion. These *premières* I should have to conduct myself.

I should be very grateful if you'd 'pass on' my answer. I'm afraid of doing it too undiplomatically and shouldn't like to offend Milhaud, who is, after all, a nice person.

How are you? Have you quite recovered? Yes, packing is a frightful drudge. We nearly didn't go to the country because I've reached the stage where I simply can't bring myself to start packing.

[..........]

ARNOLD SCHÖNBERG

40. TO ANTON WEBERN   *Traunkirchen*, 7 *July* 1922
My very dear fellow,
First and foremost my warmest congratulations on your appointment as conductor of the Konzertverein.[3] May it turn out to be a permanent and flourishing appointment, in keeping with the musical interests of Vienna! Hearty congratulations.

---

[1] The widow of Gustav Mahler. See also postscript to Letter 262.
[2] The idea of dancing *Pierrot lunaire* evidently originated with Leonid Massine, the distinguished Russian dancer.
[3] It was the popular Sunday-afternoon concerts for which Webern had been engaged. Since one short rehearsal was the utmost allowed for each concert, Webern could not be satisfied with the job and soon resigned.

To Anton Webern JULY 1922

You needn't worry because your salary isn't yet fixed. *On the contrary*, I consider it a good sign, implying: 'we won't do yer dahn, guv'nor',* i.e., we'll certainly pay you enough to satisfy you.

[..........]

ARNOLD SCHÖNBERG

41. TO ALBAN BERG *Traunkirchen, 20 July* 1922

My very dear fellow,

The idea of having 'Wozzeck' lithographed on your own account seems to me a *very good* one, even if Zemlinsky (who's spending the summer in Bad Aussee — couldn't you play 'Wozzeck' for him?) takes a different view. Only you mustn't imagine that it's going to guarantee you a performance. (Zemlinsky, by the way, is more in favour of playing it to people!) In any case it'll take a long time to recoup the printing expenses. Fräulein Keller — my cordial regards to her and to your wife — must of course face the fact that her loan is likely to be a long-term one! — One thing though: mightn't it be possible, in the circumstances, to come to an agreement with U.E.? Or perhaps it wouldn't be such a good thing?

Helene's[1] being so unwell is really too bad — of course it is a rotten summer — so far anyway. [..........] — After a short break I shall start working at 'Jacob's Ladder' again. All the very best. Ever,

ARNOLD SCHÖNBERG

42. TO WASSILY KANDINSKY[2] *Traunkirchen, 20 July* 1922

My dear Kandinsky,

I'm very glad to have heard from you at long last. How often I've thought of you with anxiety during these eight years! And how many people I have asked about you, without ever getting any definite and reliable information. You must have been through a great deal!

I expect you know we've had our trials here too: famine! It really was pretty awful! But perhaps — for we Viennese seem to be a patient lot — perhaps the worst was after all the overturning of everything one has believed in. That was probably the most grievous thing of all.

When one's been used, where one's own work was concerned, to clearing away all obstacles often by means of one immense intellectual

---

* Schoenberg here uses the standard Viennese dialect expression, 'mir wern kan Richter brauchen', literally: 'We shan't need a judge' (i.e., to go to court about it). [TRANS.]

[1] Berg's wife.   [2] The painter.

effort and in those 8 years found oneself constantly faced with new obstacles against which all thinking, all power of invention, all energy, all ideas, proved helpless, for a man for whom ideas have been everything it means nothing less than the total collapse of things, unless he has come to find support, in ever increasing measure, in belief in something higher, beyond. You would, I think, see what I mean best from my libretto 'Jacob's Ladder'* (an oratorio): what I mean is — even though without any organisational fetters — religion. This was my one and only support during those years — here let this be said for the first time.

I can understand your being surprised by the artistic situation in Berlin. But are you also pleased about it? Personally, I haven't much taste for all these movements, but at least I don't have to worry that they'll irritate me for long. Nothing comes to a standstill sooner than these movements that are brought about by so many people.

For the rest, all these people aren't peddling their own precious skins, but ours — yours and mine. I find it perfectly disgusting, at least in music: these atonalists! Damn it all, I did my composing without any 'ism' in mind. What has it got to do with me?

I hope you'll soon be able to get down to work. I think it's precisely these movements that can do with your putting some hindrances in their way. — What are your plans? — How is your book 'Das Geistige in der Kunst' ['Art and Intellect'] getting on? I think of it because it appeared at the same time as my Harmonielehre ['Theory of Harmony'], a much revised new edition of which I am just sending to the printers. — It may interest you to know I am at present working on 'Jacob's Ladder'. I began it several years ago, but had to break off work (at one of the most rapt passages) in order to join the army.[1] Since then I've never got back into the mood to go on with it. It seems, however, that it is meant to go ahead this year. It will be a big work: choir, solo voices, orchestra. Apart from that I plan to write a smaller theoretical book, 'Lehre vom musikalischen Zusammenhang' ['Theory of Musical Unity'], which has also been in my mind for several years and which is always being postponed — probably because it hasn't yet matured. For the rest: chamber music etc. Further, I am thinking about a Theory of Composition, for which I've been making preliminary studies for years now.

Well, now I've gone jabbering on like a small child, which I actually stopped being some decades ago. But that's the way it is with letter-writing: by the time one's warmed up, one is also worn out.

* Shall I send you the book? I'd like to know what you think of it. [S.]
[1] See Letter 28.

To Wassily Kandinsky   JULY 1922

Will you be able to come to Austria one of these days? I'd very much like to see you.

In any case I hope to hear from you more often now; it does me a lot of good. [. . . . .]

                                                     ARNOLD SCHÖNBERG

43. To PAUL SCHEINPFLUG   *Traunkirchen*, 29 *July* 1922

Dear Herr Generalmusikdirektor,

I was convinced that your performance[1] would be a particularly fine one, from the moment that Universal Edition, in answer to my question whether a sufficient number of rehearsals had been agreed on, gave me news far surpassing my expectations: that you had yourself arranged many more rehearsals than I demanded. The fact is, this is my yardstick: the more exactly a musician knows what he wants to effect, the more he is bound to find fault with what the orchestra and the singers offer him, and he is therefore all the more *capable* of keeping on and on with rehearsals in order to make the performance approximate to his idea of it. Anyone who can do with few rehearsals has either *no* idea or one that is *no more than moderately clear*, or else he is incapable of noticing the divergences between his idea of it and the reality, and thus of identifying them and rectifying them.

In my view it is no proof of skill to manage with few rehearsals, since it is always done at the cost of the work. What is a proof of skill is to have the material for many rehearsals, to go on being dissatisfied with oneself and the others, always finding a way of improving something more, not being able to bring oneself to present a thing until one has brought it as close to perfection as possible.

That is an ideal, and I cannot admit the existence of any of the higher moral and artistic qualities in those practical people who contrive to come to terms with things more easily.

Yes, you're right when you say in your letter that you were royally rewarded for all your trouble, for in art a good servant finds a good master; anyone who gives service worthy of a king is rewarded in kingly fashion; but anyone to whom time — rehearsal time — is money shall ever be rewarded with no more than money (which may, after all, please him more), and it is fitting that he should save time in order to make money, for his time will soon be over, and if by then he hasn't at least *money* . . . . !

[1] Paul Scheinpflug had conducted the *Gurrelieder* in Duisburg.

AETAT 47 *To Marie Gutheil-Schoder*

Your very kind letters have made me more sorry than ever not to have been able to hear this performance. It is especially the very kind and cordial tone in which you write that has given me an idea of your musical qualities! Please accept my heartfelt thanks for all the goodness and kindness you have shown towards my work and myself. I am not really dismayed at not being able to thank you properly for your trouble, your achievement, and your devotion; for the fact that the *royal* reward comes from within oneself is something I know too well from my own experience not to rejoice with you on that account, and not to know that one no longer needs another's thanks when one has already received the best thanks there are. Please do also convey my very warm thanks to the many others who contributed and gave me of their best for so long.

[. . . . .]

ARNOLD SCHÖNBERG

44. TO BERNARD SCHUSTER[1] *Traunkirchen, 31 July 1922*

Dear Herr Kapellmeister Schuster,

I congratulate you very warmly indeed on the revival of 'Musik'. It was sadly missed in these grievous years, and I hope, indeed fervently wish, that it may turn out as distinguished as it was.

I gladly promise that as soon as I have something for publication again I shall think *first* of 'Musik'. With kind regards, Yours sincerely,

ARNOLD SCHÖNBERG

45. TO MARIE GUTHEIL-SCHODER *Traunkirchen, 5 August 1922*

My dear Frau Gutheil,

It occurs to me again — for the 100th time — that you may be angry with me, and it impels me — at last I am doing it — to break off work and write to you. Please do not assume that I meant to treat you in any way badly, to offend you or hurt your feelings. Please do assume that there is some misunderstanding. I no longer recall exactly what happened, but I did discuss the whole thing in detail with Stein[2] at the time and shall ask him to refresh my mind about it so that I can explain to you. Believe me, nothing is further from me than an attitude

[1] The editor of the well-known Berlin music periodical, *Musik*.
[2] Frau Gutheil had in the autumn of 1921 begun studying the *Sprechstimme* in *Pierrot lunaire* with the editor of this selection of Schoenberg's letters. But since she could not find enough time to rehearse, Frau Erika Wagner was engaged for the performances due to be given by the Society for Private Concerts.

To Marie Gutheil-Schoder   AUGUST 1922

that could call forth your disapproval; there is nothing I wish more than to keep my good old friendship with you as untarnished as my admiration for you, which is ever new, ever the same.

Do trust me: I am not deceitful!

Now I hope you are well-disposed to me again, or at least neutral, and have regained my peace of mind.

With warmest, devoted regards, Yours sincerely,

                                                        ARNOLD SCHÖNBERG

46. TO MARYA FREUND[1]   *Traunkirchen, 16 August* 1922

My dear Frau Freund,

We expected you — alas, in vain — all day on Sunday and Monday. (Incidentally, I had written to you (via Honegger) a week before the 'Music Festival'.) I am delighted to hear that you are now coming to Traunkirchen after all, in about a week. What a pity, though, that you are thinking of staying only *one* day. It would be nice, and also useful, if you could stay a little longer. There are a number of things regarding the performance of my works that I should like to talk over with you. I am anxious to explain to you why I cannot allow any will but mine to prevail in realising the musical thoughts that I have recorded on paper, and why realising them must be done in such deadly earnest, with such inexorable severity, because the composing was done just that way. I should very much like to do some thorough rehearsing with you, so that you should get to know the way to solve the musical picture-puzzles that my works constitute. I am quite convinced that you will soon feel at home with them: you would only have to hear it once directly from me [..........]

                                                        ARNOLD SCHÖNBERG

47. TO JOSEF STRANSKY[2]   *Traunkirchen, 23 August* 1922

Dear Herr Kapellmeister Stransky,

What a pity I missed seeing you in Mödling!

So far I have arranged 2 Bach chorale preludes. These are No. 35 (Peters edition), 'Come, God, Creator, Holy Ghost', for large orchestra, and No. 49, 'Adorn thyself, O my soul', for solo 'cello and large orchestra.

It is uncertain whether I shall do anything more of this kind in the immediate future, but it is not quite impossible.

[1] The singer.
[2] The conductor of the Philharmonic Orchestra, New York.

AETAT 47   *To Fräulein Goldbecker*

I should be very pleased to let you have these pieces for performance and should therefore like to know: 1. if you care to have them. 2. if you are absolutely set on having the rights for the first performance (for since I did not hear from you, I have already more or less given my consent to Zemlinsky in Prague and Webern in Vienna, without however being bound by this, since neither of them insists on first-performance rights and both merely need to know the date). 3. In the event of your wishing to give the first performance, please inform me of the date of the concert. . . . . . .

Would you not like to look at scores of works by Dr. Anton von Webern and Alban Berg, two real musicians — not Bolshevik illiterates, but men with a musically educated ear!

U.E.[1] have published a Passacaglia of Webern's that has been repeatedly performed with unmitigated success and which is not yet such a 'dangerous' work.* Among Berg's things there are three very interesting orchestral pieces: 'Reigen' (Round Dances), approximating to the dance, but *quite* modern. They are unpublished and unperformed. [. . . . .]

                                                         ARNOLD SCHÖNBERG

* also several series of orchestral pieces and orchestral songs. [S.]

48. TO FRÄULEIN GOLDBECKER   *Traunkirchen*, 31 *August* 1922
Dear Fräulein Goldbecker,

Not merely for the sake of responding to your mode of address, but rather because from your letter and the intentions that gave rise to it one receives the picture of a dear and kind lady, one feels moved to begin at once by saying something especially in kindness to you. So then: Dear and kind Fräulein Goldbecker, your letter gave me much pleasure, and it is possible for a musician to feel pleasure only when he sees that music — perhaps, indeed, his own — has enabled another human being to live in a dream world, and when from that dream world greetings come to him and a wish is sent to him that is a wish not in that it demands anything but in that it grants, wishing only that what others wish may be fulfilled, and contents itself with going on dreaming about that in as much detail as possible (and, for that reason, agreeably).

I shall gladly see to it that this dream becomes as much reality as possible and therefore shall pass on your donation as you wish. I am sending it to two young musicians,[2] both as poor as they are gifted, as

[1] Universal Edition, Vienna.
[2] Hanns Eisler and Karl Rankl, both at that time Schoenberg's pupils. See the following letter.

To Fräulein Goldbecker   AUGUST 1922

ardent as they are sensitive, and as intelligent as they are imaginative, so that they will be truly encouraged by your gift and in their gratitude worthy of the giver's delight in giving. They will write to you in a few days.

    Once more with warmest thanks, dear Fräulein Goldbecker,
                Yours sincerely,
                            ARNOLD SCHÖNBERG

49. TO HANNS EISLER[1]   *Traunkirchen, 31 August 1922*

Dear Eisler,

Letter enclosed[2] from a nice probably very ill person whose relatives presumably keep her in the dark about present-day conditions (perhaps in order not to agitate her) and who therefore has no notion of the value of money. I shouldn't like to destroy her dream, so I haven't made the slightest attempt to explain the situation to her; on the contrary, I have written to say that I am passing on the *sum* to two musicians (you and Rankl). Please *both* write her a short and cordial letter (not too fulsome, lest she suspect something). Really tactfully; write and say what you are working at, briefly, but in such a way as to interest her.

Perhaps you will both send me the drafts of your letters. But it must be done quickly; even before you get the money, otherwise it'll drag on too long.

Return the enclosed letter to me.

I shall write to you in a few days about the matter of your lessons.
                            ARNOLD SCHÖNBERG

50. TO PIERRE FERROUD[3]   *Traunkirchen, 31 August 1922*

Dear Herr Ferroud,

I shall gladly provide all the answers required and only ask you to give score-references for specific questions. Unless I am mistaken, I have throughout entered metronome markings in the score, which give a good picture of the *tempi*.

The main difficulty in the chamber symphony is the great amount of

---

[1] See note 2 to Letter 48.

[2] See the previous letter to Fräulein Goldbecker, who had got in touch with Schoenberg on her own initiative. She obviously knew nothing of the inflation in Austria, for her donation amounted to a very small sum owing to the depreciation in the value of money. Many of the following letters, written in 1922/23, reflect the hardships caused by the inflation.

[3] Composer and music critic, Paris.

AETAT 48 *To H. Hinrichsen*

polyphony. In order to cope with this one must pay very careful attention indeed to getting *all* dynamic signs (from *ppp* to *fff*, etc.,) rendered as exactly as possible. What is particularly important, however, is the *p* in the *fp*. This *piano* is *much more important* than the *forte*, since otherwise all the instruments would be swamped. It is therefore advisable to have *individual, separate* rehearsals; the best would be to have a *solo-*rehearsal with each player, in order to reach an exact understanding with him as to how he is to play.

[..........]

After having, as I hope, answered all your questions, I should just like to say that I was delighted with your very *kind* letter. With all my heart I wish you luck in your splendid undertaking. It would give me much pleasure to get to know your own music, too. Has anything yet been published?

Please remember me cordially to your teacher, Florent Schmitt.

With very kind regards,

ARNOLD SCHÖNBERG

51. TO JOSEF STRANSKY *Traunkirchen, 9 September* 1922

Dear Herr Kapellmeister Stransky,

Kindly conduct all further negotiations regarding my Bach arrangements with Direktor Hertzka (Universal Edition).[1]

I am much more in the habit of refusing requests even when made in fitting terms; I often give orders, but never take them; and I make a special point of never doing business: not merely because I dread everything connected with it, but: because nothing brings people so close together as business. My own taste, however, is for keeping my distance.

[..........]

ARNOLD SCHÖNBERG

52. TO HERR HINRICHSEN[2] 29 *September* 1922

Dear Herr Hinrichsen,

What you are doing is all splendid and pleases me very much indeed. In this case, after all, it really isn't a matter of actual mistakes, but

---

[1] See Letter 47. Schoenberg was indignant at the tone of Stransky's letter of 6th September, which said: 'Give orders for the material to be copied at once. The performance in New York *must* be given at the beginning of November.... So it means making all haste....'

[2] Proprietor of the publishing house C. F. Peters ('Edition Peters'). The letter refers to Peters' publication of Schoenberg's *Five Pieces for Orchestra*, op. 16.

To H. Hinrichsen SEPTEMBER 1922

simply of improvements, making the work easier to understand. I am very grateful to you for tackling it in such a thorough manner and for not shrinking from the expense in these difficult times.

Please do convey my warmest thanks to your proof-reader for having taken on this laborious job of making a list of errors. It has really been done with the utmost care. If you think it fitting and not too 'feudal' a gesture (and I am, I'm sorry to say, far from resembling a feudal lord), I would ask you to give him the enclosed card.* [1]

Of conductors — you asked about this — who have performed the Orchestral Pieces I can (off-hand) mention only some: Wood (London), Stokowski (Philadelphia), Damrosch, Stransky (New York), Stock (America?), Concertgebouw (Amsterdam), Paris — I can't recall either the names or the orchestras. Boston and Chicago, also San Francisco, were, I think among them. Also some (?) in Germany — as yet *none* in Austria — Zemlinsky (Prague).

With many kindest regards and all good wishes,
I am, yours very sincerely,
ARNOLD SCHÖNBERG

* May I also enclose one for you? [S.]

53. TO EDGAR VARÈSE[2] *Mödling, 23 October* 1922
Dear Herr Varèse,

I hope you received my telegram saying that I do not know your objects. But that is not the only reason why for the present I cannot join. There are also several others:

I: Above all: from your manifesto and the programmes of three concerts I gather that you have hitherto attached no importance to German music. No single German among 27 composers performed! So then you have been international to the exclusion of the Germans!

II. What offends me equally, however, is that without asking me whether you *can and may* do so you simply set a definitive date for my 'Pierrot lunaire'. But do you even know whether you can manage it? Have you already got a suitable speaker [*Sprecherin*]; a violinist, a pianist, a conductor ... etc.? How many rehearsals do you mean to hold, etc... etc.? In Vienna, with everyone starving and shivering, something like 100 rehearsals were held and an impeccable ensemble achieved with my collaboration. But you people simply fix a date and

[1] Probably a photograph.
[2] The composer, chairman of the International Composers' Guild. He had asked Schoenberg to join the Guild.

think that's all there is to it! Have you any inkling of the difficulties, of the style; of the declamation; of the *tempi*; of the dynamics and all that? And you expect me to associate myself with it? No; I'm not *smart** enough for that! If you want to have anything to do with me, you must set about it quite differently. What I want to know is: 1. How many rehearsals? 2. Who is in charge of rehearsals? 3. Who does the *Sprechstimme*? 4. Who are the players? If all this is to my satisfaction, I shall give my blessing. But for the rest I am, of course, powerless and you can do as you like. But then kindly refrain from asking me about it.

I regret not being able to say anything more obliging. But I must reject this exclusively business approach. I sincerely hope that another time I may have occasion to be more cordial.[1]

ARNOLD SCHÖNBERG

54. TO ALEXANDER ZEMLINSKY[2] *Mödling, 26 October 1922*
Dear Alex,

The day before yesterday I wrote to you, about the Society[3] among other things, and now here today I get a letter from you: with reproaches. What I don't know above all is: are these aimed at the President of the Vienna Society or the Honorary President of the Prague Society?[4] As I know from 'very well informed quarters', the former's decisions were indisputably independent; I therefore assume that you people are not addressing yourself to the President of my Society, but merely to the Honorary President of yours, whose position has, I must admit, always been somewhat obscure to me, becoming still more obscure as a result of these reproaches. As I know, however, from the quarters above-mentioned, he too hasn't taken his task at all lightly; has done far more than what he formally agreed to do; in so far as he is at all capable of learning from the bitter lessons of the past, he has brought to the arrangements for this programme all the experience gained in years of organising concerts; went on changing and revising all these arrangements down to the last detail until finally they seemed to him such as to be in keeping with all the Society's principles and in part to express them, and is doing more than was required by the agree-

---

* Schoenberg here uses the English word, obviously in the then modish German sense of 'quick to take advantage', 'ingenious to the point of dishonesty', 'slick'. [TRANS.]
[1] Schoenberg and Varèse subsequently became friends.
[2] See note 1 to Letter 38.
[3] The Society for Private Concerts.
[4] Schoenberg was President of the Vienna Society and Honorary President of the Prague Society.

To Alexander Zemlinsky OCTOBER 1922

ment. The undersigned Honorary President of the Prague Soc. f. Pr. Con. has three witnesses to this: 1. the ordinary President of the Viennese Soc. f. Pr. Con., 2. the two musical directors of the Vienna Soc. f. Pr. Con., Erwin Stein and Anton Webern.

With reference to the matter itself I should like to let the following figures speak: In our prospectus of Nov. 1921 you will find, on page 2, the figures on which our discussions were based. I noted that although you wish for repeats in Prague, you do not consider such frequent ones possible.

I. Thus, if in Vienna we had 151 first performances among 360 items in the programmes of 112 concerts, 209 were repeats (360–151).

II. Accordingly the figures in Prague should be: in 10 concerts (112/11): first performances (151/11): 13 (–14); repeats (209/11); 19; total of programme items (360/11): 32 (–33).

III. So far we have had 4 concerts: at these we performed 15 items. Of these the first performances were: 12; repeats 3.

[..........]

I think these figures speak for themselves: If we repeat only half as much, we might well do 10 works twice; but, taking 32 works as the basis, we shall be repeating only 6·4 works. Here it must also be borne in mind that the Prague programmes are from $\frac{1}{3}$ to $\frac{1}{2}$ *longer* than the Vienna programmes, which as rule have *at the most* 90 minutes of music. Thus the repeats are here to be regarded *purely as something 'thrown in'*. Just as people once used to demand a 'da capo', so here, where it is universally not demanded, but for educational reasons, for the sake of which the Society exists, repetition is included in the programme from the very first. It would be a very good thing if you would keep on telling your members this! People will, after all, put up with everything, even with what is good and right, if one can only talk them into it. Perhaps one must give them to understand that it is wrong, or beautiful, or high-flown?

Now as to the 'insignificant' Milhaud. I don't agree. Milhaud strikes me as the most important representative of the contemporary movement in all Latin countries: polytonality. Whether I like him is not to the point. But I consider him very talented. But that is not a question for the Society, which sets out *only to inform*. It was actually primarily on your own account that I did Milhaud once again, hoping that he would interest you. — Reger must in my view be done often; 1, because he has written a lot; 2, because he is already dead and people are still not clear about him. (I consider him a genius.)

[..........]

AETAT 48 *To Marya Freund*

We are concerned about your not being well. Still, it's reassuring to hear that it has taken you so long to decide to see a doctor: so far, at least, no one has done you any harm! We hope you'll very soon be quite all right. [..........]

ARNOLD SCHÖNBERG

55. TO PAUL VON KLENAU[1] *Mödling, 13 November* 1922

Dear Herr von Klenau,

Very many thanks indeed for your kind letter. I am much looking forward to conducting my chamber symphony under your auspices on the 30th January 1923 and agree, furthermore, to all the terms you mention. Especially that I can have as many rehearsals as necessary! Then I can, I suppose, have as many as ten? But if the gentlemen of the orchestra prepare well on their own beforehand, I am sure to be able to manage with less (probably 7–8). Of course, in that event each of them would have to have worked out each rhythm with the utmost exactitude (mathematically!), to have got all the dynamic and technical aspect beyond reproach and perfectly under control, and to have achieved very pure tone. Then I shall need still fewer rehearsals. But I know quite well it's idle to expect that. In my experience only the best musicians are capable of preparing in such a way, and all instrumentalists, no matter how good they may be, learn only at rehearsals. In any case it would be a good thing to draw the attention of the gentlemen of the orchestra to the fact it is *chamber music* and must therefore be *played very exactly*, because every note can be heard! — As for the fee, I put myself entirely in your hands. [..........] The dates of the rehearsals and so forth we shall, I dare say, be able to decide later. It will also have to be decided whether anything else is to be done and, if so, what. — I hope we shall meet soon! When is your concert? Won't you come and see me again? I should also like you to hear our Pierrot-rehearsing. About the visa I shall doubtless hear direct from Copenhagen.

Hoping to see you soon, I am, with kind regards, [..........]

ARNOLD SCHÖNBERG

56. TO MARYA FREUND[2] *Mödling, 30 December* 1922

Frau Marya Freund, Paris

[..........]

What you write about the last Paris performance of Pierrot[3] perturbs me. In Geneva and Amsterdam I notice for the first time that

[1] The Danish composer and conductor. [2] See Letter 46.
[3] *Pierrot lunaire* contains 21 poems, among which are those named.

To Marya Freund DECEMBER 1922

'Madonna', 'Red Mass' and also 'Crosses' somehow give religious offence. Such a possibility never before crossed my mind and nothing was ever further from me in all my life than any such intention, since I have never at any time in my life been anti-religious, indeed have never really been un-religious either. I seem to have had an altogether much naiver view of these poems than most people have and am still not quite uncertain that this is entirely unjustified [sic]. Anyway I am not responsible for what people make up their minds to read into the words. If they were musical, not a single one of them would give a damn for the words. Instead, they would go away whistling the tunes. But as it is, the modern musical public understands at best the WORDS, while for the rest it remains completely deaf to music — on that point no amount of success in the world can delude me.

Now for once I've written to you at length. And that is because my pupils have given me a typewriter for Christmas. Now I dare say I shall for a while write somewhat more frequent letters.[1]

Now to conclude by reciprocating with all my heart, and also on behalf of my wife and children, your good wishes for the New Year.

MUCH HAPPINESS AND MUCH SUCCESS in the New Year!

To our next meeting before long, first in Copenhagen and then perhaps in Prague too!

My kindest regards to my friends, as to yourself.

ARNOLD SCHÖNBERG

57. TO THE SOCIETY FOR PRIVATE CONCERTS IN PRAGUE[2]

Mödling, 14 *January* 1923

For the attention of the Secretary, Georg Alter

I ought probably to have informed the Prague Soc. for P.C. some time ago that I have agreed with Herr Erwin Stein that I shall leave the direction of the Vienna Society, and thus also all business on behalf of the Prague Society, to him, entirely at his discretion, in the same way as I did on one occasion previously, during my visit to Holland. My main reason for hitherto refraining from communicating this decision to you was that, being constantly in touch with Herr Stein personally, I have in any case continued to have a very considerable influence on all decisions in the Society's affairs. Recently, however, its claims on my attention

---

[1] From the beginning of 1923 the letters are typed, unless otherwise stated.
[2] See Letter 38.

AETAT 48 *To Alexander Zemlinsky*

increased to such an extent that there was no time left for my own concerns: my work.[1] So I had to retire.

Naturally I shall not withdraw my interest from the Society, which I founded myself! But neither the Vienna nor the Prague Society can any longer expect me to do any work for it. I am very sorry that your Society will henceforth have an Honorary President who is no use at all. But for this very reason I mean to try and polish up the lustre of my name: by trying to write some new works.

ARNOLD SCHÖNBERG

58. To ALEXANDER ZEMLINSKY *Mödling*, 12 *February* 1923
Dear Alex,

I am engaged in some work for the first third of which, for financial reasons, I have allowed myself one month, which will be up in about three weeks from now. If I were to break off at that point, which I should gladly do in order to be able to come and see you again in Prague, I could, always assuming that I don't get behind with the job, set out on the 4th March at the earliest, in other words be ready for a performance by about the 20th.

Frankly, however, I shouldn't at all care to risk such an interruption, for I have very often found that it may be fatal to me (e.g., 'Jacob's Ladder') to lose the thread. In this case it is not only that I ought to get something finished again at long last after so many disturbances, but also a matter of a, for me, very large fee to be paid me for 2 works that are only just begun. Now, Hertzka has waived his rights in this case solely on condition that I deliver him 2 works, which are, however, still further from completion. So I have to compose 4 works: 2 series of piano pieces, of which not much more than half is finished, the serenade, with 6–7 movements of which 3 are almost finished and 3 sketched out, or rather, begun, and a septet for strings or a violin concerto, both of which are also only just begun. So there's a long road ahead of me, and I should be glad to get the money soon, so long as it still has any value at all.[2]

[1] The Presidency of the Society had taken up excessively much of Schoenberg's time. The Society soon went out of existence as a result of the progressive decline in the value of money.
[2] The four works turned out to be: *Five Pieces for Piano*, op. 23; *Serenade*, op. 24; *Suite for Piano*, op. 25; and Quintet for Wind Instruments, op. 26. The first two works were published by Wilhelm Hansen, Copenhagen, the other two by Universal Edition, Vienna. Opp. 25 and 26 are the first works written according to Schoenberg's technique of 'twelve-note composition'.

To Alexander Zemlinsky   FEBRUARY 1923

Apart from this, I want without fail to come to the performance of 'Erwartung' ['Expectation'] and find it humiliating that your Herr Kramer,[1] who can pay fees to Strauss and others, offers me only my expenses. I should in no circumstances accept this. If Herr Kramer can make a profit out of me, then let him pay, let him pay exactly as much as everyone else pays everyone else. If he cannot make a profit out of me, then I shall gladly come without receiving any recompense, for the sake of seeing you and yours. Of course I should then be delighted if you would conduct, for not only is it very instructive and pleasant for me to hear my works conducted by you and to be able to attend your rehearsals, but I also realise how valuable it is when someone of your authority, your standing with the orchestra and the public, identifies himself with the work, while I am all the more at the mercy of the wild beasts because they would think your not conducting meant you had refused: 'Even his own brother-in-law doesn't like the stuff!'

I should very much like to hear this performance, I should very much like to see you all; but I think it better for me to come all the more definitely to 'Erwartung', to my own to-the-utmost-tensed expectation.[2]

[. . . . .]

                                                       ARNOLD SCHÖNBERG

59. TO ERWIN STEIN[3]   *Mödling*, 1 *March* 1923

Dear Stein,

Some time ago you got someone to ask if I was angry. I am very sorry about your accident[4] and am certainly very sympathetic; nevertheless I cannot deny that it was absolutely wrong of you (and from this point of view I am naturally very angry with you) to go off on a journey in that state, leaving the matters entrusted to you [. . . . .] in the lurch. I fail to understand how you could bring yourself to risk all that and your own reputation and my trust in you, without thinking of the very probable danger that you might very well not yet have got over your injury: I was really horrified when you rang up to tell me you were going away, and began to make some kind of protest, but you didn't catch what I said and I couldn't make myself repeat it, in order not to be perpetually playing the big bow-wow — still, I think you must have noticed — even if you hadn't thought the same thing yourself!

[1] Director of the German Theatre in Prague.
[2] The performance under discussion was that of the *Five Pieces for Orchestra* to be given in April. The performance of *Erwartung* did not take place until the following year.
[3] The editor of these letters.
[4] A knee injury that long remained troublesome.

AETAT 48 *To Professor Bandler*

But what am I to do about you now? Although you don't ask it, there's obviously nothing for it but to forgive you! Very well then: perhaps you've paid dearly enough by now anyway. Of course I'm awfully sorry about that, and apart from the pain, I can imagine it must be frightful being chair-bound, even if one has a sturdy conscience.

[..........]

I'll tell you about Copenhagen when we meet in Vienna. I at least was very satisfied; more than usual, for I was dealing with very charming people. Besides, I have come back with a very satisfactory offer from the Hansen publishing company, which looks as though it will almost certainly come to something. — One thing, though: those were better days when you were able to accompany me on such journeys. We shan't see them again; but you mustn't forget that you could only do it because you were young; apart from money, it couldn't be done nowadays anyway, because every older man has someone else to think of besides himself!

[..........]

ARNOLD SCHÖNBERG

60. TO PROFESSOR HEINRICH BANDLER[1] *Mödling, 2 February* 1923

Dear Herr Professor Bandler,

Many thanks for the very kind invitation to perform Pierrot with your ensemble. I'm afraid I can't accept it at the moment, but that does not mean I am saying no. For perhaps in the meantime conditions will have changed for the better. Today, I must admit, I make every effort to avoid such opportunities as that proposed. For I do not care to become the victim of politicians whose taste for sensationalism does not draw the line even at real art; if even before the war I had no liking for exposing myself to the judgment of those who hiss in places where, whatever one may say, at least supposedly artistic interests were to some extent being supported, nowadays, when it is certain to be solely a matter of politics, I have less wish than ever to offer myself as a victim. All the more because I do not wish completely to deny the justification for such politics.

But by then the times will perhaps have changed, perhaps people will have calmed down again at least enough to make it possible for one to speak to them again as if to human beings. Then I shall very gladly come and also declare my agreement with the terms you have proposed.

[1] Leader of the Hamburg Philharmonic Orchestra and also of a string quartet known by his name.

To Professor Bandler   FEBRUARY 1923

I am gladly prepared to conduct in Germany without a fee, because nowadays Germany cannot pay. And even if I do not happen to be precisely the person who earned particularly high fees as a conductor in Germany before the war, I do think one must never forget what Germany did for art while it was still in a position to do so.

[..........]

                                                                 ARNOLD SCHÖNBERG

61. TO PAUL STEFAN[1]   *Mödling, 24 April 1923*

Dear Dr. Stefan,

I have suggested Herr Hauer (Josef Matthias) among others to the 'Friends' Relief Mission' and am now asked for his address, which I do not know. Can you let me have it, or will you write directly to the F.R.M.?

I have a bone to pick with you, Herr Biograph!*

You translate (with salutations to Casella that are linguistically impossible and themselves need to be translated; one can translate with a sense of language or with belly-ache, or even with the aid of a dictionary; but not the way you go about it!) an article on this composer in which the portrayal of Casella's greatness is effected particularly by means of reducing me in stature.[2] And this, Herr Biograph, with your assistance and with the collaboration of your salutations. And as if that were not enough, you actually go and publish this in Anbruch, where it should surely be easy for you, Herr Biobaron, to tell the author of this article that a certain Herr Schönberg, on the point of being biobeknighted by you, is sacrosanct, and that it must surely be possible, considering the undoubtedly existent greatness of Herr Casella, to represent that greatness even if I remain great; because it may after all be that Herr C.'s is an absolute greatness only when it is independent of any relation to me. This since (Herr Bio-Prince) I am much too unimportant for others to need to compare themselves with me!

But now seriously: I find the whole thing utterly impossible. You know that although I thoroughly detest criticism (and have only con-

---

[1] Dr. Paul Stefan, writer on music and editor of the journal *Musikblätter des Anbruch*, Vienna, wished to become Schoenberg's biographer.

* I.e., Mister Biographer. There is no means of translating the pun 'Biograf' (Graf = count, earl), on which Schoenberg then embroiders. [TRANS.]

[2] The article (in *Musikblätter des Anbruch*, March 1920) contains the passage: '... the nature of Casella's art is as far removed from the impressionism of a Debussy as from the barbarism of a Stravinsky and the cerebralism of Schoenberg.' At the end of the article there is a note saying: 'Freely translated, with salutations to Casella from Paul Stefan'.

tempt for anyone who finds the slightest fault with anything I publish: this, you see, Herr Bio-Duke, is my rank of nobility: the fact that I believe what I do and only do what I believe; and woe to anyone who lays hands on my faith. Such a man I regard as an enemy, and no quarter given! You cannot keep in with me if you also get on with my opponents. I tell you this in all seriousness, now, in good time, when you can still withdraw from the biography or from compromising friendships.

Don't wait until it is too late! — it is only here that I end the long parenthesis begun above), I am nevertheless utterly indifferent to what is said about me. Whether good or bad is said about me in Anbruch is a matter of such indifference to me that I cannot even summon up the enthusiasm to try to find an epithet for this indifference. But I do not associate with those who cannot think rightly about me. And you would certainly not be able to remain a bio-nobleman acknowledged by me, but would decline into a bio-burgher, butcher, beggarman, if your artistic faith were in fief elsewhere.

Do you too only what you believe if you want to uphold your bio-nobility!

Perhaps nobody has ever yet said such things to you. But perhaps some day you will thank me for it.

Meanwhile yours etc.,

ARNOLD SCHÖNBERG

62. To Professor Wilhelm Klatte, Berlin

Mödling, 24 April 1923

Dear Sir,

On the 17th March I wrote to you expressing my thanks and accepting with much pleasure the invitation to join the German and Austrian Honorary Committee for the American Relief Fund for German and Austrian Musicians.[1] At the same time I asked to be informed when and to what address I should send statements of cases of extreme need in Austria. Perhaps you have not yet received my letter or have not yet had time to have an answer sent. May I therefore herewith inform you of some cases of need known to me? It goes without saying that I personally vouch unreservedly for the artistic worthiness of those concerned, as also for the genuineness of their need.

[1] The aim of the Fund was to give material help to musicians suffering especial hardship as a result of post-war conditions and the inflation then prevailing in Austria and Germany.

To Professor Wilhelm Klatte APRIL 1923

The names are:

Alban Berg, composer, Vienna XIII, Trautmannsdorfgasse 27; Dr. Anton von Webern, composer, Mödling near Vienna, Neusiedlerstrasse 58; Josef Matthias Hauer, composer and musicologist, whose present address I do not know at the moment but shall have in a few days.

I can also supply further suggestions, but have for the moment mentioned those that appear to me most urgent.

[..........]

ARNOLD SCHÖNBERG

63. TO WASSILY KANDINSKY[1] *Mödling, 20 April 1923*

Dear Herr Kandinsky,

If I had received your letter a year ago I should have let all my principles go hang, should have renounced the prospect of at last being free to compose, and should have plunged headlong into the adventure. Indeed I confess: even today I wavered for a moment: so great is my taste for teaching, so easily is my enthusiasm still inflamed. But it cannot be.

For I have at last learnt the lesson that has been forced upon me during this year, and I shall not ever forget it. It is that I am not a German, not a European, indeed perhaps scarcely even a human being (at least, the Europeans prefer the worst of their race to me), but I am a Jew.

I am content that it should be so! Today I no longer wish to be an exception; I have no objection at all to being lumped together with all the rest. For I have seen that on the other side (which is otherwise no model so far as I'm concerned, far from it) everything is also just one lump. I have seen that someone with whom I thought myself on a level preferred to seek the community of the lump; I have heard that even a Kandinsky sees only evil in the actions of Jews and in their evil actions only the Jewishness, and at this point I give up the hope of reaching any understanding. It was a dream. We are two kinds of people. Definitively!

So you will realise that I only do whatever is necessary to keep alive. Perhaps some day a later generation will be in a position to indulge in dreams. I wish it neither for them nor for myself. On the contrary, in-

---

[1] Kandinsky, who had been on terms of close friendship with Schoenberg before the first world war, had asked him to come to Weimar to help in founding an artistic and intellectual centre at the Bauhaus there. Schoenberg had heard it said that there were antisemitic tendencies among members of the Bauhaus.

deed, I would give much that it might be granted to me to bring about an awakening.

I should like the Kandinsky I knew in the past and the Kandinsky of today each to take his fair share of my cordial and respectful greetings.

ARNOLD SCHÖNBERG

64. To WASSILY KANDINSKY *Mödling*, 4 *May* 1923

Dear Kandinsky,

I address you so because you wrote that you were deeply moved by my letter. That was what I hoped of Kandinsky, although I have not yet said a hundredth part of what a Kandinsky's imagination must conjure up before his mind's eye if he is to be my Kandinsky! Because I have not yet said that for instance when I walk along the street and each person looks at me to see whether I'm a Jew or a Christian, I can't very well tell each of them that I'm the one that Kandinsky and some others make an exception of, although of course that man Hitler is not of their opinion. And then even this benevolent view of me wouldn't be much use to me, even if I were, like blind beggars, to write it on a piece of cardboard and hang it round my neck for everyone to read. Must not a Kandinsky bear that in mind? Must not a Kandinsky have an inkling of what really happened when I had to break off my first working summer for 5 years, leave the place I had sought out for peace to work in, and afterwards couldn't regain the peace of mind to work at all?[1] Because the Germans will not put up with Jews! Is it possible for a Kandinsky to be of more or less one mind with others instead of with me? But is it possible for him to have even a single thought in common with HUMAN BEINGS who are capable of disturbing the peace in which I want to work? Is it a thought at all that one can have in common with such people? And: can it be right? It seems to me: Kandinsky cannot possibly have even such a thing as geometry in common with them! That is not his position, or he does not stand where I stand!

I ask: Why do people say that the Jews are like what their black-marketeers are like?

Do people also say that the Aryans are like their worst elements? Why is an Aryan judged by Goethe, Schopenhauer and so forth? Why don't people say the Jews are like Mahler, Altenberg, Schönberg and many others?

Why, if you have a feeling for human beings, are you a politician?

---

[1] Schoenberg had gone to spend the summer in Mattsee, Salzburg, where he was given to understand that Jews were not welcome.

To Wassily Kandinsky   MAY 1923

When a politician is, after all, someone who must not take any count of the human being but simply keep his eyes fixed on his party's aims?

What every Jew reveals by his hooked nose is not only his own guilt but also that of all those with hooked noses who don't happen to be there too. But if a hundred Aryan criminals are all together, all that anyone will be able to read from their noses is their taste for alcohol, while for the rest they will be considered respectable people.

And you join in that sort of thing and 'reject me as a Jew'. Did I ever offer myself to you? Do you think that someone like myself lets himself be rejected! Do you think that a man who knows his own value grants anyone the right to criticise even his most trivial qualities? Who might it be, anyway, who could have such a right? In what way would he be better? Yes, everyone is free to criticise me behind my back, there's plenty of room there. But if I come to hear of it he is liable to my retaliation, and no quarter given.

How can a Kandinsky approve of my being insulted; how can he associate himself with politics that aim at bringing about the possibility of excluding me from my natural sphere of action; how can he refrain from combating a view of the world whose aim is St. Bartholomew's nights in the darkness of which no one will be able to read the little placard saying that I'm exempt! I, myself, if I had any say in the matter, would, in a corresponding case, associate myself with a view of the world that maintains for the world the right view of the 2–3 Kandinskys that the world produces in a century — I should be of the opinion that only such a view of the world would do for me. And I should leave the pogroms to the others. That is, if I couldn't do anything to stop them!

You will call it a regrettable individual case if I too am affected by the results of the antisemitic movement. But why do people not see the bad Jew as a regrettable individual case, instead of as what's typical? In the small circle of my own pupils, immediately after the war, almost all the Aryans had not been on active service, but had got themselves cushy jobs. On the other hand, almost all the Jews had seen active service and been wounded. How about the individual cases there?

But it isn't an individual case, that is, it isn't merely accidental. On the contrary, it is all part of a plan that, after first not being respected on the ordinary conventional road, I now have to go the long way round through politics into the bargain. Of course: these people, to whom my music and my ideas were a nuisance, could only be delighted to find there is now one more chance of getting rid of me for the time being. My artistic success leaves me cold, you know that. But I won't let myself be insulted!

AETAT 48 *To Wassily Kandinsky*

What have I to do with Communism? I'm not one and never was one! What have I to do with the Elders of Zion? All that means to me is the title of a fairy-tale out of a Thousand and One Nights, but not one that refers to anything remotely as worthy of belief.

Wouldn't I too necessarily know something of the Elders of Zion? Or do you think that I owe my discoveries, my knowledge and skill, to Jewish machinations in high places? Or does Einstein owe his to a commission from the Elders of Zion?

I don't understand it. For all that won't stand up to serious examination. And didn't you have plenty of chance in the war to notice how much official lying is done, indeed that official talk is all lies. How our brain, in its attempt to be objective, shuts down on the prospect of truth for ever. Didn't you know that or have you forgotten?

Have you also forgotten how much disaster can be evoked by a particular mode of feeling? Don't you know that in peace-time everyone was horrified by a railway-accident in which four people were killed, and that during the war one could hear people talking about 100,000 dead without even trying to picture the misery, the pain, the fear, and the consequences? Yes, and that there were people who were delighted to read about as many enemy dead as possible; the more, the more so! I am no pacifist; being against war is as pointless as being against death. Both are inevitable, both depend only to the very slightest degree on ourselves, and are among the human race's methods of regeneration that have been invented not by us, but by higher powers. In the same way the shift in the social structure that is now going on isn't to be lodged to the guilty account of any individual. It is written in the stars and is an inevitable process. The middle classes were all too intent on ideals, no longer capable of fighting for anything, and that is why the wretched but robust elements are rising up out of the abysses of humanity in order to generate another sort of middle class, fit to exist. It's one that will buy a beautiful book printed on bad paper, and starve. This is the way it must be, and not otherwise — can one fail to see that?

And all this is what you want to prevent. And that's what you want to hold the Jews responsible for? I don't understand it!

Are all Jews Communists? You know as well as I do that that isn't so. I'm not one because I know there aren't enough of the things everyone wants to be shared out all round, but scarcely for a tenth. What there's enough of (misfortune, illness, beastliness, inefficiency and the like) is shared out anyway. Then, too, because I know that the subjective sense of happiness doesn't depend on possessions; it's a mysterious constitution that one either has or has not. And thirdly because this earth is a

To Wassily Kandinsky MAY 1923

vale of tears and not a place of entertainment, because, in other words, it is neither in the Creator's plan that all should fare equally well, nor, perhaps, has it any deeper meaning at all.

Nowadays all one needs is to utter some nonsense in scientifico-journalistic jargon, and the cleverest people take it for a revelation. The Elders of Zion — of course; it's the very name for modern films, scientific works, operettas, cabarets, in fact everything that nowadays keeps the intellectual world going round.

The Jews do business, as business men. But if they are a nuisance to their competitors, they are attacked; only not as business men, but as Jews. As what then are they to defend themselves? But I am convinced that they defend themselves merely as business men, and that the defence as Jews is only an apparent one. I.e., that their Aryan attackers defend themselves when attacked in just the same way, even though in somewhat other words and by adopting other (more attractive???) forms of hypocrisy; and that the Jews are not in the least concerned with beating their Christian competitors, but only with beating *competitors*! and that the Aryan ones are in exactly the same way out to beat *any* competitors; and that any association is thinkable among them if it leads to the goal, and every other contradiction. Nowadays it is race; another time I don't know what. And a Kandinsky will join in that sort of thing?

The great American banks have given money for Communism, not denying the fact. Do you know why? Mr. Ford will know that they aren't in a position to deny it: Perhaps if they did they would uncover some other fact much more inconvenient to them. For if it were true, someone would long ago have proved it is untrue.

WE KNOW ALL THAT! THAT'S THE VERY THING WE KNOW FROM OUR OWN EXPERIENCE! Trotsky and Lenin spilt rivers of blood (which, by the way, no revolution in the history of the world could ever avoid doing!), in order to turn a theory — false, it goes without saying (but which, like those of the philanthropists who brought about previous revolutions, was well meant) — into reality. It is a thing to be cursed and a thing that shall be punished, for he who sets his hand to such things must not make mistakes! But will people be better and happier if now, with the same fanaticism and just such streams of blood, other, though antagonistic, theories, which are nevertheless no more right (for they are of course all false, and only our belief endows them, from one instance to the next, with the shimmer of truth that suffices to delude us), are turned into reality?

But what is antisemitism to lead to if not to acts of violence? Is it so difficult to imagine that? You are perhaps satisfied with depriving Jews of their civil rights. Then certainly Einstein, Mahler, I and many others, will have been got rid of. But one thing is certain: they will not be able to exterminate those much tougher elements thanks to whose endurance Jewry has maintained itself unaided against the whole of mankind for 20 centuries. For these are evidently so constituted that they can accomplish the task that their God has imposed on them: To survive in exile, uncorrupted and unbroken, until the hour of salvation comes!

The antisemites are, after all, world-reforming busybodies with no more perspicacity and with just as little insight as the Communists. The good people are Utopians, and the bad people: business men.

I must make an end, for my eyes are aching from all this typing. . . . . . . I had to leave off for a few days and now see that morally and tactically speaking I made a very great mistake.

I was arguing! I was defending a position!

I forgot that it *is not a matter* of right and wrong, of truth and untruth, of understanding and blindness, but of power; and in such matters everyone seems to be blind, in hatred as blind as in love.

I forgot, it's no use arguing because of course I won't be listened to; because there is no will to understand, but only one not to hear what the other says.

If you will, read what I have written; but I do ask that you will not send me an argumentative answer. Don't make the same mistake as I made. I am trying to keep you from it by telling you:

I shall not understand you; I cannot understand you. Perhaps a few days ago I still hoped that my arguments might make some impression on you. Today I no longer believe that and feel it as almost undignified that I uttered any defence.

I wanted to answer your letter because I wanted to show you that for me, even in his new guise, Kandinsky is still there; and that I have not lost the respect for him that I once had. And if you would take it on yourself to convey greetings from me to my former friend Kandinsky, I should very much wish to charge you with some of my very warmest, but I should not be able to help adding this message:

We have not seen each other for a long time; who knows whether we shall ever see each other again; if it should, however, turn out that we do meet again, it would be sad if we had to be blind to each other.[1] So please pass on my most cordial greetings.

ARNOLD SCHÖNBERG

[1] Schoenberg and Kandinsky subsequently became friends again.

To Alma Mahler-Werfel MAY 1923

65. TO ALMA MAHLER-WERFEL *Mödling, 11 May* 1923

My very dear lady,

In my view you should not tell [——] and [——][1] that I've heard from you whose spiritual brothers they now are. What would suit them both best would be not to admit their guilt, but to make an accusation: against you! Anyone who is in the wrong looks for a chance to scream; don't give them that chance! Let them stammer and for the future say only things that everyone, and especially I, may hear of.

There's the point, besides, that I might really have happened to hear, even without your telling me, the way they now think in Weimar. There are five people I know there! But there are other ways in which I come to hear of everything that people are thinking: perhaps I haven't heard it first from you at all, but by means of my wireless connections! I should write to them:

'I know of the letter that Sch. wrote to Kand.! Why do you ask whether I told him about it? Are you trying to cover up? Are you afraid of Schönberg, who is the most helpless person one could possibly imagine, because he has never wanted to take revenge. Do you believe that opinions such as those you hold can be kept a secret? Sch. has no need to hear from me what you think: if he didn't guess it for himself, it would be borne to him on every wind that blows.'

Evidently you know only my first letter, but not the second. The latter is certainly even much stronger than the former, but it doesn't exclude the possibility of a reconciliation.

[..........]

ARNOLD SCHÖNBERG

66. TO PAUL PELLA *Mödling, 15 May* 1923

Dear Pella,

I am astonished to find that you don't take me more seriously. You must surely have realised that if I don't want to come to Berlin[2] it isn't merely a prima-donna-ish whim! Now you even want me to conduct! For your sake; and what am I to do for my sake? Apart from the fact that only one Song for Orchestra has never been performed at all, I do not consider it to anyone's advantage that anything more of mine should be done here. Besides, it is sheer provocation to do only works of one

---

[1] The names have been suppressed for personal reasons.
[2] Paul Pella and Heinrich Jalowetz were organising an Austrian Music Week in Berlin.

tendency in a Viennese music festival. In your place I should definitely have done something by *Bittner* (! who has very great need of it) and Marx or Schmidt or Prohaska. Off-hand I suggest something by Bittner and Marx, and in that case I should allow Steuermann to play his two-hand arrangement (transcription) of my chamber symphony (which is a brilliant 'display' piece). In this way you will gain rehearsal-time for the orchestral stuff, and with the chamber symphony alone will have filled 22 minutes of the programme, with plenty of variety.

[..........]

Let me know about the progress of rehearsals. I should also very much like to know the date of the performance; perhaps I shall be present 'incognito'!

Webern and Berg also complain that they have heard nothing 'official', for written invitations are needed if one is to get a visa! Here's wishing you and Jalowetz (from whom I hear absolutely nothing more at all!) the best of luck and all success.

ARNOLD SCHÖNBERG

67. To PAUL PELLA[1] *Traunkirchen, 9 June* 1923

Dear Herr Pella,

On the 7th there was the first, yesterday the second, and today I suppose the third performance of the Gurre-Lieder in Berlin, and so far no one has thought it worth the trouble of even letting me know whether the performance took place or not. In consideration of the circumstance that I did, after all, go to some trouble and expend many words in order to persuade Hertzka to let you have the performing rights, it should not have seemed too much trouble or too much expense to send me a few words of news about it.

And I suppose I'm expected to go on preserving the utmost amiability about everything, and if I don't, people shrug their shoulders . . . ! I'm sure you have gone to a great deal of trouble with the concerts and have proved yourself deserving of praise. But why don't you think of such things? After all, there is also the author to consider and not just always the performance. I'm all for abstraction and highmindedness in their proper place; but the human aspect also makes certain demands, which you people all fulfil to the limit so far as they happen to be your own; why am I already treated as if I were merely my own monument?

In the meantime with regards as kind as I can bring myself to make them, but not without anger.

ARNOLD SCHÖNBERG

[1] See the previous letter.

To Hermann Scherchen JUNE 1923

68. TO HERMANN SCHERCHEN *Traunkirchen, 23 June* 1923

Dear Herr Scherchen,

I should of course very much have liked to come to your concerts of modern music,[1] but I'm afraid I can't. For the first time for some years I once more find myself able to work for a while without interruption, and this only because I have resolved not to let myself be diverted at any price; neither by invitations to concerts nor by any other sort of activity. For some time at least all I want is to compose. Even the fact that I write so many letters is a very harmful deviation from this principle. And though anyone who means well by me should certainly write to me as often as possible (for I'm always glad of that), it should be in such a way that I don't have to answer! And without being offended: anyone who is my friend must wish me to fulfil at last certain long overdue obligations, completing long awaited works.

Now let me wish you much luck and all success with your splendid festival. Please give your choir my warmest thanks for the very kind words they sent me after the rehearsal. Tell them that my chorus 'Peace on Earth' is an illusion for mixed choir, an illusion, as I know today, having believed, in 1906 (?), when I composed it, that this pure harmony among human beings was conceivable, and more than that: would not have thought it possible to exist without perpetual insistence on the required elevation of tone. Since then I have perforce learnt to yield, and have learnt that peace on earth is possible only if there is the most intense vigilance as to harmony, in a word; not without accompaniment. If human beings are ever to reach the stage of singing peace at sight, without rehearsal, each individual will first have to be immune to the temptation to sink!

Once more warmest congratulations and many thanks for the kind words;

Yours sincerely,

ARNOLD SCHÖNBERG

69. TO MAX TEMMING[2] *Traunkirchen, 28 June* 1923

Herr Max Temming, Hamburg

Herr Rufer[3] is a pupil of mine and has worked for more than two years in the Society for Private Concerts, seeing and hearing everything

[1] The Music Festival of the German Musical Society (*Allgemeiner Deutscher Musikverein*) at which Scherchen conducted Schoenberg's *a cappella* chorus *Friede auf Erden* ('Peace on Earth'). Scherchen was at that time conductor of the Frankfurt museum concerts.

[2] A Hamburg patron of the arts, who was financing concerts of contemporary music.

[3] Josef Rufer was subsequently Schoenberg's assistant at the Prussian Academy of Arts in Berlin.

AETAT 48   *To Reclam's Universum, Leipzig*

there was to see and hear. I think there is no possible doubt that he must in this way have acquired an unusual amount of knowledge and experience. Accordingly I am entirely hopeful that Herr Rufer will prove a completely satisfactory choice for the appointment he is to take up. Of Herr Stuckenschmidt[1] I have had very satisfactory accounts from Herr Rufer, who has also kept me generally informed about the Hamburg project. I do not know him myself, and if he does indeed call himself my pupil, then undoubtedly all he means by it is that he associates himself with what is called my school. There is no other information that I can give about him.

I am very glad that something similar to my Vienna Society is now being started in Hamburg. I am convinced that it will soon be apparent what a blessing such an activity is, and congratulate you with all my heart on the very promising beginning.

                                              ARNOLD SCHÖNBERG

70. To EDITORIAL DEPARTMENT, RECLAM'S UNIVERSUM, LEIPZIG
                                       Traunkirchen, 28 *June* 1923

The best way for me to answer your circularised question: 'What sounds beautiful?', is, I think, to refrain from saying anything new. The old saw, 'Truth, to him who can recognise it', will here serve all the better since I myself intend making use of it by honestly telling you what prevents me from answering your questionnaire in any other way.

Your periodical is published by the famous Reclam-Verlag, to which every German reader owes the greatest part of his education and in whose taste and good will people therefore have almost boundless confidence: thus with their literary mother's milk imbibing ideas, judgments, and opinions proclaimed by the authors published in Reclam, they are utterly at the mercy of those ideas until they acquire some of their own or otherwise acquire different ones.

Now, this same publisher produced an excellent little history of music; by Nohl, a highminded, clever, and gentle person possessed both of education and of historical perception, wherefore, instead of vying with journalists in writing the history of the day, he wrote that of the years, and this not for his own day alone but for the century. By virtue

[1] H. H. Stuckenschmidt, writer on music, and a Schoenberg biographer (see note *, p. 244).

To Reclam's Universum, Leipzig JUNE 1923

of its pleasing qualities this book might have proved of permanent value, had not the Reclam-Verlag deprived it of the chance by having it brought up to date by a certain unclean spirit, one Herr Professor Chop, a journalist in whom the qualities of his calling are developed to a rare degree, with innumerable qualities of a stylistic nature that are of far too little concern to me to be cited in detail. It is now this gentleman's views that the young German reader encounters when he seeks information about the music of his time. Look up what this gentleman writes about me and my circle and then judge for yourselves whether it would really be as you say in your very cordial letter, 'Our readers would certainly feel it to be an omission if your name and ——'s were not to appear in this number'; whether those, at least, who acquire their musical taste from the Reclam-Verlag's history of music (taste that is lower than any acquired from daily newspapers, even if it originates in journalism), must [not?] be of the opposite opinion: that it is entirely unfitting to set beside the views of famous composers, virtuosos, singers, etc., those of an author so contemptible as I have the honour of being in the eyes of Chop-worshippers. In any case, having always prized honour above any sort of advantage, I do not wish to expose myself to being judged by such standards of taste, or rather, do not wish to expose myself to it yet again, since in this respect it has several times in the past been my sorry experience to find that I had been approached in a very polite and very flattering letter asking for a contribution, only for it then to be printed with malicious, indeed, insulting remarks by the grateful editor (among others, by the above-mentioned Herr Chop!!).

It goes without saying that I perfectly realise that not even the Reclam-Verlag, to say nothing of the editor of Universum, is responsible for the views proclaimed by Karl Moor, Max Stirner, and the Buddha in works published under their imprint. So munificent a host cannot probe to the furthest recess of each guest's soul, and above all it is more difficult for him than for smaller fry to rid himself of unbidden guests; I am indeed prepared to overlook the fact that Herr Chop is not, like Schiller or Schopenhauer, an unbidden even though welcome guest. He was probably bidden to the feast; probably because of the reputation he has managed to make for himself he was asked by Reclam to revise Nohl's work. I am also ready to grant that a business man does not enquire into his authors' views, but lets his own view of an author be dictated solely by the demand for his work. But I, *I* do not happen to be a business man, am not in a position to go in for lucrative broadmindedness, but am destined by the Lord my God to act only according to honour, and that is why to my very great regret I cannot do you the favour for which you ask.

I am, yours very faithfully,
ARNOLD SCHÖNBERG

71. TO RENÉE HENDSCH[1]   *Traunkirchen, 9 July 1923*

My dear Frau Hendsch,

    Short as — to my very great regret! — your visit in Mödling was, still, it did give me the feeling of having succeeded in being kindly remembered in Geneva. I am very glad about this, and it is what especially encourages me to try to arouse your interest on behalf of Dr. Anton von Webern, my former pupil and my friend, who I am sure is known to you as being both one of the most vilified and one of the most esteemed of those who believe in a new art. But he is, I am sure, one of the most highly distinguished. He is now very badly off; our country is undergoing an economic cure, which means that its finances will get well, but its artists will fall ill! Who still has any money left, these days, for modern art? Would it be possible for you and your friends to do something for him? This is the worst time of all for him, having a family of four children to provide for: the holidays are here, lucrative work comes to a standstill, and instead of being able to send the children to the country for their health, he has to worry about the most immediate necessities. It is very sad! Can you do something?

    Would you, in the event, get in touch with him yourself, or shall I pass on a message to him?

[..........]

ARNOLD SCHÖNBERG

72. TO A DUTCH PATRON OF THE ARTS   *Traunkirchen, 9 July 1923*

Dear Mr. Boissevain,

    I myself have received many a proof of our friendship, yet I cannot help feeling somewhat diffident about now asking you for yet another. This time it is, into the bargain, a matter of financial support. It is for my former pupil, my friend, Dr. Anton von Webern. He is in very dire need. He is the father of four children and every summer, when private lessons stop, he finds himself without any income, without any prospect of earning anything. In earlier days there was frequently help from abroad. But now, with the ever rising cost of living, the sums he receives

[1] A Swiss patron.

To a Dutch Patron   JULY 1923

scarcely cover a quarter of what he needs. Since I myself have very few rich acquaintances, I have myself repeatedly helped him out with fairly large sums (far beyond what I can afford). At the moment I could scarcely do more. And indeed I think my resources would not stretch to it.

You know Webern; you know that he is an extraordinarily gifted composer. I don't have to introduce him to you. You undoubtedly have a flair for remarkable people and must long ago have realised that he is one of them: Do help to keep him going! Perhaps by means of a collection you can raise a sum sufficient to relieve him of all worry for some time: from my own experience I know all too well what it means to be able to breathe freely again even if only for a short time. I know that I shall not be appealing in vain to your goodness of heart.

[..........]

At long last I am working again, and pretty hard too! It is doing me a lot of good, except for one thing: I am getting rather fat! I hope all is well with you and yours. I should be very glad if you could fairly soon let me have a favourable answer to my request on Webern's behalf.

[..........]

                                                               ARNOLD SCHÖNBERG

---

73. To WERNER REINHART[1]   *Traunkirchen, 9 July* 1923

Dear Herr Reinhart,

Warmest thanks to you and your brother Hans, to whom I shall write at more length in a few days, for the kind words you sent me in connection with the Frankfurt Festival of New Music. I may say that for the present it matters more to me if people understand my older works, such as this chorus 'Peace on Earth'. They are the natural forerunners of my later works, and only those who understand and comprehend them will be able to hear the latter with any understanding beyond the fashionable minimum. And only such people will realise that the melodic character of these later works is the natural consequence of my earlier experiments. So I am truly delighted by your friendly words. I do not attach so much importance to being a musical bogy-man as to being a natural continuer of properly understood good old tradition!

[..........]

There is one other thing I must speak of: Webern is in a bad way. He is at the moment without any income whatsoever. The rise in the cost of living is terrible; Austrians cannot help him permanently, and we do

---

[1] The well-known Swiss patron of the arts.

AETAT 48 　　　　　　　　　　　　　　　*To Fritz Windisch*

not know any rich people. I know you have already done a great deal for him. That is why I have so long hesitated to mention the matter. But since I cannot help him in any other way, it does seem right to do so. Could you do something for him again? Summer has always been a great worry to anyone who lives by giving lessons; and now it is 10 times worse. And especially for a modern musician. I know this from more than 25 years' experience.

[..........]

　　　　　　　　　　　　　　　　　　　　　ARNOLD SCHÖNBERG

74. TO WERNER REINHART 　　　　*Traunkirchen, 22 August* 1923

Dear Herr Reinhart,

Since the Salzburg Festival I have had an almost uninterrupted stream of (congenial) visitors. That, and the fact that I hoped to have a visit from you as well, is the reason for my not yet having thanked you for your speedy and generous response to my message about Webern. I am very glad indeed that he will be able to take things easy again for a time now, and I devoutly hope and trust that he will write much new stuff, showing that we too still exist. I hope you will take another opportunity, perhaps soon, to have a look at the Traunsee and some of its admirers. With grateful regards and all good wishes, I am, yours sincerely,

　　　　　　　　　　　　　　　　　　　　　ARNOLD SCHÖNBERG

75. TO FRITZ WINDISCH[1] 　　　　*Traunkirchen, 30 August* 1923

Dear Herr Windisch,

Even during our personal discussion I doubted that such a programme could be rehearsed for the beginning of October.[2] Today it is too late to doubt it; it only remains to state it as a certainty. A new work of mine requires 30–40 rehearsals; the Serenade perhaps even more, because one can't yet judge at all how the mandoline and the guitar will cope with the unusual task set them. The quintet for wind is only half finished. The inherent difficulties are very great. In addition there is the problem of digestion: Who can so quickly digest so much entirely new music?

If the festival was to be in October, a beginning ought to have been made in July at the latest.

I find your courage and your energy very gratifying, but I think you

[1] Organiser of concerts in Berlin.
[2] Fritz Windisch's plan was to give performances of Schoenberg's chamber music in Berlin.

To Fritz Windisch AUGUST 1923

underestimate the difficulties. Your appeal to my energy is certainly worth taking to heart. Only unfortunately my energy is a very insubordinate entity, which is not the least of the reasons why it exists at all. It is so disobliging that it won't take orders even from me: it's either there or not there, and does just as it pleases. Into the bargain, it has taken on obligations elsewhere for the present; it considers it high time for me to get some more things finished, and since I have a fair degree of respect for it, I cannot wish it to slacken off!

[*Here follow exact instructions as to the players to be provided for the various works and how they are to be rehearsed.*]

[..........]

Now I think I have said everything. You can see it isn't easy to get on with me. But don't lose heart because of that!

ARNOLD SCHÖNBERG

76. TO ROBERTO GERHARD[1]   *Mödling, 4 November* 1923

Dear Sir,

At present I have no time to look into your compositions more closely. But a fleeting glance and your letter give me a very good impression. Frankly: The final decision whether I take someone on as a pupil usually depends on the personal impression I get of him, and that is why I prefer to see people first. Can you manage to come to Vienna? I think I am certain to accept; and I also think I shall be able to help you a bit, since I understand your depression.

Before coming, do please find out whether I am in Vienna. Preferably by telegram. With kind regards and looking forward with much interest to making your acquaintance,

ARNOLD SCHÖNBERG

77. TO ALMA MAHLER-WERFEL   *Mödling,* 11 *November* 1923

My very dear lady,

At the moment[2] the idea of spending a more or less interesting afternoon with people who are practically strangers is so distressing that all this time I have been wondering whether I couldn't refuse. So you can imagine how relieved I was when you postponed it to a day on which I already have another engagement that cannot be broken. I'm sure you won't insist on my using sentimental expressions: You know quite well

---

[1] The Spanish composer, who became Schoenberg's pupil and friend.
[2] Schoenberg's first wife, Mathilde, had died on the 22nd October.

how I should like being in your company and that there are not many people with whom I can, quite without strain, have a conversation that is all good acoustics. But at present the Casellas really are too much like strangers; at present I really couldn't keep up talk about the things we have in common for long enough for it not to be embarrassing for any of those present (certainly for me). I'm sure you'll understand that to me any innocent laughter that deprives a dead person of some of the mourning one owes to him seems a crime. For in any case one doesn't mourn for as long as the dead person would deserve, the person for whom everything has now come to an end and for whom there is nothing left but what we give him. I have the feeling, and don't want to fight against it, that this withdrawal from mourning is brutal and inconsiderate, selfish and cowardly, and the most loathsome quality with which man has been endowed: The God who bestowed it on us had no respect for us! I'm sure you won't be angry with me, but will let me soon take an opportunity of telling you personally and in more detail — well, perhaps nothing more about it at all.

With very best wishes, your very devoted,

ARNOLD SCHÖNBERG

78. To JOSEF MATTHIAS HAUER[1]   *Mödling*, 1 *December* 1923
Dear Herr Hauer,

Your letter gave me very, very great pleasure. And I can give you proof of this. The fact is that about $1\frac{1}{2}$ or 2 years ago I saw from one of your publications that you were trying to do something similar to me, in a similar way. After coming to terms with the painful feeling that someone else, by also being engaged in something I had been thinking about for pretty well 15 years, was jeopardising my reputation for originality, which might cause me to renounce putting my ideas into practice if I do not want to pass for a plagiarist — a painful feeling, you will admit — after having come to terms with this feeling and having come to see wherein we differ from each other and that I was in a position to prove the independence of my ideas, I resolved to make the following suggestion to you:

'Let us write a book together, a book in which one chapter will be written by one of us, the next by the other, and so on. In it let us

[1] The composer Josef Matthias Hauer, whose compositions are, like Schoenberg's, based on the twelve notes of our system, though not related to a key. Schoenberg, however, whose 'twelve-note composition' developed out of decades of creative work, *invents* a new, appropriate series (note-row) to be the basis of each piece, whereas Hauer's theory establishes a number of series, from among which he then makes his choice for each work. See also Letter 143.

To Josef Matthias Hauer DECEMBER 1923

state our ideas, exactly defining the distinctive elements, by means of objective (but courteous) argument trying to collaborate a little bit in spite of these differences: because of what there is in common a basis can surely be found on which we can get along smoothly with each other.'

And I meant to say also: 'Let us show the world that *music*, if nothing else, would not have advanced if it had not been for the Austrians, and that *we* know what the next step must be.'

Then, however, I had qualms (there are always mischief-makers and gossips) lest I would be exposing myself to a refusal, and so the letter was never written. Perhaps, now, your suggestion of a school is even better. Above all, because in that way an exchange of ideas would come about spontaneously, more frequently, and without the agitatory contributions of a public maliciously looking on and provoking one to stubbornness. But the idea of the book, for the purpose of establishing the present point of view, should not be completely rejected either.

We are perhaps both in search of the same thing and have probably found related things. My point of departure was the attempt to replace the no longer applicable principle of tonality by a new principle relevant to the changed conditions: that is, in theory. I am definitely concerned with no other theories but the methods of 'twelve-note composition', as — after many errors and deviations — I now (and I hope definitively) call it. I believe — for the first time again for 15 years — that I have found a key. Probably the book to be entitled 'The Theory of Musical Unity', originally planned about 10 years ago, often sketched out and just as often scrapped, time and again newly delimited and then again enlarged, will in the end have just the modest title: 'Composition with Twelve Notes'. This is as far as I have got in the last approximately two years, and frankly, I have so far — for the first time — found no mistake and the system keeps on growing of its own accord, without my doing anything about it. This I consider a good sign. In this way I find myself positively enabled to compose as freely and fantastically as one otherwise does only in one's youth, and am nevertheless subject to a precisely definable aesthetic discipline. It is now more precise than it has ever been. For I can provide rules for almost everything. Admittedly I have not yet taught this method, because I must still test it in some more compositions and expand it in some directions. But in the introductory course for my pupils I have been using a great deal of it for some years in order to define forms and formal elements and in particular in order to explain musical technique.

Please do believe that my wish to reach an understanding with you

AETAT 49   *To Josef Matthias Hauer*

springs above all from the urge to recognise achievement. This is something I have proved often enough; among other cases, also where you were concerned (I mention this in order to show you that the two occasions when you tried to find an approach to me were, after all, not wasted): in my Theory of Harmony I argue (on page 488 of the new edition) against the concept 'atonality'* and then continue with an appreciation of you personally: you will realise that I did that for no one's sake but my own, out of my own need to be fair: and this makes the value of my praise objectively even greater! My friends will be able to confirm, too, that although I have put my head down and charged like a bull at what I am opposed to in your ideas, in conversation I have acknowledged your achievements at least as much as I have done in my book.

It is a pleasure to be able to give you proof of all this, for your amicable advance is of a kind that should remove all misunderstandings and all grudges; and so I shall gladly contribute a share as large as yours. I should be very pleased if we could now soon also have a personal discussion about further details. It is in particular the project of the school that I have a good deal to say about, having long been turning over the idea of starting a school for the development of style. Perhaps you will yourself name some afternoon next week when you would care to visit me (excepting Tuesday and Friday). Although I may be in Vienna next week, I do not know whether I shall then have time.

I am looking forward very much to the further development of our understanding and remain, with kindest regards, yours sincerely,

                                       ARNOLD SCHÖNBERG

N.B. This letter was not dictated, but written by me personally on the typewriter, thus respecting your wish that for the present I should not mention our discussions to any third person.

              * against the term, I mean, not against the thing itself! [S.]

79. To JOSEF MATTHIAS HAUER   *Mödling, 7 December* 1923

My dear Herr Hauer,

I very much look forward to your visit and shall expect you, as you suggest, on Monday, 10.xii, in the afternoon, in the certainty that this conversation will produce much good.

Although we have both been doing so, as it seems, unconsciously so far, it seems very useful that we should set about our discussion like former belligerents now wishing for peace: we make declarations that

To Josef Matthias Hauer   DECEMBER 1923

reveal the chances of peace and define them exactly, thus safeguarding ourselves on many sides from the necessity of 'having to dig up the buried hatchet'. Let me contribute yet something more to this; clarity can only be beneficial to us, can only bring us closer together.

1. 'We have both found the same thing.' But it isn't quite the same thing, for we are, after all, of different opinions and will perhaps always remain so. Yet in a certain respect it is the same thing, and it will perhaps only be a matter of recognising the most important elements in common and setting them in the right light. By doing this, however, we may incidentally arrive at a basis for smooth collaboration. You must not overlook one thing: I am almost fifty, with nothing but years of warfare behind me, and am unfortunately still given to getting very worked up about a great many things although there is nothing I need more than peace! What I suggest is therefore: Let us take what is common to our results and regard it as 'possibilities of achieving logical form by the use of 12 notes'. They are also possibilities even for someone who considers them necessities; this logic you could perhaps (solely within the framework of our relationship) let stand instead of the complex for which you use the term 'nomos'.* About the rest we are sure to be in agreement; so the only question is whether you can bring yourself to accept the reduction that approaches my standpoint. But in considering this do bear in mind that I too am making a concession. For behind the term 'logical' there is, for me, a complex that says: logic = human thinking = human world = human music = human ideas of nature and law and so forth. So you see that I too would have liked to go somewhat further than I propose to do for the sake of reaching agreement, and refrain from bringing up the rest, the controversial rest, in the discussion at all.

2. Should we reach agreement in this way or, alternatively, in some way to be proposed by you, it seems to me that yet another step would be possible, in so far as we would say more or less this: 'Each of us has discovered the possibility of a new form of composition and we agree that it is advisable, not to say necessary, to proceed thus and thus. On the other hand, we differ in this and that respect.' Assuming we had found a way of representing musical thoughts that was comparable to the fugue, the logic and inner necessity of which can be demonstrated just as conclusively as those of a natural body, then certain parallel phenomena would be discoverable, and plenty of them, and I should be no more deprived of the chance to maintain my opinion 'that we are at the beginning of a development for which there are analogies in the

* I.e., 'law'. [Trans.]

history of music' than you would be deprived of that to maintain your views on earlier methods of composition. For our task could then easily be localised: We would both have to make known, as well as we can at the present time, our technique of composition, our methods of representing musical thoughts (as I prefer to call it). It seems to me that would be very useful: you will, I am sure, notice that I too have the passion for teaching!

3. A third possibility occurs to me, which might guarantee a thorough and calm discussion and lead to still better results for the general public. There are 2 forms:

(a) to continue and then publish the written discussion that we have begun;
(b) to conduct this discussion right out in public by addressing open letters to each other in a musical journal.

What do you think? We can of course discuss the details, if necessary, when we meet.[1]

[Written by hand:] Since it is now 10 o'clock and my eyes are beginning to ache from typing, I shall break off here. I look forward to Monday. With v. best wishes,

ARNOLD SCHÖNBERG

80. TO THE EDITOR, *Courrier Musical*, PARIS

Mödling, 5 December 1923

The Editor,
Courrier Musical,
Paris.

I am very pleased to accede to your wish and will let you have either a short article or some aphorisms on modern music.

May I, however, suggest a reciprocal gesture that would be a fine act of artistic chivalry?

Namely:

Like perhaps the whole of the rest of the world, Austrians feel deep pity for the sad plight of German artists.

As everywhere else, so here too in Mödling endeavours are being made to alleviate this by raising as large a sum as possible.

No doubt you intend to offer me, who seldom consent to write for newspapers, a suitable fee for this contribution. Would you be prepared to make over this sum, whatever it may amount to, to the municipality of Mödling for its German Relief Fund (I shall in due course let you

---

[1] Nothing came of the discussion.

To Editor, Courrier Musical, *Paris*　　　　　　　　　DECEMBER 1923

know the exact address), informing that body that you do so in recognition of an article that I have given you [?]

And: will you also make this procedure known to your readers in a short note at the beginning of your article? Perhaps this might lead to the winning of more friends for German artists, who are glad to give money to alleviate hardship and pour oil on seas of hatred, and who would in this way give a fine and courageous sign of their humanity?[1]

ARNOLD SCHÖNBERG

81. TO PRINCE EGON FÜRSTENBERG[2]

Mödling [*No date, but evidently April* 1924]

May it please Your Highness,

May I, first and foremost, most respectfully thank you from the bottom of my heart for the extremely gratifying words that Your Highness has had the goodness to address to me?

The splendid enterprise in Donaueschingen is something I have long admired: this enterprise that is reminiscent of the fairest, alas bygone, days of art when a prince stood as a protector before an artist, showing the rabble that art, a matter for princes, is beyond the judgment of common people. And only the authority of such personages, in that it permits the artist to participate in the distinctive position bestowed by a higher power, is able to demonstrate this demarcation in a sensuously tangible manner to all those who are merely educated, who have merely worked their way up, and to make manifest the difference between those who have become what they are and those who were born what they are; between those who arrive at a position and occupation by indirect means and those who are directly born to it. If I may really be permitted to respond to this summons, it would, I must confess, be very much to my own liking to do so with my latest work, the 'Serenade' and, in accordance with your wish, to conduct it myself. It must however be mentioned that this unfortunately cannot be actually a first performance, since the latter will take place — though privately, not in public — on the 2nd May, a performance for which we are just now having the final rehearsals. Yet I will — if Your Highness attaches importance to it — do all that is in my power to secure my publisher's agreement that it shall at least be the first public performance in Germany.

[1] The sequel is not known.

[2] Handwritten draft of a letter to Prince Egon Fürstenberg, who had invited Schoenberg to conduct his *Serenade* at the Music Festival at Donaueschingen. The performance took place that summer.

AETAT 49 *To Paul Bekker*

Once more thanking Your Highness most respectfully for all your flattering and kind words, I remain, with deep veneration and respect,

ARNOLD SCHÖNBERG

82. TO PAUL BEKKER[1] 1 *August* 1924

Dear Herr Bekker,

Intercourse between artists and critics is bound to be somewhat risky for both sides. Now, since I in particular cannot tolerate any criticism whatsoever (for I should not like to think I had written anything that would justify adverse criticism, but cannot, on the other hand, see why I should always be expected to be considerate towards those who understand nothing yet rush in where angels fear to tread, who have not enough insight to suppress lesser or greater qualms about an author of evident merit, and seldom the courage not to intersperse their praise with qualifications, securing their strategic position on several sides), I have up to now as a rule preferred not to become personally acquainted with critics.

However, I too have become somewhat calmer in the course of recent years and have a milder attitude to much of that sort of thing. Today I realise that I cannot be understood, and I am content to make do with respect. That, however, does not mean one can overlook the fact that respect is the very thing that has not been shown me, and this to a quite incredible degree, although at least that stage is now in the main a matter of the past. The most favourable formula was as a rule: 'Whatever one may choose to think of Schönberg', which of course I cannot but regard as great presumption.

Now I don't mind confessing that at our meeting I received a very pleasant impression of your personality and your ideas, and felt that you have indeed the capacity to behave respectfully to one who deserves respect. It seems to me that the only people who can do this are those who respect themselves, and the real sceptics are above all those who do not believe in themselves. On the other hand, someone who believes in himself and respects himself is the one and only person capable of respecting and honouring merit. For this reason I also find association with the aristocracy very pleasant to one who thinks something of himself.

Your desire for independence is something that no one can sympathise with more than I, who, as you may not be unaware, have made

[1] Music critic of the *Frankfurter Allgemeine Zeitung*, subsequently Intendant of the Prussian State Theatre in Wiesbaden.

To Paul Bekker   AUGUST 1924

the greatest of sacrifices for the sake of my independence. Yet I think one should not let such considerations interfere with the pleasure of devoting oneself to a cause or a person. For such pleasure is in my experience not outweighed by even the gravest disappointments. Unfortunately the better sort of people become enemies faster than friends because everything is so serious and important to them that they are perpetually in a defensive position. They are driven to this by the great, indeed ruthless honesty with which they treat themselves and which makes them adopt the same attitude to other people as well. It is very wrong, really, for we human beings are far too much in need of tolerance for any thoroughgoing honesty to be helpful to us. If only we could manage to be wise enough to put people on probation instead of condemning them, if we could only give proven friends such extended credit! — I am speaking of my own defects, knowing very well why I have often been more lonely than could well be pleasant.

Perhaps you will gather from all this that I am no longer the bugaboo I used to be. I do not think it means that I stick to my principles less tenaciously than before, but I have come to acquire patience and some knowledge of human nature and am now able to believe that, however sacred I hold my faith, it is no longer so difficult to get on with me as it used to be. So I firmly hope and trust that neither of us will have cause to regret having begun a personal exchange of ideas, and I look forward with the greatest of interest to receiving your book. Very many thanks for it in anticipation.

                                                                   ARNOLD SCHÖNBERG

83. TO ADOLF LOOS[1]   *Mödling, 5 August* 1924

My dear Loos,

Your telegram missed me in Donaueschingen but was forwarded to me in Mödling. It was sent on the 22nd, but I had already left for the Salzkammergut and only came back to Mödling nearly a fortnight later. What a pity!

I had actually hoped to see you in Donaueschingen. It was very nice there and would certainly have interested you very much. A festival like that, under the aegis of a man who is not doing it as a means of becoming anything, but who, because he has always been something in himself, is capable of really bestowing honours, further reinforces my distaste for democracy and that sort of thing.

[..........]

                                                           ARNOLD SCHÖNBERG

[1] The famous Viennese architect.

AETAT 49   *To Hermann Scherchen*

84. To Hermann Scherchen[1]   *Mödling*, 12 *August* 1924

Dear Herr Scherchen,

Your delightful plan gives me really very great pleasure. Let me waste no words: you will know for yourself how beautifully this thing has been thought out and that it comes from your hearts and that it therefore cannot fail to have the corresponding effect on me: I rejoice with all my heart!

Well then, to the point!

I shall be delighted to join in!

I must, however, mention some difficulties and make some suggestions.

[. . . . .]

Now let me thank you once again most warmly and ask you to tell Hindemith too that I am *extremely pleased with him*. By doing this he is making a splendid sign of a proper attitude to his elders, a sign such as can be made only by a man with a genuine and justifiable sense of his own worth; only by one who has no need to fear for his own fame when another is being honoured and who recognises that precisely such an honour does honour also to him if he associates himself with it. I once said: only he can bestow honour who himself has a sense of honour and deserves honour. Such a man knows what is due to him and therefore also what is due to his peers.

Please also answer this soon so that the matter is kept constantly in my mind, lest I neglect it amid the many concerns keeping me busy at the moment.

                                                     Arnold Schönberg

[1] Answer to a letter, in connection with Schoenberg's 50th birthday on the 13th September, part of which reads as follows:

'... Paul Hindemith and I have organised a festival in Frankfurt-am-Main from the 15th to the 18th September:

    I. The Hanging Gardens   II. 1st Quartet
       2nd Quartet (Frau Freund and the   Piano Pieces (Steuermann)
       Amar Quartet).   Chamber Symphony (etc.).
  III. Serenade   IV. Pierrot lunaire
       Wind Quintet   (played by your Ensemble, with
       Serenade (your Ensemble, con-   Frau Erika Wagner).
       ducted by you).

Our wish in doing this is to honour you, as musicians, out of our own resources, entirely without the aid of any committee of ignorant financial backers. Please write immediately and tell me — and please do let it be in the affirmative — that it is all right to start everything with all speed. It would do if you were here from the 16th–18th (please, you must contrive to slip away from Vienna for those few days), — and I shall rehearse the Chamber Symphony so thoroughly as to leave no technical work for you to do so that musically you will be able to do just what you wish with the Ensemble. Dear Herr Schönberg, make this festival possible for us by coming. Paul Hindemith begs this of you as earnestly as I do. We musicians want to acclaim and honour you! That is more important than municipal festivals — at least that's the way I see it. With very cordial regards,

                          Yours,   Scherchen

To Chairman, Austrian Association   DECEMBER 1924

85. TO CHAIRMAN OF THE COMMITTEE, AUSTRIAN ASSOCIATION OF TEACHERS OF MUSIC   *Mödling*, 11 *December* 1924

I wish herewith to announce my resignation from the Ass. Teach. Mus., asking you to be good enough to note my reasons:

In order to save myself all superfluous annoyance, I have long sought to keep any sort of newspaper criticism concerning myself from entering my house: Since membership of the Society is now linked with regular delivery of a journal publishing music criticism, I see no other means of closing my doors against this intruder (the very first number of which carries personal abuse of me surpassing the grossest that even I have hitherto had to put up with) than to resign from the Society.

        Yours faithfully,

               ARNOLD SCHÖNBERG

Registered

86. TO THE EDITOR, NEUES WIENER JOURNAL

               Mödling, 26 *September* 1925

Herr J. Bistron,
Editor,
Neues Wiener Journal[1]

Dear Sir,

Many thanks for your kind suggestion. I am afraid, however, that just at the moment I am on the one hand too busy with work of my own, on the other so overwhelmed with requests for articles (which would indeed interest me, as does your own question), that I see no way out but to write none at all, because I should otherwise have no time left for anything else.

Allow me to take this opportunity of answering another question: I have been told you wished to publish an interview with me. I must ask you, however, to abandon this proposal. For it is my most intense desire to depart from Vienna as unnoticed as I have always been while I was here. I desire no accusations, no attacks, no defence, no publicity, no triumph!

     only: p e a c e !

               ARNOLD SCHÖNBERG

---

[1] Schoenberg's appointment to the Berlin Academy of Arts had caused a stir in Vienna.

Section III
BERLIN — BARCELONA
1926 – 1933

BIOGRAPHICAL NOTES

At the beginning of January 1926 Schoenberg moved to Berlin, where he took up his teaching appointment as director of a class in musical composition at the Prussian Academy of Arts. In order to assure him adequate leisure for his own creative work, he was not obliged to spend more than six months of each year in Berlin. By virtue of his appointment he became a member of the Senate of the Academy, the President of which was at that time the painter Max Liebermann. Schoenberg also took an active interest in general artistic, educational, and administrative problems at the Academy (see Letters 93 and 98), and his suggestions were usually accepted.

1927: Schoenberg conducted concerts in Berlin, Paris and Spain, and delivered a lecture in French at the Sorbonne.

1928: Conducted the *Gurrelieder* in London. *Die glückliche Hand* was performed in Breslau (see Letters 102 and 103). Furtwängler conducted the first performance of the *Variations for Orchestra*, op. 31 (see Letters 104, 105, and 109). *Von heute auf morgen* ('From Today till Tomorrow') composed.

1930: First performance of *Von heute auf morgen* at the Frankfurt Opera House; shortly afterwards broadcast by Radio Berlin, Schoenberg conducting. The association with Dr. Flesch, Intendant of Radio Berlin, became a fruitful source of ideas (see Letters 112 and 115). *Erwartung* and *Die glückliche Hand* performed at the Oper am Platz der Republik in Berlin (see Letter 114). Schoenberg began composing *Moses und Aron*.

1931: Schoenberg conducted *Erwartung* for a broadcast by the B.B.C. His poor health forced him to move to a warmer climate: first to Territet, in Southern Switzerland, and then, on his doctor's very strong recommendation, to Spain, spending the winter in Barcelona (see Letter 130).

1932: The second act of *Moses und Aron* finished on the 10th

Biographical Notes

March. At the beginning of June Schoenberg left Barcelona, returning to Berlin (see Letters 137-142). The general election gave the National-Socialist Party a majority in the German Reichstag. Although the cold northern climate was bad for his health, Schoenberg decided to spend the winter in Berlin.

1933: At the beginning of the year Schoenberg went to London and to Vienna. After the National-Socialists assumed power the President of the Academy, Max von Schillings, announced at a meeting of the Senate that he was directed by the Minister of Education to proclaim that 'the Jewish influence at the Academy must be eliminated'. Having declared that he never stayed where his presence was not welcome, Schoenberg left the meeting. On the 17th May he left Berlin.

WORKS

1926: *Four Pieces* for mixed chorus, op. 27.
Three Satires for mixed chorus, op. 28.
1927: Third string quartet, op. 30.
1926/28: *Variations for Orchestra*, op. 31.
1928/29: *Von heute auf morgen*, opera in one act, op. 32.
Piano Piece, op. 33a.
1929/30: *Accompaniment to a Film-Scene*, op. 34.
Six Pieces for male chorus, op. 35.
1931: *Piano Piece*, op. 33b.
1930/32: *Moses und Aron*, opera, acts 1 and 2.
1933: *Three Songs* for low voice, op. 48.
1928: J. S. Bach, Prelude and Fugue in E flat major, arranged for large orchestra.
1932: G. M. Monn, Concerto for harpsichord, arranged for 'cello and orchestra.
1933: G. F. Handel, *Concerto grosso*, op. 6, No. 7, arranged as Concerto for string quartet and orchestra.
1926/27: *Der biblische Weg* ('The Biblical Way'), drama (see Letter 153).

87. TO THE PRUSSIAN MINISTER FOR SCIENCE, ART AND EDUCATION
Mödling, 24 September 1925

Your Excellency,
 Today I received the formal letter of appointment,[1] which had been forwarded from one address to another, and wish most respectfully to express my warmest thanks for the great honour and distinction accorded me by this appointment to such an eminent position.
 I am fully aware of the responsibility that this imposes upon me, and wish to pledge myself herewith to exert all my energies in order to prove myself not unworthy of the distinction bestowed on me. And should it be granted me in this position to achieve what is expected of me, it would be a matter of the deepest satisfaction to me.
 Originally it had been my intention to use the many plans that have occupied my mind for years in order to evolve a more or less detailed programme, and to place this in Your Excellency's hands. On further consideration, however, I decided in favour of first becoming acquainted with the given conditions and the situation arising out of my appointment, and only then to act as the situation may demand. That in doing so I shall not spare myself is perhaps sufficiently vouched for by my past record.
 In once again expressing my respectful thanks, I should like, in conclusion, to emphasise that they specifically refer also to the generous way in which my wishes have been granted, and I remain,
 Your obedient servant,
 ARNOLD SCHÖNBERG

88. TO PROFESSOR LEO KESTENBERG   *Mödling, 24 September* 1925
Herr Professor Leo Kestenberg,
Prussian Ministry of Science, Art, and Education, Berlin

Dear Herr Professor,
 I enclose copies of my letters to the Minister and to the President of the Senate, hastening to tell you *that I am delighted.* Recognition does

---

[1] As director of a class in musical composition at the Prussian Academy of Arts in Berlin.

To Professor Leo Kestenberg SEPTEMBER 1925

one good, and it has not escaped me that you yourself took up this matter with great pleasure, and your pleasure, and the warmth with which you expounded the whole thing to me, communicated themselves to me and, as you must, I am sure, have noticed, at once made me feel I wanted to drop all my preconceived opinions and accept the appointment.

So, once again, I am quite delighted!

I am not clear about one thing: am I expected to present myself before the Senate on the 1.x. in person, which I would do if it were absolutely necessary, or can this be postponed to some later occasion? It would be very kind of you to let me know about all this. Especially, besides: when am I expected actually to take up my appointment? Should I perhaps come to Berlin beforehand? Do I have to apply by letter to the offices (treasurer's etc.) mentioned in the Minister's letter (last paragraph), or does all that take its official course without action from me?

I shall — if I don't have to go to Berlin — be staying in Mödling for at least about another 6 weeks, in order to finish some jobs, and hope in the meantime to receive all necessary information from you.[1] May I also ask you to have the enclosed letters forwarded to the exact addresses, which I do not know?

With many very warm thanks for the pleasure you have given me and which you have shown me. . . .

ARNOLD SCHÖNBERG

89. TO MAX BUTTING[2] *Berlin, 4 February 1926*
Dear Herr Butting,

Frankly, I should think it more profitable, at the present juncture, to make the Berlin public acquainted with my earlier works rather than with my latest. For to me it matters more that people should understand my work than that they should take an interest in it. In any case, however, I do not think it advantageous either to me or to Schnabel (as was indeed quite evident in Venice)[3] for us both to appear in one programme. The most stylish programme is arrived at by setting about it

---

[1] Schoenberg's move to Berlin was delayed until the beginning of the new year (see Biographical Notes, p. 62).

[2] Composer, chairman of the Berlin section of the International Society for Modern Music.

[3] At the Festival of the International Society for Modern Music in 1925 performances were given of both Schoenberg's *Serenade* and a piano sonata by Artur Schnabel.

with a thorough disregard for style, simply seeing to it that there is variety and contrast. Stylistic affinity only produces a sense of monotony in a sensitive listener!

ARNOLD SCHÖNBERG

90. To ALEXANDER ZEMLINSKY *Berlin, 3 March* 1926

Dear Alex,

Since Herr Eisler[1] claims that you must have misunderstood him when you both had your talk about twelve-note composition in the train, I'd be very grateful if you would answer the following questions.

Please just write your answers in beside the questions.

I. Did Herr E. say he is turning away from all this modern stuff?
II. that he doesn't understand twelve-note music?
III. that he simply doesn't consider it music at all?

That is what you told me at the time, and since E. denies it, it would interest me to know the truth. You will perhaps also recall the praise you bestowed on him, saying he was the only independent personality among my pupils, the only one who didn't 'repeat after me'.

ARNOLD SCHÖNBERG

91. To HANNS EISLER[2] *Berlin, 10 March* 1926

Dear Eisler,

In informing me of an essay in preparation (which you have begun), knowing even before you have finished it that I shall completely reject (your words!) the little that you have to say, you are, after all, presenting me with the intellectual and moral foundations of your remarks to Zemlinsky, which you nevertheless wish to have regarded as merely a casual 'chat in the train'! But then this is the way it is: you hold opinions deviating from me, wherefore I shall presumably reject them out of hand, and on the basis of these opinions, as on the basis of everyone's right to freedom of speech, you spoke about them freely to Zemlinsky. It was not much more you were reproached with; so you should never have denied it. What I find wrong is that you announce this essay as containing statements of 'complete loyalty' towards me 'personally' and to my 'cause'. Although it is actually no more than I am entitled to demand, if I were to offer you no more than that, if I were to propose

[1] The composer Hanns Eisler was a pupil of Schoenberg's (see Letters 92 and 49).
[2] See the foregoing letter.

To Hanns Eisler MARCH 1926

merely granting you the application of the letter of the law, you would surely be dissatisfied. Well, so am I; because the standard I am accustomed to apply in establishing the laws of loyalty within the circle of my friends is that of my own conscience.

I can only approve of your wishing 'not suddenly to appear meek as a lamb', since you are nothing of the sort. I have also vainly tried to talk myself into regarding the matter so, and endeavoured to make myself believe that it was only that cynicism and nihilism of yours, successful solely in café-haunting circles, which tempted you to fling off a snap judgment even where it condemns you — a view that would have enabled me to show clemency, since I do not go quite so far as to regard that state of mind as amounting to a skin disease, but at the most as a sorry condition the clothing is in, and clothing can be changed.

You write: 'I was nonplussed by your opinion of me personally. I reproduce it (with some exaggeration): a ... young puppy from Suburbia bursting with modish jargon ... etc.' You know very well that my verdict was much harsher. That I described your proceedings as treason. But I now consider it was not me you betrayed, it was *yourself* you betrayed in a 'chat in the train'; in such chat, in fact, you were not capable of not betraying your opinion of me, you actually had to blazon it abroad, although a change of mind on your part is *not yet* perceptible in your works, although you were only *intending* to put this abrupt change of attitude into operation in your future works, so that it is not a creative act at all; although the mode of composition that was to document this volte-face did not yet exist; although there would, therefore, still have been plenty of time and no need to take advantage of the first railway-carriage chat you happened to have.

I am sincerely sorry that I cannot take any other view of this; perhaps because I cannot think any other way, or for some other reason: admittedly I had had a premonition of your behaviour. Nevertheless I should gladly have built a bridge for you. But you have made it too difficult for me to discover the facts, and so I have cooled off to such an extent that even I would not have been able to help betraying one of the two of us if I had shown you more cordiality. But you are perhaps right in having 'utmost confidence in the next few years', and so I will have it too. And you may be sure that I shall be very glad if this confidence leads to no disappointments for either of us.

May all go well with you, and much luck for the future. And if there is any way I could help you, you do know, don't you, that it would be doing me only another injustice if you didn't tell me. Best wishes.

ARNOLD SCHÖNBERG

AETAT 51   *To Hanns Eisler*

92. To Hanns Eisler[1]   *Berlin*, 12 *March* 1926

Dear Herr Eisler,

Although I must say I find your remark about 'if you had discovered that I resented your views' diverging from mine, you would not have tried to say anything about it', pretty arrogant, still — I must write to you once more. For I cannot leave you the slightest loophole.

Quote the sentence from which you gather that! Views diverging from my own are something I should never resent, as little as I resent anyone's having any other disability! one short leg, a clumsy hand, etc. I could only be sorry for such a person, but I couldn't be angry with him. But the sentence on which you seem to base your remark reproaches you with having had to talk to Zemlinsky about it, and further on I point out that at a stage in which there was still no necessity (for perhaps I should have found your opinion very interesting, have approved it, indeed perhaps even accepted it!) you managed to convey [it] to a person where [sic] it was likely to meet with a very favourable reaction, but where you would have done better to remain silent. At the age of 25 I had completed the 'Gurre-Lieder', which Zemlinsky at that time thought bad, and yet it never occurred to me that I held opinions different from his, although even that work pointed ahead to what I only became conscious of much later. In any case, however, I should at every period have had enough tact not to speak of an already existing or developing divergence of views to someone who himself differed from Zemlinsky, and did so, what is more, in quite another way than I. For please be good enough to realise that the way Zemlinsky differs from me nowadays is of quite another kind than your way; and that your divergences from me would not infallibly have amounted to opposition if you had not created the opposition by taking this attitude. I have written differently from Mahler and Zemlinsky, but never felt any need to take up opposition to them. And only if there is opposition is it necessary to state one's attitude in good time.

I cannot know, of course, whether you are still capable of wanting to understand me: for this reason this is to be the last word on the subject. I have built you several bridges, at least footbridges. If you do not see your way to using them, then I must regard you as remaining on the further bank. Can regret it but not change it. So: best wishes and keep well.

                                               ARNOLD SCHÖNBERG

[1] See Letters 90 and 91.

To Max Liebermann   JUNE 1926

93. TO MAX LIEBERMANN   *Berlin, 14 June 1926*
J.No. 505

ACADEMY OF ARTS IN BERLIN

The Minister of Education has in principle approved my suggestion that we should establish the award of a medal at the Academy of Arts in Berlin to especially talented students sitting for the examinations of the Prussian art academies (for the visual arts and music). Before submitting to the Ministry a draft of the conditions on which such an award would be made, I should like to learn the views of all the art schools concerned, in order to consider any specific wishes that they may have. I wish to emphasise that the medal is to be awarded only to students who pass their examinations with distinction in *all* subjects. Before announcing a competition for the most suitable design for the medal, I herewith call upon all concerned to inform me of any specific wishes as to the terms of the award, which will be made by the Prussian Academy of Arts, Berlin, on the recommendation of the presiding bodies of the relevant institutes of higher education.

         M. Liebermann
         President

17 June 1926

Dear Herr Präsident,

In reply to the question raised in your circular letter J.No. 505 of the 14.vi.1926 I should like to make the following points:

The condition that the medal shall be awarded only to students who pass their examinations with distinction in *all* subjects strikes me as somewhat too narrow and not wholly proof against misinterpretation. Narrow: because in this way departments such as the advanced classes in musical composition, where there is only *one subject*, could not enter their students. Further, it is comparatively seldom that distinction is achieved in all subjects, nor is it always a sign of creative talent; on the contrary, it is more often a sign of vigorous mediocrity. Since, furthermore, it is in some circumstances quite possible for a mediocre student's examination results to stand out among inferior results, without absolutely deserving the distinction under discussion, I should like to suggest a formulation leaving less scope for misinterpretation:

The award shall be made only to students whose talent and ability are such as to warrant the expectation that their future achievements will surpass the average.[1]

         Yours faithfully,

         ARNOLD SCHÖNBERG

[1] Schoenberg's proposal was accepted.

AETAT 51   *To Geheimrat H. Hinrichsen*

94. To Professor Gustav Singer[1]   *Berlin, 7 August* 1926

Dear Herr Professor,

My wife* this year insists on taking me to a resort where something can be done for my asthma.

[..........]

We should like to collect the necessary information as soon as possible, in order to be able to start out at once. It can be somewhere abroad; only if possible not in Germany, for everything is much dearer here and not so pleasant.

May I take this opportunity of giving you a brief account of myself: I now have less difficulty in breathing when going to sleep, and I don't so often start up gasping for breath. The cough (except when I get another attack of influenza, which means a rise of temperature) is less frequent and does not cause such shattering spasms. I must admit I would sometimes rather cough more, in order to get rid of the mucus. On the other hand, in the morning, after being in a horizontal position, I feel somewhat exhausted and breathless, and at other times too I tend to get out of breath more than before. So this strikes me as somewhat less good now. Recently I have not been running so many temperatures, but I am not sure whether it isn't merely the deadening effect of habit and that I have lost my sensitivity to it. As a result, i.e. since I no longer notice my temperature as much as formerly, I have recently not been taking it: from which you will perhaps observe that I am not a hypochondriac.

I think I have now said everything that seems important, and hope I haven't bored you excessively with it.

[..........]

                                                      Arnold Schönberg

95. To Geheimrat H. Hinrichsen[2]   *Berlin,* 12 *February* 1927

Dear Herr Geheimrat,

Above all thank you very much for your very charming letter, from which I gather with pleasure that you take an interest in my work. I should have liked to be able to send you a definitive answer at once, and have been waiting more than a week for a letter from Universal Edition. Now, however, I hear that Herr Direktor Hertzka is said to be ill, and

---

[1] Physician, professor at the University of Vienna.

* Schoenberg had married again. [TRANS.]

[2] Geheimrat ('Privy Councillor') H. Hinrichsen was proprietor of the publishing house of C. F. Peters. See also Letter 52.

To Geheimrat H. Hinrichsen FEBRUARY 1927

so it may still be some time before I can give you more details. So I will perhaps first answer the questions you have asked, begging you then to let me know whether in the circumstances as they appear from these answers you are still prepared to consider further negotiations: which of course I *sincerely hope*!

First of all, then: the works are of very recent date, which means, it goes without saying, what is commonly called 'atonal'; music of the future, which has, after all, hitherto proved itself to be not entirely hopeless! I usually answer the question why I no longer write as I did at the period of 'Verklärte Nacht' by saying: 'I do, but I can't help it if people don't yet recognise the fact'. In the case of some works about which I have been asked this, e.g. my 2nd String Quartet (incidentally, at the first performance there were the most tremendous scenes I have ever experienced), people are actually beginning to recognise this even now and to forgive me for composing not only as beautifully as before but also very much better than then. But I cannot and of course do not want to blame anyone who is nevertheless not yet capable of feeling complete confidence in it.

With reference to your offer of remuneration, I must say that I hope for a better one when you have examined my statement of the position...

[..........]

ARNOLD SCHÖNBERG

96. To ERWIN STEIN[1] *Berlin, 8 April* 1927

Dear Stein,

I have nothing against the F sharp minor Quartet's being included in the Library of String Orchestral Works.[2] It does certainly astonish me to hear that Berg has a score of it, since I ought to have one myself. Nor can I remember whether I really put in double-basses. Anyway, ask Webern about this. I'm afraid I can't look it up among my stuff, since it's all in crates with the removals people. Incidentally, the division of each 4/4 bar into two 4/8 bars where I have indicated it in the last movement is on no account to be let stand. In my view it has not passed the test. For it only meant even more accents being given than otherwise. The 8/8 bar must therefore be restored, as it is in the original edition.

[1] The editor of this collection of letters was at that time artistic adviser to Universal Edition and editor of the periodical *Pult und Taktstock* ('Music-Desk and Baton'), which was published by the same firm.

[2] Published by Universal Edition. The work under discussion was an arrangement of the Quartet for string orchestra (see note 3 to Letter 33). The arrangement was made by Schoenberg.

AETAT 52(?) *To Max Liebermann*

As for the problem of a reduced score of 'Pelleas' for provincial orchestras, I am inclined to think it would be fairly difficult to do it in a *valid* form. Are you quite sure that the 'Gurre-Lieder' reduction turned out well? You know I haven't heard it, but I don't know whether such attempts to make things easier don't merely increase the difficulties. The lay-out of the scores is certainly larger than I should make it now; on the other hand the instrumentation has really been done very well within this system, and with a fine sense for the sound, and, what is most important of all: tried and tested on the basis of experience! Naturally it would be better to put something cut-and-dried into these people's hands, rather than leave it to the musical directors, for those gentlemen to do it on their own. But I do think it very difficult. I know I often have to think about it for a very long time when I try out something of this kind. And then in the end it doesn't always work out completely, despite all the experience that's gone into it. The difficulty is in fact this: one would also have to keep the sound-proportions [*Klangproportionen*] in mind and therefore actually reduce it even in places where no instrument is missing: and can one really take it on oneself to destroy a sound that has been proven?!

But if you think it can be done well, I won't make any objection. Just as of course all I say here isn't in the remotest meant to suggest distrust of you!

Well, think it over, and if you find it works, then do it.

Tonight I'm conducting a broadcast of 'Pelleas'. Although I had only 3 rehearsals, it will turn out pretty well. Not so polished as I should have liked, but a fairly clean job.

ARNOLD SCHÖNBERG

97. TO MAX LIEBERMANN [*undated draft*][1]

Dear Herr Präsident,
Revered Master,

Pray permit me, one who has known and admired your work ever since the first exhibition organised by the Vienna Sezession,[2] one who, even if only as a musician, was also active in the struggle to establish modern painting, and to whom, as to so many others, you were a prophet and guide not only in your paintings but also in the magnificent

---

[1] Handwritten draft of a letter to the painter Max Liebermann on the occasion of his 80th birthday on the 20th July 1927. Liebermann was at that time President of the Academy of Arts in Berlin.

[2] The 'Sezession' was a Viennese group of modern artists (painters, sculptors, etc.) round about 1900.

To Max Liebermann UNDATED DRAFT

words that you pronounced — permit me to convey to you, on the occasion of your 80th birthday, my heartfelt congratulations, my very great admiration and veneration, and my very, very best wishes for your welfare.

ARNOLD SCHÖNBERG

98. TO THE ACADEMY OF ARTS IN BERLIN

Pörtschach, 21 *July* 1927

Ref. J. No. 861.

I believe it right to record that I am *against* making it compulsory for students at the academies of art to participate in gymnastics.

Students at academies of art are as a rule under the necessity of earning a living, so that this measure might very well be damaging to them. Further, most of them are of an age and at a stage of development such as to make such compulsion appear scarcely suitable, perhaps indeed not in keeping with the status of a university.

A decline in interest is certainly to be feared if gymnastics of the old-fashioned kind are to be held in gymnasia, either as pure gymnastics or with apparatus.

If on the other hand some modern sport, especially if of a competitive kind, were to be introduced: boxing, rowing, swimming, football, hockey, tennis, polo, etc., etc., it seems to me highly probable that compulsion would be entirely obviated, as is indeed demonstrated by the examples of England and America.

It is highly probable that students would here regard it as a matter of prestige to produce good teams in as many spheres of sport as possible, just as students do at English and American universities. For ambition is an authority to which obedience is accorded voluntarily and spontaneously!

ARNOLD SCHÖNBERG

99. TO ERWIN STEIN *Pörtschach, 5 August* 1927

Dear Stein,

I have already outlined the answer I would give to your questionnaire.[1] What is uncertain, however, is whether and, if so, when I shall work it up. Recently I have revised my play[2] again and again, but it still isn't

---

[1] In the periodical *Pult und Taktstock* (see note 1 to Letter 96).
[2] The unpublished drama, *Der biblische Weg* ('The Biblical Way').

finished. In the last few days, besides, I was very depressed. I was foolish enough to read it aloud to H. (fortunately only the first act), and he had the bad taste to give me his really hopelessly amateurish, conventional opinion. He didn't understand a word of it, and obviously applied to it the standards he applies to ballet-pantomimes by Wellesz, Hofmannsthal, Wassermann and Casella. Stupid as what he said was, still it did show me that not everybody is going to like this thing either. And since I have not the same technical sureness in literary work that I have in my musical work, it upset me even more. Incidentally, for years now I have never shown any music to anyone who presumes to have an opinion about it. H. has of course become somewhat overbearing as a result of the servility of the authors published by his firm, and is now very given to laying down the law. My anger may astonish you. But perhaps you will be even more astonished by the grounds I give for it: that I have in fact really not done any more work on the thing since then!

Perhaps you will regard this as namby-pamby from one who has put forth his work despite the world's opposition. But perhaps you will see from this that each time I was actually surprised by the dissent, having expected approval.

But enough now of this sentimentalising: it was foolish to show it, and I shall try to avoid that for the future.

I'll see if I can finish writing the wireless talk for you.

ARNOLD SCHÖNBERG

100. To WINFRIED ZILLIG[1] *Berlin, 20 October* 1927

Dear Zillig,

This is an *excellent piece*. If *I* were allowed to conduct, *I* should instantly take up the cudgels for it. But you know, don't you, I am not allowed to. But I am convinced, today, when musicians and conductors are beginning to be able to read this sort of thing more easily, you will soon find someone to perform the piece. I also think that people are sure to like it very much.

Well now I've written you a letter here. Next time I'll go back to my own writing-paper.

Very best wishes, yours,

ARNOLD SCHÖNBERG

[1] Schoenberg wrote this 'letter' on the title-page of the Overture for large orchestra by Winfried Zillig, who was at that time his pupil, and sent Zillig, with the score, to Klemperer.

To Anton Webern   OCTOBER 1927

101. To ANTON WEBERN   *Berlin*, 31 *October* 1927

My very dear fellow,

Not much news for the moment. We have no flat of our own, only three furnished rooms with board. But I have at last got my study fitted up. And the furniture-moving etc. that this involved took up a lot of my time.

You may know that I am going to conduct the Gurre-Lieder in London this year (in January).[1] In December I shall probably be conducting an orchestral concert given by Frau Freund (Waldtaube, Bach chorales, Pelleas and Pierrot); also, under the aegis of the S.M.I., the new Suite and Pierrot, and piano pieces as well (Steuermann). In February Pierrot, in Basle and Berne, and in March, in Chemnitz, Bach chorales, Verklärte Nacht and Pelleas. Quite a fresh start after years of neglect.

In Berlin there'll be an evening devoted to your new string trio (to which I am looking forward with much curiosity), Berg's Lyric Suite, and my 3rd Quartet.

I hope I can get down to work again soon. At the moment I have to prepare a lecture that I want to give in Paris, at the Sorbonne (in French); subject (approximately): criteria of musical value, or something like that.

If you knew that I would have to spend at least two hours a day writing letters if I were to get through my correspondence, you would forgive my long silence. In addition, my dislike of letter-writing increases daily. I find it more and more difficult to produce something as imperfect as an unrevised letter is, improvised as to both form and content. If it were not for the typewriter, which still gives me a certain amount of pleasure, I'm sure nothing would ever get answered. As it is I do answer about a fifth, some of it on matters that are of importance to me.

It would be very good if you could get out of Vienna again too for once. Perhaps we could try to find a way of getting up a concert here for you. Only there isn't much hope of it, for the concerts are all run at a very great loss!

Please write to me very often; I'm always so glad to get news from Vienna. Do you find time for work? And how about your Concerto? [. . . . .]

                                                                 ARNOLD SCHÖNBERG

---

[1] 1928!

SCHOENBERG IN 1927

AETAT 53 *To Intendant Turnau, Breslau*
102. To HERBERT GRAF[1] *Berlin, 14 March* 1928
Dear Sir,
   I agree to your proposals for the fee.
   But if you take the line that the author isn't wanted at rehearsals, I cannot have anything at all to do with it. I could not have granted the rights for such an important performance[2] without reserving to myself a certain amount of influence on the final form my work would take. Should you not be able to meet me on this point, I should, however much I regretted it, have to dissociate myself from your production, just as I did not attend that of 'Erwartung' in Wiesbaden, where Herr Bekker likewise invited me to the dress-rehearsal.
   It is perhaps taking a risk if I now postpone the attempt to draft a lecture until I receive your answer; but it strikes me as much more of a risk to announce a lecture by me without considering the possibility that I may not approve of the production (let us assume e.g.: the chorus's performance) and yet by virtue of this very lecture am so to speak authorising the whole enterprise. If you think that the work has been sufficiently well done at your end, then you need have no fear of the author's presence. He still understands enough to recognise that, anyway. He is satisfied if he sees there is seriousness and good will. But he is affronted if there is any attempt to pass him over, any idea that anyone else knows best. Knows what best? Everything!
   Do not believe that I am trying to exert pressure on you: read the letters I have written on this matter, and you will have to admit that I insisted on all this from the very beginning: I take this opportunity of reminding you that I wished to make a suggestion about the arrangement of rehearsals, another suggestion that you did not think it worth considering!
   Here is my minimum demand: put the 23rd at my disposal for a rehearsal, which must last until I am satisfied: then I shall come.
                                                     ARNOLD SCHÖNBERG

103. To INTENDANT TURNAU, BRESLAU[3]   *Berlin, 29 March* 1928
Herr Prof. Turnau,
Municipal Theatre, Breslau

My dear Herr Generalintendant,
   Let me first of all say what particularly gratified me at the Breslau

[1] Producer at the Municipal Theatre, Breslau.
[2] *Die glückliche Hand* ('The Lucky Hand'). See the following letter.
[3] Handwritten draft, which Schoenberg kept, as in similar cases, as a record of a handwritten letter.

I   S.S.L.

To Intendant Turnau, Breslau MARCH 1928

performance of my 'Glückliche Hand': the intense enthusiasm with which every individual threw himself into the work.

I must say that even with my more 'popular' works, e.g. the Gurre-Lieder, I have never yet had to such a degree the feeling that my work was being treated with respect and indeed with affection.

And this was, I think, the source of all the qualities that this production had: All those in charge were dedicated to the matter in hand, and more than that: they were capable of communicating their own enthusiasm to the others, capable of evoking an achievement of sheer artistic will, the one and only means of so perfectly overcoming the difficulties inherent in the material; causing them to be so far forgotten that even in writing this letter I had forgotten that Breslau is not Berlin and that I ought to apply a relative standard, not an absolute one: in other words, one felt one was in an artistic capital. So I should like first and foremost to thank you and the management: Dr. Graf, Herr Cortolezzi, Herr Prof. Wildermann, and then the 'soloists', among whom I must actually indeed count not only Herr Andra, Frl. Swedlund and Herr Gargula, but all the rest as well: above all the six ladies and six gentlemen but not least the orchestra, whose admirable performance was a great surprise to me.

ARNOLD SCHÖNBERG

104. TO WILHELM FURTWÄNGLER *Berlin, 30 May 1928*
Dear Herr Dr. Furtwängler,

Herr Stein informed you quite correctly: I did indeed three-quarters finish an orchestral work, 'Variations on an Original Theme', *two* years ago. But since then I have not been in a position to complete it. Meanwhile I have finished and also published a great deal else; and although I am sure it would not take me much more than a fortnight to finish this work, I simply cannot say when it will be done.

In any case I thank you very much indeed for your kind interest and your charming letter. Should I finish the work, I shall let you know. Only one thing I should like to say at once: I would not let a new work have its first performance in Vienna. The fact is I am the only composer of any reputation at all whom the Philharmonic have not yet performed. And it may as well rest at that!

With all good wishes and very kind regards, I am, yours very truly,

ARNOLD SCHÖNBERG

105. To WILHELM FURTWÄNGLER

Roquebrune Cap Martin, 21 September 1928

Dear Herr Furtwängler,

Today I wrote the last bar of the score[1] and hasten to answer your letter at once. What I still have to do is revise the score and have it photographed. I hope to be able to send it to you then in about 5–6 days.

The Berlin performance will be the first, and it is a great pleasure to me to put it into your hands. The work will probably take 12–15 minutes to perform (unfortunately I have no metronome here to work it out more exactly), according to whether the 'full' tempi can be taken (which depends, after all, on whether the orchestra can manage it); this is without really taking account of the time needed for ritardandi etc. With regard to the Vienna Philharmonic: I should like to forestall any possible misunderstanding at once! It is like this: I shall have to insist on the Philharmonic's fulfilling a condition, on which it will depend whether I let them have any works to perform or not. What I allude to is: making up for damage done, i.e. they will have to make good their omission before there can be any talk of anything else.

I am sure I do not need to make a point of asking you to regard this problem as something that has nothing to do with you personally. But you will appreciate the fact that the great injury done me by the Philharmonic precisely in the years of my hardest struggles cannot be allowed to remain unatoned for!

A word more about the 'Variations for Orchestra'. I do not think the work excessively difficult from the ensemble point of view. Easier indeed than e.g. 'Pierrot lunaire' or 'Erwartung'. On the other hand, the individual parts are for the most part *very* difficult, so that in this case the quality of the performance depends on the *musicianship* of the players. I am very probably going to say something that you will certainly also have been doing for a long time and which you have probably known longer than I have: in such cases I have found it very useful to read the piece through once with the players a fair time beforehand. They then see which parts they must practise, and they do so. And I think the piece is so orchestrated (at least that was my intention) that the sound depends on the players' playing exactly what I have written.

In a few days, then.

ARNOLD SCHÖNBERG

[1] The *Variations for Orchestra*, op. 31. See previous letter.

To Professor Leo Kestenberg   JUNE 1928

106. TO PROFESSOR LEO KESTENBERG, BERLIN

Temporarily: Vienna, 18 *June* 1928

In connection with a conversation that I had with Schreker[1] some weeks ago about the Kleiber-Klemperer-Walter-Bodanzky intrigue, I wished to show him my own attitude to all that kind of thing: that I do not take the slightest notice of intrigues and the like; that I feel the like of us are in any case no match for that sort of thing and do best not to let themselves be in any way lured into taking sides; and told him, as an example of intrigue on the one hand, and, on the other hand, of my indifference to that sort of thing, how in the early days of my appointment in Berlin, when there was some hostility to his holding the position he did, I was given more or less obvious hints about my chances of becoming Director of the Hochschule. Now Schreker has written to tell me that he has raised the question with you. However, since I mentioned no names to him and most scrupulously avoided giving any hint as to who the four people involved were, and since, furthermore, even now, after giving the matter some thought, I cannot definitely say whether you were present when the matter arose, it cannot of course be my fault if Schreker has had the idea of raising the question with you.[2] In any case I wish this letter to be regarded as establishing the original form of my remarks and as a declaration that I did not make those remarks in order to cause mischief, but on the contrary: in order to demonstrate how one best holds aloof from that sort of commotion: with the effect *that it now besets me*!!! I dare say that is how it is with all worldly wisdom: in dodging one waggon bearing down on me, I run smack into the other! It goes without saying that what I said was not intended to be passed on: it was foolish of me not to reckon with that; and it is a lesson to me *to do exactly the same in future*; for I do not see what concern of mine the consequences are! I am sending a copy of this letter to Schreker, hoping and trusting that it will help to bring about an understanding between you both. I should be glad to achieve that!

I shall soon be leaving here. Probably for France, where I have the advantage of understanding the language even less than what is called the language in this country, and where I am in a position to imagine things quite different from what people are actually saying to me: That is why I always so much like being abroad.

[. . . . .]

ARNOLD SCHÖNBERG

[1] The composer Franz Schreker was Director of the Hochschule für Musik in Berlin.
[2] At the bottom of the carbon copy of this letter there is a note written by hand: 'The

AETAT 54

107. TO HEINRICH JALOWETZ

To Paul Bekker
Berlin, 18 April 1929

Dr. Heinrich Jalowetz,
Municipal Opera House, Cologne
[..........]

Première rights[1] have not yet been given to anyone. (But would you only do the première? I think I can guarantee that the work itself wouldn't change as a result of having been used once already.) The piece is in one act, lasts roughly 45–55 minutes and has only one scene; a room, no difficulties with lighting or other apparatus, no costumes, modern dress. It is a cheerful to gay, sometimes even (I hope at least) comic, opera; not grotesque, not offensive, not political, not religious. The music is as bad as mine always is: that is, appropriate to my intellectual and artistic condition. But it is also appropriate to the subject and therefore continually produces self-contained forms that are interrupted and linked by distinct (but naturally 'non-tonal') recitatives that do not set up to be melodic. There are several ensembles: duets and quartets. But there are only four characters: a soprano, say Gutheil-Schoder, but somewhat brighter and lighter; a second soprano, higher and still lighter, perhaps like Lotte Schöne; a baritone, somewhat like Duhan in Vienna, but I should have nothing against Bohnen; then a sweet, thin, lyric tenor such as Tauber or Naval, whose vocal sweetness might even produce a touch of involuntary comedy; i.e., if he is not capable of appearing comic in spite of it.

Now I think I have said everything important. The best thing would be for your Intendant to entrust you with the honourable task of looking at the music; then we should see each other again after all this time.

ARNOLD SCHÖNBERG

108. TO PAUL BEKKER[2]

Berlin, 22 June 1929

Dear Sir,

I enclose the libretto, by Max Blonda,* of an opera, 'Von heute auf morgen', which I recently finished composing.

At the moment I am still in a position to grant the rights for the first performance. Since, however, owing to some dissension with Universal Edition I cannot have it published for the present, I shall have to have

four persons were Kestenberg, Schünemann, Schnabel and Gmeindl. — I do not want to cause any mischief.'
'I answered that I would never take over such a job.'
    [1] Of the opera *Von heute auf morgen*.
    [2] Generalintendant, Wiesbaden.
    * Pseudonym of Schoenberg's second wife. [TRANS].

To Paul Bekker JUNE 1929

the copying done myself and should like to spread these heavy expenses over several theatres, actually not granting first-performance rights, but trying to place the performing-rights with about ten theatres for a period of one year, in return for a share in the cost of the copying, without setting a definite date for the first performance.[1]

For these reasons I cannot yet send you either a score or a piano arrangement. What I could perhaps do is to have a photographic copy made of the very legible first draft (in short-score form).

[..........]

ARNOLD SCHÖNBERG

109. WILHELM FURTWÄNGLER   *Berlin, 4 June* 1929
Dear Herr Doktor,

Let me say before all else that when an artist like yourself expresses a wish to me, it is of course a pleasure to say 'Yes!' and this also means saying I am very glad to give you the rights for the first performance of my Bach arrangement (Prelude and Fugue for Organ in E flat major for large orchestra).

But may I also now say that I am somewhat disappointed at your not having done my orchestral pieces[2] again after the scenes in Berlin, considering, after all, that the hissing was at least as much of an oafish impertinence towards you as towards me. Frankly, I expected that you would repeat the piece at the next concert, showing the rabble that *you only do what you consider right*! Indeed several journalists wrote something to this effect, saying that the fact that you conducted the work amounted to identifying yourself with it, acknowledging its value.

It is not my intention, in saying this, to try to make any conditions; for nothing is right in any such case but what one does of one's own free will.

Yet if I am to give praise honestly, I must also be able to do the opposite just as honestly.

[..........]

ARNOLD SCHÖNBERG

110. TO INTENDANT FLESCH, BERLIN   *Berlin, 4 October* 1929
Radio Berlin
Dear Herr Intendant,

On the 23.ix., that is, more than a week ago, I addressed a letter to 'The Musical Management, Radio Berlin', saying: 'My First String

---

[1] The first performance was given at the Opera House in Frankfurt-am-Main in January 1930; shortly afterwards (in February) the opera was broadcast by Radio Berlin.

[2] Schoenberg means the *Variations for Orchestra*, op. 31 (see Letter 105).

AETAT 55(?)   *To Intendant Flesch, Berlin*

Quartet was recently broadcast by you with two cuts. Please inform me whether you were aware of this violation of my artistic rights.'

  The 'Musical Management' has not thought it necessary to answer. If it were merely a matter of my ambition, I might be perfectly satisfied with this sign of disesteem. Since, however, there is little doubt that it will turn out to be a legal matter, I cannot content myself with expressions of disesteem on both sides and am therefore now raising my question with 'higher authorities', hoping to meet with higher civility in that quarter, although indeed this is a matter in which the most ordinary civility would have sufficed.[1]

ARNOLD SCHÖNBERG

111.   [*No date; presumably* 1929]

Answers to a questionnaire[2]

1. Are you satisfied with the present German educational system?

   No.

2. What defects strike you as as most serious?

   The way the young are stuffed with 'ready-made' knowledge and acquire only 'tangible' qualifications.

3. What is your idea of good educational methods?

   Encouraging young people to look at things for themselves, to observe, compare, define, describe, weigh, test, draw conclusions and use them.

4. What cultural ideal should modern youth strive to attain?

   (*a*) knowledge in the sense of understanding,
   (*b*) skill that is constantly refreshed and enlarged from the depths of the knowledge that is understanding.

5. Can and should teachers try to influence the young in this direction?

   Yes.

---

[1] The matter was in due course settled to Schoenberg's satisfaction.
[2] Handwritten draft; the name of the author of the questionnaire cannot be deciphered.

Answers to a Questionnaire   PRESUMABLY 1929

6. By what methods?   By training the mind. By bringing the pupil (according to the stage he has reached) face to face with the difficulties, problems, and inherent terms of the given material; by helping him to recognise them; by forcing him to help himself in this respect, which means letting him make his own mistakes and correcting them afterwards, but also being of assistance to him in finding the solution.

[..........]

                                                            ARNOLD SCHÖNBERG

112. TO INTENDANT FLESCH, BERLIN

[*Handwritten draft, no date (probably February or March* 1930)]

I have played through the records of my opera[1] several times and — for artistic reasons — prefer not to conceal from you the fact that these sounds depress me extremely. I cannot bring myself to believe that it is my fault, either as composer or as conductor; but, even while admitting that I do not know, I really must say: my music must not sound like this. Either *I* must change, or the *performance* or the *reproduction* must.

In connection with these reflections I have now (by the following chronological process) developed an idea that I should like to put to you.

First I thought: perhaps one has to get one's ear in, and I intended suggesting that you should make an agreement with me entitling you to repeat the individual pieces several times as recorded concerts (separately).

Then I got the idea that it might perhaps be better to do at least one or two of the recordings again.

Then I thought this might be done in a mixed programme, since after

---

[1] *Von heute auf morgen* was broadcast by Radio Berlin in February 1930, with Schoenberg conducting. This draft letter refers to records made on this occasion. There is no evidence whether the letter was sent in this form, but Dr. Flesch was in the habit of accepting Schoenberg's suggestions, and regular broadcasts of new music were in fact established by Radio Berlin.

AETAT 55   *To Alban Berg*

all the cost of a short repetition is not very great once the orchestra has been rehearsed anyway.

And then I came straight to what I think is a very good idea. It is this:

The Radio could (e.g., once or twice a week), after concluding its evening programme (about 11.30 p.m.) do a series of half-hour to one-hour broadcasts with the title *Propaganda* for New Music, and for this purpose, by

A. (*a*) partly using records already existing,

    (*b*) partly, say, using an orchestra or the given ensemble and soloists,

    (*c*) partly using piano,

        1. with the aid of *elucidatory talks*,

        2. [by] *playing passages*, section, bars, themes, motifs (of any required length),

        3. in conclusion perhaps [by] performing the whole or part of the piece discussed,

help to create a basis of understanding for either an already given or a forthcoming performance; and at the same time turn to account

B. (*a*) both this demonstration itself and also

    (*b*) such rehearsals as might be required, beforehand, in order (by repeated listening, regulating, and altering of instrumentation and players, as also by making any such slight revisions as might seem necessary) to

        1. find a style of *performance* and of *broadcasting* for modern music,

        2. establish the laws or at least approximate rules to be observed.

I shall be glad to discuss the matter with you in detail and would also be prepared to organise such a series of programmes, possibly indeed to take charge of it.

                                                                            ARNOLD SCHÖNBERG

113. To ALBAN BERG, VIENNA[1]   *Baden-Baden*, 10 *April* 1930

[..........]

After a year of very strenuous work I too was in real need of a holiday and I'm busy playing tennis instead of working as I'd meant to. — Shortly before leaving Berlin (and this is what I'm mainly writing to you

[1] The letter is written by hand.

To Alban Berg APRIL 1930

about), I was rung up by Schreker, who wanted me to sound you about something on his behalf. I had to refuse, since I did him such a service once before (Frau Gutheil), but was then left looking a fool because after receiving her consent he failed to follow the matter up. I have to explain this first, so that this question shouldn't again raise hopes that may then not be fulfilled, and I must tell you that you must still face this possibility even if *Schr.* makes you an offer directly. For they make these things very easy for themselves here: they ask a number of people *without prejudice*, and it's only when they've got them to agree that they make their final choice, and apply to the Ministry for official approval!!! Well anyway, the question is to be this: whether you would accept an appointment as a teacher of composition at the Hochschule [Berlin]. Salary 8–900 Marks a month; teaching also of subsidiary subjects. (You would have to insist on long holidays — to be discussed with me!) — If you were to ask my advice: Yes! Very definitely: Yes! You would be able to breathe freely here. And after all it's a very considerable step towards security. True, the salary isn't high and one can't afford much in the way of luxuries. But one can manage very nicely. You would have to insist *absolutely* on a guarantee of somewhere to live. And in fact preferably in such a way that the Ministry pays 1. the cost of moving, 2. whatever has to be put down for premium or mortgage, and 3. a monthly bonus of about 2–300 Marks for the beginning, until you have a place to live in.

But now I must tell you: since I refused to ask you, Schreker said he would do it himself, as he was going to Vienna anyway. Perhaps he won't really do it. I am telling you about it so that you have time to think. Otherwise one isn't prepared to deal with such things. So I hope Schreker asks you. I should be overjoyed to have you in Berlin. NB: You know that such approaches have to be kept secret, so one must not tell *anyone*.

Now before finishing this letter I just want to congratulate you with all my heart on your opera.[1] I was very pleased indeed about it. . . . Finally, one more thing: Heinrichshofen are soon to publish my 'Accompaniment to a Film-Scene', for small orchestra, and Bote & Bock: a cycle, six male-voice choruses. But what I'm going to write now I still don't know. What I'd like best is an opera. Actually I have some plans, even for my own libretto, and have also thought of Werfel, whose novel (which you gave me — did I ever thank you for it? Anyway I do so now!) I liked very much. Do you think he would do something *together* with me? For with my last opera I did collaborate a lot. But

[1] *Wozzeck*.

AETAT 55   *To Intendant Legal, Berlin*

perhaps I shall do 'Moses and Aaron'. — Now: all very best wishes to your wife and yourself. Also from my wife.

Yours ever,
ARNOLD SCHÖNBERG

114. TO INTENDANT LEGAL, BERLIN, OPER AM PLATZ DER REPUBLIK
Baden-Baden, 14 *April* 1930

Dear Herr Intendant,

I am answering so quickly because I think this *letter might encourage you to make a little Easter trip* here in your handsome motor-car. I myself am not likely to be back in Berlin before the 15th May [. . . . .] — But what I can say about the production problems even now is this:[1]

The most important thing is: I believe that you are *not* one of the producers who look at a work only in order to see how to make it into *something quite different*. Such a wrong could never be greater than if done to me, since while I was composing I had all the scenic effects in mind, seeing them with the utmost precision.

In 'Erwartung' the greatest difficulty is this:

I. It is essential for the woman to be seen always *in the forest*, so that people realise that she is *afraid of it*!! For the whole drama *can* be understood as a nightmare. But for that very reason it must be a *real* forest and not merely a 'conventional' one, for one may loathe the latter, but one can't be afraid of it.

II. In composing I left almost no time for the three transformations, so that they must be managed without bringing down the curtain.

III. Further, it is only in the last (4th) scene that the back of the stage plays any part, during which the front of the stage must be *empty*, so that anything disturbing a clear view must be removed. —

The first two transformations can be done by merely shifting the light indicating the path along which the woman must go, so that she enters from different sides, and for the rest one can manage by merely representing another part of the forest by using some movable or revolving scenery. In the 4th scene the house in the background must become visible and the forest must have disappeared.

This problem isn't easy to solve. — At home I have begun making a little model in an attempt to fit up two little revolving discs on the stage, so that by turning them to the side everything that's no longer wanted

[1] Schoenberg's operas *Erwartung* and *Die glückliche Hand* were produced at the Oper am Platz der Republik later that year.

To Intendant Legal, Berlin   APRIL 1930

can be removed. On the groundplan that would perhaps look somewhat as shown by the enclosed paper model. Here there are two little discs. But one can perhaps fit up some more. The size is a matter for the technicians. There are four sections, each built up differently. By setting the axial points eccentrically one can get a narrow strip quite empty for the 4th scene. The discs may be so small that they can be revolved by hand. — What do you think of the idea?

In the 'Glückliche Hand' the main thing is:

I. The use of coloured lights. Strong lights are needed, and *good colours*. The set must be painted in such a way that it *takes on* the colours!

II. For an infinite number of reasons the construction of the stage and the set must be carried out to a T in accordance with my directions, otherwise nothing will work. I did once make drawings for this, which I would have to look for. Anyway I ought to be sent the sketches in plenty of time to have a look at them.

III. I have also exactly fixed the positions of the actors and the lines along which they have to move. I am convinced that this must be exactly kept to if everything is to turn out all right.

IV. Lighting up the 12 faces in the 1st and 4th scenes, making them disappear and appear again (and instantly!) is very difficult and must be discussed.

V. The mythical animal must be very big. The experiment made in Vienna and Breslau, of having a human being to do it, has so far turned out to be no good at all. Above all at the end of the 3rd scene, where the boulder begins to shine and topples on the man and then turns into the mythical animal. Above all no performer has been able to jump so far (about 8-9 feet). But anyway a jump like that doesn't look like toppling. Here it would probably be best to come back to my description.

VI. At the end of the 1st scene the curtain should *tear*. So far not even a suggestion of this has been managed anywhere. My wife thinks [it could be done] by projection. I think a skilled upholsterer ought to be able to contrive it with a system of blind-cords.

VII. Likewise, at the end of the 1st scene 'black veils' descend on the man. Hitherto not solved either.

VIII. The 'sun' in the second scene isn't easy to do either. It must be low down!

I think I have indicated most of what has caused difficulties so far.

I have no liking for what is called 'stylised' decorations (what style?)

AETAT 55 *To Intendant Flesch, Berlin*

and always want to see a set done by the good old experienced hand of a painter who can draw a straight line straight and not model his work on children's drawings or the art of primitive peoples. The objects and settings in my pieces *also play their parts*, and so they should be just as clearly recognisable as the pitch of the notes. If the people in the audience are confronted with a picture-puzzle ('Where is the hunter?') and have to begin by asking what it means, they miss hearing part of the music. Although this may suit them, it is not what I want.

This has become a long letter, but I hope it isn't too long. I am very interested in this production and am entirely at your disposal. And: everything should be done in good time! For in the end there is always a rush anyway.

[..........]

ARNOLD SCHÖNBERG

115. To INTENDANT FLESCH, BERLIN *Baden-Baden*, 14 *June* 1930

Herr Intendant Dr. Flesch,
Radio Berlin

I have just seen that the problem of criticism is being discussed over the wireless.

Here is a suggestion I have long had in mind:
confrontation of divergent opinions and the author's remarks on them.

In the following form:

Three critics first talk for three minutes each, the talk properly worked out and in writing, approximately 1½ pages of typescript.

Then the author: answer. Also in writing (the critics' manuscripts having previously been shown to him), about five to six minutes.

Then free discussion:

The three critics reply in the same way, each having 2–3 minutes. Final remarks by the author or some objective person (if such exists), 5–6 minutes.

The whole thing to last scarcely half an hour.[1]

For the sake of variety one might also consider: One critic only, another specialist, a member of the public, and the author.

Further one could occasionally also interpolate, for variety, singly, the views of members of the public, well sifted, interestingly arranged, if necessary with comments by author or critic.

In a general way I have for years had the idea of getting someone to

---

[1] Schoenberg's suggestion was adopted.

To Intendant Flesch, Berlin JUNE 1930

start a periodical in which the public could express opinions in the manner described above.

ARNOLD SCHÖNBERG

116. TO THE DEUTSCHE ALLGEMEINE ZEITUNG *Berlin, 18 June* 1930
Herr Raffael da Costa, Vienna
Deutsche Allgemeine Zeitung

For someone as unpopular as I am to answer the question about 'musical life and a shift of the centre of gravity from Vienna to Berlin' means running the risk of making himself still more disliked.

I shall avoid this risk by trying to express unpopular opinions in an unpopular way:

Even before the war people in Vienna were rightly and wrongly proud and ashamed of being less active than Berlin.

Even at that time Berlin showed a lively and intense interest in recognising and explaining the symptoms of a work of art, something that was missing in Vienna, thanks to centuries of experience in composing.

Even in those days whatever was new was derided after several performances in Berlin, whereas in Vienna it needed only one performance. In extreme cases — in both places — no performance at all.

Even in those days, in both cities, the public had discovered that there is always plenty of time to honour a great man after he is dead. Presumably it had been recognised even in those days that it can then be done more effectively and decoratively and, what is most to the point, more lucratively.

The Society for Private Concerts in Vienna[1] had three hundred members, two hundred of them good ones. But they could not keep it afloat.

1/10,000th of 2 millions is 200;
1/10,000th ,, 4 ,, ,, 400.

Perhaps four hundred can keep an artistically pure enterprise going?

I am looking for a centre of *gravity* and find them all too light.

What didn't get shiftily shifted during the inflation! Perhaps, behind my back, some lighter centres of gravity as well?

ARNOLD SCHÖNBERG

117. TO ALBAN BERG *Lugano, 5 August* 1930
My dear fellow,

Above all hearty congratulations on your car and all good wishes for much pleasure with it. Many thanks for your news about your adapta-

[1] See Biographical Notes, p. 61.

tion of 'Erdgeist' and 'Büchse der Pandora'.[1] The arrangement is sure to be very good: that much one can gather even now. I am very eager to see it as a finished work and entirely understand your point of view in wanting to show it only at that stage. What a third person imagines about a house that isn't built yet is, after all, unfortunately so irrelevant that one can't quite understand how artists of earlier times could discuss their unbuilt houses with their friends, though one does sometimes long to be able to do the same thing.

So I also appreciate (your hint in your last letter, evidently meant to warn me in good time) that you are still anxious about my 'Moses and Aaron'. I suppose, because you have seen some similarity to some other work treating the same subject; something to which, as you write, 'it might have a certain external similarity'. You are obviously thinking of Strindberg.[2] A whole year ago I looked into that play for this reason. There is in fact a certain similarity in so far as we both go in for somewhat Biblical language and even use many outright quotations. As a matter of fact I am now, among other revisions, removing these Biblical echoes. Not because of the likeness to Strindberg; that wouldn't matter: But because I am of the opinion that the language of the Bible is mediaeval German, which, being obscure to us, should be used at most to give colour; and that is something I don't need. I cannot suppose, considering your thoroughness and the confidence that I am sure you have in my inventive gifts, that you have found any other similarity. I don't at the moment remember what idea Strindberg was presenting. But mine, both my main idea and the many, many subsidiary ideas literally and symbolically presented, is all so much tied up with my own personality that it is impossible for Strindberg to have presented anything that could have even an external similarity. You would have been sure to find this on looking through the work again, all the more if — which is, after all, as you know, absolutely necessary with my work — you had looked at every word and every sentence from several points of view. Today I can really scarcely remember what belongs to me: but one thing must be granted me (I won't let myself be deprived of it): Everything I have written has a certain inner likeness to myself.

I have already finished the first page, have sketched out a lot and hope soon to be getting up speed. I hope I'll soon be able to produce a

---

[1] *Earth Spirit* and its sequel, *Pandora's Box*, two plays by Frank Wedekind, out of which Berg made the libretto for his opera *Lulu*.

[2] Strindberg's *Moses* is the first part of his posthumous *Cosmic Trilogy*. The other two parts are entitled *Socrates* and *Christ*.

To Alban Berg AUGUST 1930

decent definitive libretto. Then you shall have it. Meanwhile: all very best wishes.

ARNOLD SCHÖNBERG

118. TO THOMAS MANN[1] *Berlin, 1 November* 1930

Dear Sir,

Unfortunately I have not the honour of knowing you personally. If I nevertheless approach you with the request that you should sign the enclosed appeal, it is because I know that Adolf Loos[2] wishes for nothing more dearly than that six or seven of the outstanding men of the day should sign it and so exert their influence in order that his longing to teach may be fulfilled.[3]

I would most warmly urge you to comply with this request if for no other reason than that Loos is so ill that one may be doing it for a dying man.

But I can say better than that; and if I am right in claiming that people of a certain standing have a sense of that standing, which teaches them who is their peer and who is not, then you will believe me when I say that Loos is one of the Very Great — if you do not already know this better than I!

ARNOLD SCHÖNBERG

119. TO THOMAS MANN *Berlin, 8 November* 1930

Dear Herr Mann,

Not only do I appreciate your scruples, not only did I foresee them, I must even confess that in your place I should not have been able to do otherwise. And the difference in our relation to Loos is neither my merit nor your fault. For Loos himself, who has taken up the cudgels for many artists, has neglected to do for his own work even as much as is done by those who hold most aloof from the world: he has not let his work be either exhibited or photographed, and it is only here and there that something has slipped through on which one might base an opinion. If I had not been a friend of his for 35 years, I should scarcely know more than everybody else does.

It strikes me as an omen that yesterday, while trying to arrange my books after moving house, I came across a volume by Adolf Loos: 'Ins Leere gesprochen, 1897–1900' [literally: 'Words spoken to the Void']. I do not want to influence you (I have not that presumption) but: I do

---
[1] The writer.   [2] The architect.
[3] The purpose was to found a Loos school.

AETAT 56   *To Theodor Wiesengrund-Adorno*

want to carry out my mission to the best of my ability. I therefore take the liberty of posting this book to you.

Since it is a copy signed by the author, I must apologetically put you to the trouble of sending it back. I should be very glad if it enabled you to gather some impression of Loos: what he knew before 1900![1]

With deep respect and regard, I am, yours very truly,

                                        ARNOLD SCHÖNBERG

120. TO PROFESSOR ALEXANDER AMERSDORFER

                                        Berlin, 6 November 1930

Herr Prof. Dr. Alexander Amersdorfer,
Academy of Arts in Berlin

For some days I have been hoping to call on you. But for the last three weeks I have been unable to shake off an attack of influenza, and so I must after all appeal to you by letter.

Adolf *Loos* will be sixty in December. At the moment he is in the Lakatos Sanatorium, in Baden near Vienna, gravely, perhaps dangerously, ill.

In the almost forty years of his activity as a reformer and an artist he has, to the best of my knowledge, never received any public honour.

[..........]

I speak of this at such length because it seems to me that the Academy of Arts in Berlin might consider an exhibition, unless some other honour, such as for instance electing him to membership, might strike you as more fitting.

Do not think it presumptuous of me not to stick to my last. But I have known Loos for 35 years and wherever I have gone in the world during the last 15 years: in Germany, Holland, Switzerland, France, Italy, Spain, Denmark, etc., I have seen Loos-like buildings, yet they were not by Loos, but by imitators. And it seems to me that once again it is the original who ought to be honoured.

[..........]   ARNOLD SCHÖNBERG

121. TO THEODOR WIESENGRUND-ADORNO[2]

                                       Berlin, 6 December 1930[?]

Herr Dr. Wiesengrund-Adorno,
Frankfurt-am-Main

[..........]

I should like to propose compiling a dictionary of musical (aesthetics

[1] Thomas Mann's answer was positive: 'A man with a vigorous, independent, distinguished mind, no doubt of that!'
[2] The musicologist.

To Theodor Wiesengrund-Adorno DECEMBER 1930(?)

or) theory. Such a work might, by analogy with say a philosophical dictionary (or any other such), trace the significant development of each subject through the whole of history.

The historical section could be compiled by specialists on the basis of the original sources, perhaps not without some labour, but without difficulty, so as to create a platform on which the more modern concepts could then be established. Here I should consider it rewarding to illustrate the various tendencies and views by letting their original exponents speak for themselves, so that the reader would find the various views collected under one heading. E.g. (e.g.!!!): Schenker, Howard, Mersmann (??), Schönberg, Wiesengrund, Stein, Wellesz (??), Hauer, etc., etc. Probably one would have first to find a publisher or a financial backer or subscribers; perhaps also to get up a committee: for the structure, the execution, the uniformity, but also for the practical problems.

What do you think?[1] [..........]

ARNOLD SCHÖNBERG

122. TO ADOLF LOOS, PRAGUE[2]　　　*Berlin, 10 December* 1930

In the service of ideas the lesser and greater achieve their best by living and working so as to serve as a model to those who strive towards the same goal. But how often is a great man to be found like you, Adolf Loos, of whom one can be sure even today that in a hundred years his name will ring, what he said be quoted, what he did be recounted, in countless citations of your words, your work and the way you lived. In intense admiration and unchangeable friendship, very best wishes.

[..........]

ARNOLD SCHÖNBERG

123. TO ANTON WEBERN　　　*Berlin, 22 January* 1931

My very dear fellow,

Your plan for the Mondsee courses I think excellent in principle. Only I would recommend your possibly arranging the analyses in such a way (by the choice of works) as to show the logical development towards 12-note composition. Thus e.g., the Netherlands School, Bach for counterpoint, Mozart for phrasing but also for handling of motifs,

---
[1] This letter remained unanswered.
[2] Letter-telegram for Loos's 60th birthday.

Beethoven but also Bach for development, Brahms and possibly Mahler for varied and complex treatment. I think this outlines the most important points.

The title could then be: 'The road to twelve-note composition'.

[..........]

What a pity you didn't hear 'Erwartung'.[1] I think it was very good. I have never before worked so well with an orchestra, never before rehearsed so well, heard so well, kept such a good beat, as this time. Admittedly I was (not unmindful of your curtain-lecture) much better prepared this time than usual. [..........] So far I have no more concerts for this season. I can't get the better of those who make a good thing out of calling me a bad conductor.

I'm now taking up my work again, which has been laid aside since October. I hope to be in full swing soon.

[..........]

Arnold Schönberg

124. To Heinrich Jalowetz[2]   Berlin, 1 February 1931

My dear Jalowetz, friend, Doktor, and Kapellmeister,

So I gave you a title that you prefer not to hear from my lips or my typewriter, did I? Or what *are* you reproaching me for?

But please, sir, I didn't do it on purpose, cross m' heart I didn't.*

I really can't remember doing it: but such things do happen when one has so little chance to speak to someone from whom one hears so rarely. It happened to me recently with Berg too: for some time I just kept on saying 'Sie' to him! And it certainly wasn't intentional, for as soon as I noticed it I began uttering such a vast quantity of '*du*'*s*' that I must have laid in an advance supply to cover a great many accidental '*Sie*'*s*'. Well: so what am I to do? Or: what can you do to stop me from doing it again? Write to me often, not counting on immediate answers and not not-writing until I answer. For my correspondence is terrifyingly huge and I can hardly cope with anything but what's urgent.

What you told me about the performance pleases me very much. I've

---

[1] Schoenberg had conducted his *Erwartung* ['Expectation'] for a B.B.C. broadcast in London at the beginning of January.

[2] *Kapellmeister* at the Municipal Opera House, Cologne.

* The original sentence is in Viennese dialect. The cause of offence, as it appears from the similar incident with Berg reported below, was that Schoenberg not only called his old pupil 'Herr Doktor' but absentmindedly used the formal second-person pronoun, 'Sie' (you), instead of the intimate 'du' (thou). The difference cannot of course be rendered in English. [TRANS.]

To Heinrich Jalowetz　　　　　　　　　　　　　　　February 1931

not really ever heard the piece[1] except at one of Klemperer's rehearsals, for I was ill at the time of the performance. People do seem to like the piece: ought I to draw any conclusions from that as to its quality? I mean: the public apparently likes it.

Pity you couldn't do Webern's songs. He's sure to have been very upset about that, for you know he takes that sort of thing very hard and always draws conclusions from it. It has not been announced on the wireless. At least I haven't heard anything. But that doesn't prove much; for all I was able to hear of my own piece was a few notes here and there, just enough to have some notion of what part was just over. But no more than that, I'm afraid.

On the other hand we have, remarkably enough, heard a good deal of Mozart, and since I can't assume that even the radio-waves try to steer clear of my music and nevertheless have never been able to hear a piece of mine — on account of inexplicable atmospherics — I long ago decided this was the actual broadcasting technique: when playing dangerous or otherwise new music, to allow 'atmospherics' to occur in such a way as to seem natural. I must say: this is what these gentry are best at. I hope that now I shall after all hear something from you now and then, so that no disconcerting 'Doktor' escapes me again!

　　　　　　　　　　　　　　　　　　　　　ARNOLD SCHÖNBERG

125. TO ALEXANDER JEMNITZ[2]　　　　　　　*Berlin, 15 April* 1931

Dear Herr Jemnitz,

I am very glad you were able to conduct my 'Verklärte Nacht': for your sake, for I have long given up the Succession States[3] simply because they have proved themselves so utterly and completely the successors of bygone Austria that one cannot help being more amazed at the durability of such a mentality than at anything else one hears of their achievements: nowhere is there less acquaintance with my music than in former Austrian territory!

But the main thing is, I dare say, that you enjoyed doing it. And for that reason I shall make no further objections to my Pierrot's being performed, although I have considerable qualms about it with such an uneducated public. Only one thing I must say at once and quite firmly:

[1] Although this letter is actually dated 1930, Schoenberg's correspondence with Jalowetz (not published in full here) makes it evident that this was a slip. The letter refers to Jalowetz's conducting, in January 1931, of Schoenberg's *Accompaniment to a Film-Scene*, composed during 1930.

[2] The Hungarian composer.

[3] The Succession States: those states, formerly part of the Austro-Hungarian Empire, that became independent in 1918.

AETAT 56   *To Max Butting*

Pierrot lunaire *is not to be sung*! Song melodies must be balanced and shaped in quite a different way from spoken melodies [*Sprechmelodien*]. You would entirely distort the work if you had it sung, and everyone who said 'That's no way of writing for singing!' would be right. I must tell you that I was for a long time angry with Frau Freund for making the same mistake, and I am convinced that this hint will suffice to keep you from any such infringement.

[..........]
                                                              ARNOLD SCHÖNBERG

126. TO HANS ROSBAUD[1]   *Berlin*, 15 *April* 1931

My very dear Herr Rosbaud,

In all haste, before the very pleasant Frankfurt impressions that I owe to you fade (under the pressure of overwhelming obligations that threaten to absorb me wholly), I want to thank you for the pleasure you gave me by the performance of my Variations for Orchestra.

You must have seen for yourself that I was most unusually pleased by these performances and that I am capable of appreciating your achievement, having for years done all I could to get such work, such thorough study, such preparation not only of the orchestra but also of the conductor, established as the basic requirement of all playing of music in public. So what I experienced was not only a musician's satisfaction at finding his principle of study realised: over and above that it showed me that there are people who set a high artistic morality before all else and are resolved not to attain success by any means other than obedience to that supreme artistic morality.

That I am grateful to you for this is something I need not especially emphasise. But I should like to say apart from this:

I have forgotten much evil and also much good (unfortunately that too) in my life. But I do not want to forget this, for to me it is one of the finest and most reassuring signs in these unpleasing times and, as I have said: I shall make a *point* of remembering it!

[..........]
                                                             ARNOLD SCHÖNBERG

127. TO MAX BUTTING[2]   *Territet*, 5 *July* 1931

Dear Herr Butting,

You find fault with my expression 'horrified' and content yourself with being grieved; and perhaps you might as well consider that an

---

[1] At that time musical director of Radio Frankfurt.

[2] Chairman of the Association of German Composers, Berlin, which controlled performances of musical work in Germany and collected royalties on behalf of its members.

To Max Butting   JULY 1931

appropriate distribution of emotions until you receive my present letter. But perhaps now it will be the other way round, once you have had an examination made of the enclosed copy of my notes. I therefore am sincerely grieved that you neglected to take note of the contents of my letter, in which I mentioned that the number of my performances has more than doubled. And from the enclosed statement you will see that from '30 to '31 up to now they have doubled again.

I do not know who wrote the article in 'Der Schaffende Musiker' ['The Musician at Work'], and can follow the intentions better than the facts on which it is based; at least so far as my music is concerned.

I must object most strongly to the expression 'intellectual constructivism' used there. This expression has been picked up from the gutter of the most illiterate journalistic controversy; it is a sneering battle-cry, a term of abuse on a level with such earlier terms as 'North-German cerebrality' and 'music of the future',* and is not to be used in an objective publication (the organ of a professional association) against an author who, being credited with a quite respectable sum in royalties, thus makes quite a respectable contribution to the publication's support. The writer's attention should furthermore be drawn to the fact that from a more elevated point of view the author thus described would be in a position to prove justification for a demand that 'serious music' should be divided into two categories! Namely: (*a*) 'profoundly serious music' and (*b*) 'shallow serious music', and that species (*a*) would then have to be given higher royalties than species (*b*), on the principle maintained by the Ass. of Ger. Comp.'s scale for light and serious music. Just as, say, the few performances of such work as Wagner's would have to count for more than those of his many contemporaries so prolific in producing light stuff, the like of Raff, Lachner, Reissiger, Reinecke, etc.

I reserve to myself the right to come back to this impropriety.

[. . . . .]

Dear Herr Butting, I am convinced there is not one single person to blame for the mistakes and defects to which I must here take exception, but that you and all your collaborators are filled with the best of intentions and that you are all doing the very best that can be done in this regard. *For the defect is in the system!* It is impossible to deal in pearls, diamonds, radium and other expensive things in the same shop that sells pins, old clothes, and similar junk. And it will never be possible to

* *Zukunftsmusik*: an untranslatable pun. The word is most commonly used to mean 'pipe-dreams', 'castles in the air', something not to be accorded any serious attention. [TRANS.]

150

do a job that takes as much time as keeping a record of popular hits and flops and at the same time have the exactitude and delicate appreciation of rarer goods that is required for serious music. We have spoken of this before, and one example of the damage it causes is the first performance of my 'Film Music'. Do you not agree that it would not have been much trouble to get me a fee several times larger for such a work? Do you not also think that someone who has given up a lifetime to making it possible to compose the way he should — is entitled to make different demands from someone who only composes as long as the stuff is performed and because he is paid for it and who may 'turn in' the whole scribble-scribble in five years' time, as I have seen happen 100 times (shall I give names?).

            Arnold Schönberg

128. To Alban Berg   *Territet, 8 August* 1931

My very dear fellow,

 I am very glad to have heard from you again at long last. . . .

There's another thing I've always meant to write to you about: your contribution to the Loos book. I must say I really admired it and am thoroughly proud of my friends (for I also liked Webern's contribution very much). — So you have one act of an opera finished too,[1] have you? So have I.[2] Almost 1000 bars it runs to. But I've already got 250 of the second act too and am just having a slight rest (rest, indeed: I think I've gone on working for at least several hours every day during this rest), which I'm using in order to revise the second act. I think it's going to turn out not at all bad. Oddly enough I'm working in just the same way: the libretto being definitely finished only during the composing, some of it even afterwards. This proves an extremely good method. Of course — and I dare say you'll have done the same — this is possible only if one starts with a very exact notion of the whole thing, and what takes some doing is not only keeping this vision vivid all the time but intensifying it, enriching it, enlarging it, in the working out of details! All composers of opera should be advised to do this. But of course it wouldn't help much! I want to try very hard to get the opera finished before going back to Berlin. It isn't going as fast as I hoped at the beginning, when I reckoned with a daily *average* of twenty bars. I'm a long way behind with it, although with my previous opera I could count on 25 bars a day. Main reason: the libretto and the choruses. Even the writing out of the chorus parts is such a waste of time that working out a

[1] The opera was *Lulu*.   [2] Of *Moses und Aron*.

To Alban Berg AUGUST 1931

4-6/part texture is a trifle by comparison. Then I'm slowed up still more by writing out a complete score from the start, which of course takes a lot of time. But still, the advantage is that I'll have finished the whole job when I've composed the last note. There's only one thing I'm afraid of: that by then I'll have forgotten everything I've written. For even now I can scarcely recognise the parts of it I composed last year. And if it weren't for a kind of unconscious memory that always automatically brings me back to the right track of ideas, both musically and with the words, I wouldn't know how the whole thing should come to hang together organically at all.

[..........]

It's really quite incomprehensible that once again neither you nor Webern have been offered an appointment at the Academy in Vienna. But believe me: you needn't be sorry; they're the ones who're going to be sorry some day!

Glad you heard Rosbaud's broadcast talk in which he also reproduced my talk.[1] I heard him too, quite by chance!! It was really very nice the way he did it, full of warmth. What you wrote to me about your audience is delightful. But it's really surprising to hear one's own voice, although I'm anything but enthusiastic about mine. — Yes, wireless is a fine thing; but still, the greatest pleasure it gives is switching it off. Being able, on the instant, to shake off the incubus of those frightful, ghastly sounds, and after a short while having one's ear free again, is a liberation and a relief not too dearly bought by what went before.

[..........]

ARNOLD SCHÖNBERG

129. To ANTON WEBERN *Territet, 12 September* 1931

[..........]

As I said, getting a libretto[2] into shape takes a lot of time. It was a very great deal of work, for instance, getting the scene 'Dance round the Golden Calf' worked out properly. I wanted to leave as little as possible to those new despots of the theatrical art, the producers, and even to envisage the choreography as far as I'm able to. For all this sort of thing is in a very bad way nowadays, and the highhandedness of these mere minions, and their total lack of conscience, is exceeded only by their barbarity and feebleness. But now I've solved the problems of the greater part of it and hope to have it all finished soon. You know I'm not at all keen on the dance. In general its expressiveness is on a level no

---

[1] On gramophone records.   [2] For the opera *Moses und Aron*.

higher than that of the crudest programme-music; and the petrified mechanical quality of its 'beauty' is something I can't stand. Anyway, so far I've succeeded in thinking out movements such as at least enter into a different territory of expression from the caperings of common-or-garden ballet. Let's hope I shall be able to see it through. Well, now I've told you a lot about my work and should rather like to get on with it, so shall close for today. I'd like to be able to send you a book; only the fact is it isn't by any means finished yet, since I often write the definitive words only just before composing. Indeed I've often done it afterwards; when it was a matter of building a 2nd or 3rd 'strophe' (as it were).

[..........]

ARNOLD SCHÖNBERG

130. To PROFESSOR ALEXANDER AMERSDORFER
Barcelona, 17 *October* 1931

Herr Professor Alexander Amersdorfer,
Academy of Arts in Berlin

Since the bad summer has caused a considerable worsening of my asthma, my doctor insists on my spending some time longer in the South, in a warm climate.

May I ask you to be so very kind as to convey this information, and also my present address, to the relevant official quarters?

I should like to take this opportunity of asking you a question that [I] meant to discuss with you last winter (which I was prevented from doing by my affliction, which makes it almost impossible for me to go out in the morning in cold, damp weather).

I have long had the wish to expound my musical theories to a somewhat larger circle, but so far have not been able to decide in what form this should be done. I have always had the Academy in mind. But since it proves necessary for all of these lectures to be attended, not merely one or some; since, furthermore, they are addressed not merely to students as such, but rather especially to those with more theoretical training; and since, finally, they would take at least 10–12 times $1\frac{1}{2}$ hours according to the arrangement and the material, and, if I am to discuss all subjects, will amount to nothing less than a 'course', I do not quite see how this should be organised and should be very grateful to you if you would some time give me your opinion and advice. For my own part I should like to give these lectures without receiving a fee, so to speak as part of my official work. On the other hand it seems to me that those attending would have to 'put their names down', although

To Professor Alexander Amersdorfer   OCTOBER 1931

even that is of course no guarantee of regular attendance. Do you not agree?

[..........]

ARNOLD SCHÖNBERG

131. TO A GROUP OF CATALAN MUSICIANS[1]

Barcelona, 3 November 1931

Gentlemen,

You have had the great kindness to send me, on my coming to stay in Barcelona for reasons of health, words of welcome that do me great honour and cause me much pleasure. For I know that I do not deserve this on account of the wretched few pieces of music that I have presented to the public, which has received them with more distaste than thanks, in so far as it was inclined to notice them at all.

But I think I may flatter myself that you perhaps prize the attitude that my character compels me to adopt: namely that I stand by my work, always, unfalteringly.

May I — thanking you for this from the bottom of my heart — say that such appreciation also honours him who bestows it: namely *you*, you who by this compliment — regardless of all aesthetic scruples — have paid attention, purely spiritual attention, to a moral fact.

Let me once more thank you very cordially indeed. With esteem and regard from your fellow musician,

ARNOLD SCHÖNBERG

132. TO JOSEF RUFER[2]   *Barcelona, 16 December* 1931

Herr Josef Rufer,
Berlin

[..........]

... For it is really very odd that no one has yet discussed the obvious beauty of my *form*. And yet it is something that ought to be evident to many who will never be able to follow a melody or a theme by ear or in their imagination. But — and this is the reason for it — there are very few people indeed who have any notion of beauty of musical form. The older men, who still had an inkling of it, are partly intimidated, partly are gradually dying off. The few younger ones are doubtless in a position to know it from me (perhaps also from Schenker?). But there is precisely the snag: it's so difficult to say it 'in modern terms'.

[..........]

ARNOLD SCHÖNBERG

[1] Answer to a letter of welcome from Catalan musicians (Casals and others).
[2] Schoenberg's pupil and his assistant at the Academy of Arts. He lives still in Berlin and is the author of *The Works of Arnold Schoenberg* (Faber, 1962) and *Composition with Twelve Notes* (Rockliff, 1954).

AETAT 57   *To Anton Webern*

133. To Pau Casals   [*Probably end of* 1931]

[*Handwritten draft without date or address*][1]

Yesterday you asked me if I wouldn't write a 'cello piece. My answer was: I have often thought of it and countless times intended doing it. I might have said more: for I had just been thinking about it again because your playing had made me so wonderfully keen to do just that; and also might have told you what plans I have.

But now I really mean to do it and so should like to make use of the short time left before leaving to discuss a few ideas with you — for I should like to write the piece for you, and indeed 'took your measurements' long ago. To indicate some of the ideas briefly:

1. A fantasia on something of Bach's (a fine Adagio or Minuet, Gavotte or the like), possibly in the form of variations; or

2. to re-interpret for 'cello a piano suite or a trio sonata or the like.

3. One of these two works either

    (*a*) for 'cello solo, or

    (*b*) for 'cello and piano, or

    (*c*) for 'cello and orchestra.

I cannot decide without seeing the music. If I had something by Bach, I don't know whether I mightn't set about it at once.

                                              Arnold Schönberg

134. To Anton Webern   *Barcelona*, 7 *January* 1932

My very dear fellow,

I do want to answer your letter at once, even if briefly.

First of all very many thanks indeed for the score of your string quartet. It is a marvellous piece, and I see this again and again with the greatest of pleasure and pride! *How* different from the general run of stuff these days.

What surprises me very much is your moving after almost 14 years. Are you all in Vienna by now? Anyway: good luck in the new house! It's certainly a very nice district; somewhere, I suppose, near the Hadikgasse. By the way, didn't you once live in the Penzingerstrasse? Or nearby? I'm very curious to know more about the new flat.

    [1] Obviously written in Barcelona and addressed to Casals (see Letter 150).

To Anton Webern JANUARY 1932

Now for the music festival:[1]

You want me to give you my opinion honestly, or even '*mercilessly*'. And I should have to do so even if you didn't directly ask me to. For:

1. I cannot forget the treatment [I received] at the Venice Music Festival;

2. I don't want to forget it;

3. I have no wish to expose myself to comment in the newspapers;

4. I consider that being in my 58th year I am not among the *young composers* and so neither fit into the framework nor have any wish to appear within it;

5. as a not-young composer however I can scarcely be said to be properly represented by a smaller, a minor work (this only by the way: for even if they meant to perform Jacob's Ladder or all my operas, I should not change my attitude to what happened in Venice);

6. you will perhaps recall my declaring at the time that only if ——[2] were chucked out of the committee could I consider having anything to do with this society. This was not done, therefore the society does not exist for me.

Please don't be cross with me: I can't regard the matter otherwise!

How are you in health? You say nothing about it in your letter. I am now feeling better. But I'm finding the work going a bit slow. Rather over-tired; but it's bound to get going again before long.

ARNOLD SCHÖNBERG

135. To HANS ROSBAUD[3]   *Barcelona*, 19 *January* 1932

My dear Herr Rosbaud,

I ought to have answered long ago. But I have been ill and am at the moment depressed because I'm not getting on with my work the way I'd like to.

Let me first of all thank you for your very nice letter and all the pleasant things you say and report.

Now for your invitation to give a talk in February in connection with my Songs with orchestra:[4] I definitely don't think I can risk coming North during the cold season. But of course I can't urge you to postpone the performance for that reason. All the less since I have already been racking my brains about a lecture like that on the orchestral songs,

[1] Webern was at that time chairman of the Austrian section of the International Society for Contemporary Music and had asked Schoenberg to agree to one of his works being performed under the Society's aegis.

[2] To avoid giving offence to persons still alive the name has been omitted. Schoenberg felt deeply insulted by the actions of a member of the executive committee in connection with the Music Festival in Venice, in 1925.

[3] See Letter 126.   [4] Op. 22.

wondering what it should be like and so far still not having the faintest notion. It's not only that I'm almost incapable of doing a re-hash; anyway, I shouldn't want to!

So what's to be done? Your idea of giving a lecture in connection with it is so right and useful, and I know you also mean it to provide an excellent opportunity for me to be there and hear the performance, and that gives me particular pleasure! That is also why I'm particularly sorry to think I may have to forego the lecture.

For all eventualities, let me know the date of the performance. I should like to try to hear it from here. Though it's difficult to get Mühlacker here, and one can't get Frankfurt at all.

[..........]

ARNOLD SCHÖNBERG

136. TO ALBAN BERG   *Barcelona, 20 January* 1932
Herr Alban Berg,
Vienna

[..........]

To come back to your 'Wine'[1] (NB. For ages I've been meaning to answer it with a Spanish champagne that is *very good* and dirt cheap; but I'm alarmed at the thought of the Austrian Customs; up to now pretty stiff duty has been charged on everything we've sent. And it would be horrid to think it cost more there than here, which is, after all, quite possible with champagne.) Well then: I find the clarity of pattern and of handling of sounds in this score is so extraordinary that I want to stress the fact that it makes an entirely unusual impression. I know really few modern scores (including my own) of which I could say the same. The thematic invention is, to my mind, equally distinguished. By the way: what does that crab-like backward-running repetition at figure 142 mean?

I am really very glad about the piece!

[..........]

I received the libretto and was very pleased by what you wrote about it.[2] I should have liked to show you two stages of the work: the fact is, after you had read the second act, I worked it over again several times and I'm sure you'd be astonished to see how extensive the changes are (though certainly in the spirit of the thing). But in order to do that I'd have had to copy a fairly large part of it, and I'm afraid I didn't do so:

[1] Berg's concert aria, *Der Wein*.
[2] Schoenberg had sent Berg the libretto of *Moses und Aron*.

To Alban Berg JANUARY 1932

and now it's too late, because the intermediate versions have all been cancelled out by continual changes.

[. . . . .]

It would interest me to hear your impressions of the Golden-Calf scene, which I put a lot of 'meaning' into. It will probably have a playing-time of about 25 minutes. But I think enough goes on to keep the audience satisfied even if it doesn't understand a thing of all I meant by it. But: does one understand anything at all? That — if you still have it in mind — is what I'd like to know.

Yes, we were ill. But we're both all right now.

[. . . . .]

ARNOLD SCHÖNBERG

137. TO PROFESSOR LEO KESTENBERG   *Barcelona, 25 January* 1932
Dear Herr Prof. Kestenberg,

Yesterday I received from Herr Josef Rufer (my former pupil) a very agitated and rather agitating letter from which I should like to quote the following:

'Prof. Kestenberg has urged me to write to you . . . attacked from all sides on account of your absence . . . such an important appointment held and salary drawn by a teacher who has not been in Berlin for the last ¾ of a year . . . could no longer take the responsibility for continued absence . . . persuade you to return with all possible speed. . . .'

After getting over the initial agitation and after some calm reflection I am inclined to think that Rufer must have slightly exaggerated your certainly well-meant words and that he had perhaps also introduced an admixture of what 'well-meaning' other persons had whispered in his ear. For if I had violated my contract, you or the Academy would of course have called me to order directly, instead of having recourse to Herr Rufer. In any case I do not understand Rufer: he knows my contract and knows that I was specifically granted the right to choose for myself which months I wished to be in Berlin. But I think he also knows the following (of which I also *informed the Academy* at the time): namely that I have two months 'to my credit', having for two years stayed in Berlin teaching for a month longer than I was by contract bound to do. It would never have occurred to me to 'debit you' these two months except in an emergency; and even now my intention is far from petty; but it turns out that *even at the end of January* I would only arrive *one month* late, even if what I am contractually entitled to were disregarded. But why should it be, since after all nobody has suffered in any way by my absence, nor will anyone suffer. For just as hitherto I have not done less than I was under an obligation to do, but *more*, so too in future — need I give you my assurance? an affidavit? (for inst. I have never taken long holidays) — I shall not do less, but *more*: if for no other reason, out of devotion to the subject; but also from sheer conscientiousness.

[..........]

After a chill (October 30th) that whole winter in Berlin I was so ill that for weeks I could not go out. Hence, after seven months' teaching, first to Montreux. There my condition worsened to such an extent that my doctor there, Dr. Minnich, gave me an alarmingly grave warning against spending the winter in the North, indeed even went so far as to insist that I should not go back to Berlin at all except in the warm season. That was why I came here, and my emphysema, which for the first few months was so bad that I sometimes could not go out for days, has markedly improved in the last four weeks and I hope that if I do not have to return to a harsh climate immediately I shall have set myself up for some considerable time. At present I am unfortunately still bound up with the weather, i.e., when the weather is bad, so am I. And I must tell you frankly: I should on no account wish to sacrifice my improved health, which has put me to such expense, on account of a few envious persons' thoughtless mischief-making, and I am convinced that you will agree.

[..........]

I should be happy if you would also let me know your attitude to this problem, although I have the joyful hope that you will acknowledge the justness of mine.

[..........]

                                                  ARNOLD SCHÖNBERG

138. To HANS ROSBAUD   *Barcelona, 30 January* 1932

My dear Herr Rosbaud,

Your delightful letter made me very much want to try and do the lecture after all.[1]

If only I knew how to do it!!!!

For I haven't got the music here!

And it would take weeks to get from U.E.: because of spite, but also because of the local mails; a letter takes anything from three to ten days to get here!!!

[1] See Letter 135.

To Hans Rosbaud　　　　　　　　　　　　　　　　January 1932

Will you risk sending me the music yourself? Perhaps it will come in time;

and (a second PERHAPS)

perhaps, then, when I see the music, something will occur to me that'll be some use;

and (third PERHAPS)

perhaps I shall still get it done in time?

Well: will you take the risk? In that case I do ask you for the score. If we are lucky,

this letter will be in your hands on the .... 2nd Feb.

If you can send the music at once (good luck!)

I may perhaps get it on the .... 5th or 6th.

Then if something occurs to me within two or

three days, I can wire you an acceptance on the ..... 7th to 9th;

can get the lecture finished between the .... 8th and 15th,

and travel on the 16th. But shall I then be in

time for the rehearsals in Frankfurt?

Shall we risk it?

And: will you also take the risk that perhaps after all at the last moment I shall have to cry off?

Please wire me your decision.* But once more: at the moment I still can't be sure that anything'll occur to me.

All very best wishes, yours,

　　　　　　　　　　　　　　　　　　　　Arnold Schönberg

* e.g., Music sent, can await your acceptance until the ... Programme already printed, or Sorry must abandon plan. [S.]

139. To Professor Leo Kestenberg　　*Barcelona, 13 February* 1932

My dear Herr Prof. Kestenberg,

Thank you very much for your kind letter, in which I fail to see (among much that it is very good of you to write and of which I am very glad) that you pay enough attention to my illness.† Do then please permit me, since I do not seem after all to have made it quite clear in my last letter, to say with all cordiality but also with all firmness: if my contract had not entitled me to be absent from Berlin now, I should have had to take sick-leave.

I do now beg you to take *official* note of this fact: little though I generally care for official communications.

† Schoenberg actually wrote in error: 'I fail to see [...] that you pay too little attention to my illness.' [trans.]

AETAT 57 *To Hans Rosbaud*

What I should like to add privately is that I had intended broadcasting a lecture from Radio Frankfurt on the 21st, after which I should continue my journey back to Berlin. But now there have been three days of snow here, something unheard-of in these parts, and automatically I have become worse: coughing, rise of temperature, difficulty in breathing. So I have had to make up my mind to cancel the Frankfurt talk. And it had better be said without more ado: I cannot risk returning to the North before warmer weather sets in.

Since the Prussian State does not grant me any pension for my wife, you cannot very well urge me to make a widow of her any sooner than is absolutely necessary.

[..........]

ARNOLD SCHÖNBERG

140. TO HANS ROSBAUD *Barcelona*, 13 *February* 1932

Dear Herr Rosbaud,

Snow has been falling here for three days, to the utter amazement of the population; and the automatic result is that my old afflictions have returned, even if luckily not quite so badly: coughing, rise of temperature, difficulty in breathing.

For the moment I cannot face the idea of travelling, particularly since connections are very bad here and I should have to change trains several times.

At all events, therefore, I shall try to get you on the telephone about 10 o'clock tonight and if necessary about 9 tomorrow morning (your time), and am writing this letter in case I can't get through. I have the talk quite finished and should very much have liked to deliver it myself. But to be on the safe side I am posting it. I think either you or Herr Wiesengrund[1] or Herr Kahn[2] will surely be able to read it. (I suppose you did get the postcard I wrote when the bad weather began here?)

I am sending two copies of the talk (keeping the worst copy for myself, in order to wait one day longer), one to your house, the other to the wireless people.

I shall go through the talk once again, checking some places where I haven't yet catered for the possibility of its being delivered by someone else. If there should be any changes, I shall send them on. I also intend writing out the musical examples again.

What a pity not to be able to deliver it myself, now that I've gone to so much trouble and broken off my work (for it's more than a week that

---

[1] Theodor Wiesengrund-Adorno.   [2] Of Radio Frankfurt.

To Hans Rosbaud   FEBRUARY 1932

I've been racking my brains over it). Besides, I'm very anxious to hear various things in the songs.

I'm afraid there doesn't seem to be any hope of the weather improving. At the moment there's such a mist that one can't see 20 paces ahead.

I was to have started out on Wednesday: so there are still four days left. Would you feel able to give me till then? Or is to too much of a risk? Of course I don't know what the weather's like in Germany, and that's what it mainly depends on!!!!

I should like very much to have seen you and heard you play my music. Pity! I'm not very hopeful. But let's hope I can get you on the telephone tonight or tomorrow.

[..........]

                                             ARNOLD SCHÖNBERG

141. TO PROFESSOR LEO KESTENBERG   *Barcelona, 13 May 1932*

Herr Ministerialrat Prof. Leo Kestenberg.

[..........]

I had arranged to leave on the 28th April. On the 24th I telegraphed a request to my bank to telegraph me the money for the journey. On the 3rd May (that is, after I had waited more than a *week* in the greatest of agitation) I received a letter from my bank saying that they could only send me half the sum needed for my journey; the Treasury would not allow the whole sum to be sent out of the country.

With only half, however, I could not leave Barcelona. Partly because of some last-minute accounts to be settled here, and partly because in the week that had passed more money had of course been spent; but in particular because these official gentry had allotted me a sum somewhat inadequate to three people's needs.

After two days of making other vain attempts I succeeded in discovering the officially permitted device for circumventing this regulation. Too late, alas, for: we were to have left at two o'clock in the afternoon of the 7th; everything was packed and the apartment given up, when my wife suddenly began to have labour-pains (at 8 in the morning) and had to be taken to a nursing-home, where at 9 o'clock she gave birth to a girl.

Well, so we should have been in Berlin punctually on the 28th if the Treasury, in its wisdom, had not thought fit to upset the applecart for us.

Now, since I can neither leave my wife alone in a foreign country, nor

AETAT 57 *To Joseph Asch*

know whether I should be allowed to send her any money (see abovementioned wisdom), and she cannot undertake a 48-hour journey with an infant unless she has someone to help her, I have no choice but to stay here until she is fit to travel. Apart from the fact that I could not have covered these expenses with the money I have left! What I would now ask of you is the following:

We hope the doctor will let us travel in approximately a week. I still don't know how much money I shall then require from my bank. Could you therefore see to it that the sum I shall then ask for by wire is this time sent without delay? So far as I can see, it will not be more than a thousand Marks.

May I ask you to wire me if necessary? For otherwise I really don't know how to get back!

Please forgive me for bothering you, and in any case my most cordial thanks in anticipation.

[. . . . .]

ARNOLD SCHÖNBERG

142. To JOSEPH ASCH *Barcelona, 24 May* 1932

Herr Dr. Joseph Asch,
New York

It's a long time since you heard from me; the last time was when I congratulated you on having become a father. Today it's your turn to reciprocate, as you can see from the enclosed announcement of my daughter's birth.

But I am writing to you for yet another reason. For some time I have been living in the South for reasons of health, and on these grounds, but also because of political conditions, am very reluctant to go back to Germany at this juncture.

But the currency restrictions make it impossible for me to get money out of Germany. And besides, I should like to finish the third act of my opera 'Moses and Aaron' (two acts are finished, scored for orchestra).

Now just think: I am surely the only composer of my standing there has been for at least a hundred years who could not live on what he made from his creative work without having to eke out his income by teaching. And when I think how many things rich people find money for, I simply can't understand that there still isn't some rich Jew, or even several, who together or single-handed would give me an annuity so that at long last I needn't do anything but create!

Here I am in a country where I could live — modestly but not too

To Joseph Asch   May 1932

badly — if I had an assured 2,000–2,400 dollars a year. Are there not some people even nowadays, some Jews, who could get together and raise for instance 200 dollars a month for me?

I am told you have enough influence to achieve something of the sort for me. I was told that quite some time ago. But it is only today that I can bring myself to approach you about it. Will you try it, will you see if you can get some rich Jews to provide for me so that I don't have to go back to Berlin among the swastika-swaggerers and pogromists?

Please send me two copies of your answer: one here to Spain, the other to Berlin.

Will you be able to arrange something? Your good will I don't doubt, nor your being well disposed towards me. Here's luck to both of us![1] [. . . . .]

                                                             Arnold Schönberg

143. To Rudolf Kolisch[2]   *Berlin, 27 July 1932*
Dear Rudi,

I've been meaning to answer for ages and the paper has actually been in the typewriter for several days. But I am engaged in a very time-consuming, though also very interesting, job: collecting and sorting out my literary works. You'd be amazed to see how much there is. . . .

You have rightly worked out the series in my string quartet[3] (apart from one detail: the 2nd consequent goes: 6th note, C sharp, 7th, G sharp). You must have gone to a great deal of trouble, and I don't think I'd have had the patience to do it. But do you think one's any better off for knowing it? I can't quite see it that way. My firm belief is that for a composer who doesn't yet quite know his way about with the use of series it may give some idea of how to set about it — a purely technical indication of the possibility of getting something out of the series. But this isn't where the aesthetic qualities reveal themselves, or, if so, only incidentally. I can't utter too many warnings against over-rating these analyses, since after all they only lead to what I have always been dead against: seeing how it is *done*; whereas I have always helped people to see: what it *is*! I have repeatedly tried to make Wiesengrund understand this, and also Berg and Webern. But they won't believe me. I can't say it often enough: my works are twelve-note *compositions*, not

---

[1] The answer was negative.
[2] Leader of the Kolisch String Quartet, Schoenberg's brother-in-law, and his former pupil.
[3] Schoenberg's Third String Quartet.

twelve-note compositions: in this respect people go on confusing me with Hauer, to whom composition is only of secondary importance.

It goes without saying that I know and never forget that even in making such investigations you never cease to live with what is actually the source of your relationship to this music: its spiritual, auditory musical substance. Still, I can't refrain from speaking out against such an analysis, since I've always done so. E.g. in the Theory of Harmony. The only sort of analysis there can be any question of for me is one that throws the idea into relief and shows how it is presented and worked out. It goes without saying that in doing this one mustn't overlook artistic subtleties.

You may wonder at my talking about this at such length. But although I'm not ashamed of a composition's having a healthy constructive basis even when I've consciously manufactured it, i.e., when it is less good than when it is a spontaneous result, produced unconsciously, I still [don't] care to be regarded as a constructor on account of the bit of juggling I can do with series, because that would be doing too little to deserve it. I think more has to be done to deserve such a title, and actually I think I am capable of fulfilling the considerable demands made on me by those entitled to do so. — But that's enough about that. I'm glad you people are working at this quartet and am very eager to hear it.

When do you all expect to be in Berlin? The elections are over and done with, anyway. I'm curious to see what's going to come of it all. I simply can't imagine.

[..........]

We've joined the Borussia Tennis Club here and are very pleased with it. It's quite close to where we live, and I think we shall get partners.

[..........]

ARNOLD SCHÖNBERG

144. TO ANTON WEBERN Berlin, 12 *August* 1932

My very dear fellow,

I'm so glad to hear the results of your examination are so good. The main thing is: nothing organically wrong. One can't really ask for more, can one? And everything else can be put right by some treatment and taking care of oneself. You ask what causes all these states. I think (it sounds old-fashioned, but still I must say it, using the old-fashioned

To Anton Webern AUGUST 1932

expression they had for it) it's from the *heart*!* I think you get too worked up about everything. Whether it's conducting, taking rehearsals, having to gain a point, being criticised, or whatever else it may be of countless things: you always put too much heart into it. (If I didn't know this about myself, I shouldn't understand it so well in your case.) I think: if you had six months free of annoyances and agitation, that is, if there should be no occasion for such, you would be well. Naturally this isn't easy in our vocation. Still, it's not quite impossible.

It's ages that I've been meaning to write to you. But although there are days when I'm intensely busy sifting, sorting, and filing the 'little manuscripts' I've been piling up for some 15 years and collecting the printed essays and also my lectures, there are often several days at a time when I don't feel like sitting down at my desk to do anything that requires concentration. The times aren't such that one can always keep one's mind on one's work and let one's thoughts run freely. And so then weeks and days pass and one sees more and more things one would also like to do!

[..........]

I've been told a great deal about the Vienna music festival. I.e. mainly about your successes. Everyone is tremendously enthusiastic and nobody can understand how it is you still haven't been asked to Berlin. I still think very often of the two marvellous concerts you conducted in Barcelona; there's nothing that could be mentioned in one breath with that.

[..........]

We'll soon be halfway through the time I'm obliged to spend in Berlin. So far the summer hasn't been unbearable; a few very hot, many very cool [days]. At the moment it's really pretty hot and we may be in for a longish heat-wave. That isn't very pleasant in town. I'm playing a fair amount of tennis, even though always worse than people expect. Still, I enjoy it.

[..........]

ARNOLD SCHÖNBERG

145. TO ALBAN BERG *Berlin, 23 September* 1932

My very dear fellow,

I am quite appalled to hear of your wife's accident. To think of sacrificing oneself like that for someone else's stupidity and careless-

* 'Heart' is here used not for *Herz*, as elsewhere, but for *Gemüt*, an untranslatable word denoting something more or less equivalent to 'heart' or even 'soul', with 19th-century nuances of delicate sensibility. [TRANS.]

ness! For beyond doubt what happened was that the girl poured methylated spirit on the flame, or something of that kind! My wife and I were dumbfounded when we read your letter. At any rate it's lucky that at least the burns in the face are not severe. But the pain must have been simply awful. Please write and tell me very soon how your wife is getting on and give her all my wife's and my very best wishes for a very quick and complete recovery, and our hopes that she will then present to one and all the same delightful aspect as previously!!

Now let me thank you very much for the beautiful birthday-present. True, I haven't yet had time to read it, but the fact that you chose it and you recommend it make me very eager indeed. Once more very, very many thanks, and I only wish I could some day get a decent idea in time for your birthday, so as not always to be the shamefaced recipient!

It seems to be a very long time since I wrote to you. I think perhaps the main reason was my disappointment at not having been able to persuade you, despite all urgings, to come and join us in Barcelona. When you first agreed to come I was very pleased, and then bit by bit the hopes dwindled, until somehow contact seems to have been lost. But it isn't only that; there's also a sort of depression, which is undoubtedly connected with having to be in Berlin, that takes away all my pleasure in work. For here I'm constantly obliged to consider the question whether and, if so, to what extent I am doing the right thing in regarding myself as belonging here or there, and whether it is forced upon me. Even without the nationalistic hints one has been getting in recent years, naturally I know where I belong. Only such a change of milieu isn't as easy as one might think.

— (Typed letters are so hard to finish — began on the 23rd, continuing today, 26th!)[1] Of course I know perfectly well where I belong. I've had it hammered into me so loudly and so long that only by being deaf to begin with could I have failed to understand it. And it's a long time now since it wrung any regrets from me. Today I'm proud to call myself a Jew; but I know the difficulties of really being one.

But that's enough about that: the whole thing's certainly working up to a decision, and one of quite a different kind. —

Only it's a pity it so much reduces my inclination to work. Recently I began sorting out and arranging my 'literary works' (finished and unfinished). At a rough estimate they amount to 1,500 pages of print — more if anything! that makes 4–5 pretty thick books — apart from the *Harmonielehre* and the volume already published. I intend publishing some of it now — (much only after my death, and other people's) — but

[1] The rest of the letter is written by hand.

To Alban Berg SEPTEMBER 1932

it's probably going to be difficult, these days, to find a publisher who has enough money (to put into this commercially sound proposition). For I'll only let it go for a fairly large advance. —

Now I'm going to play tennis with Rudi. This is my and my wife's chief pleasure! — Write to me soon. I'll keep on writing more often too.

Once more all the very best of good wishes for your wife's recovery, also from my wife — and very best wishes from, Yours ever,

ARNOLD SCHÖNBERG

146. TO PROFESSOR MAX VON SCHILLINGS

Berlin, 27 October 1932

The President of the Academy,
Generalmusikdirektor Prof. Dr. Max von Schillings

I had intended raising another question about author's copyright at yesterday's Academy meeting, but simply could not remember what it was. If I may, I shall now repeat the question I raised yesterday and append the other.

Here they are:

I. What is the legal position if an author makes a change, a revision, or a new version of his work and the publisher refuses, or is unable, to publish it?

II. Is there any means of guaranteeing the public's (i.e., art-lovers', as also the author's) right to a good translation on a level with the original literary work? I have the following practical examples in mind:

I myself expect soon to have to let my *Harmonielehre* be translated into English (and perhaps also other languages), without being in a position to check the translation as thoroughly as is necessary; above all without being able to say whether the translation is on a level above the colloquial and the journalistic. That is to say, in the same position as e.g., Strindberg, who certainly knew more German than I know French or English. But precisely his case indicates how wrong it is to let a translator have a monopoly, perhaps for an eternity (!!). For it's now many years since I was told, by people qualified to judge, that Strindberg is one of the outstanding stylists in the Swedish language, whereas the translation rather gave me the opposite impression.

Perhaps it would interest you to raise these two questions for discussion. I think a new law should at least begin by considering how to cover such more subtle problems.

[..........]

ARNOLD SCHÖNBERG

AETAT 58

147. To ROBERTO GERHARD

To Hans Rosbaud
Berlin, 15 November 1932

Dear Herr Gerhard,

First and foremost, very many thanks for your charming letter, with all the kind and delightful things it contained. [..........]

As to when I — or rather, we — may come back:[1] by the terms of my contract I could set out on the 1st December. But I rather think it would be better for me to stay in Berlin for as long as I remain well. So for the present we plan to stay in Berlin, uninterruptedly, until the end of January. Then I have some lectures to give (Vienna, Brünn, and Frankfurt-am-Main), and a broadcast concert in London on the 8th. I am just now working out the dates for this journey. Presumably I shall go to London first, then via Frankfurt to Brünn and Vienna, and from there possibly to Spain. Possibly: that is, if there should be enough concerts and possibly also lectures to give there (in German, French or English, for I shan't yet be good enough at Spanish!!!). For this year I shall have to reckon still more seriously than last year with the difficulties of the currency freeze and in Spain would have to live mainly on what I could earn there.

[..........]

As for living-quarters and tennis, the fact is these two problems are for us very closely connected. For when I'm tired after playing I would really like to be able to get home easily, and to get there easily too. Each time there's a rush, through no fault of mine, or even through my fault, it costs money, having to take a taxi: unless of course one buys oneself a car! But perhaps that's a problem there's still plenty of time to think about. At all events, anyway, I'd be grateful *if you would look around pretty near to Barcelona L.T.C.* For I think that's really a likelier prospect than a car.

[..........]

ARNOLD SCHÖNBERG

148. To HANS ROSBAUD

Barcelona, 7 January 1933

Dear Herr Rosbaud,

Please forgive me. For one thing I've been working and for another I still don't know what I'm to lecture on for you. (Two days ago I finished a 'cello concerto with orchestra 'freely adapted from a keyboard concerto by Monn [1746]', the first performance of which I should like to do together with Casals; London wants to engage me for it for next

[1] It was at Gerhard's suggestion that Schoenberg had spent the winter of 1931–2 in Barcelona.

To Hans Rosbaud JANUARY 1933

season; but if Casals has time I'd really like to do it this season. I put it to you quite frankly: Perhaps you are of the opinion that Frankfurt would be interested in it; then I'll have opened a door. But please; no obligation; on either side! For I shouldn't want to let it go at all cheaply.)

As for the lecture, it certainly is high time to decide about it.

For this purpose it would be best if you would send me the answer to the following questions as quickly as possible:

I. How long can a talk without music be?

II. What time have you fixed it for on the 11th February?

III. What is the very highest fee you can offer me (bearing in mind that I was to have written a talk especially for Frankfurt)?

IV. Can you yourself suggest a subject?

Originally I had intended giving the same talk for you as in Vienna (15th Feb.) and Cologne (10th or 12th Feb.): 'Style and Idea, or Outmoded and New Music.'*

But I'm afraid it's too long: somewhat over an hour. I couldn't shorten it though, because then I wouldn't be able to read it convincingly without the cuts in Vienna and Cologne: that is, if the cuts were good and justified.

Would you be interested in a talk on Brahms? Here I'd probably have something to say that only I can say. For though my exact contemporaries, and those who are older than I, also lived in Brahms' time, they aren't 'modern'. But the younger Brahmsians can't know the Brahms tradition from first-hand experience, and anyway they mostly tend to be 'reactionary'. But: what I have in mind is the theory of composition, not anecdotes!

But I should very much like to have your decision as soon as possible, for I must start thinking the talk out at once!!

[. . . . .]

ARNOLD SCHÖNBERG

149. TO PROFESSOR HEINZ TIESSEN *Berlin, 25 January 1933*
Herr Prof. Heinz Tiessen,
Academy of Arts in Berlin

Dear Professor Tiessen,

Since illness prevents me from attending the electoral meetings today and tomorrow, may I ask you to represent me? I am quite sure that you

* Later revised and reprinted in *Style and Idea* [1950] as 'New Music, Outmoded Music, Style and Idea'. [TRANS.]

will use my vote only as I would myself, but should nevertheless like to emphasise that I earnestly wish it to be cast in favour of Alban Berg's proposal that Dr. Anton von Webern should be elected into the place now vacant for a new Member of the Academy.[1]

With very many thanks and all kind regards, I am, Yours sincerely,
ARNOLD SCHÖNBERG

150. TO PAU CASALS *Berlin*, 20 *February* 1933

My dear and revered Maestro Casals!

About 6 weeks ago I completed a little work[2] of which I tried to send you news by various routes, only to discover that it has not reached you.

[..........]

The title of the work is:

Concerto for Violoncello and Orchestra,
After the Concerto for Harpsichord by G. M. Monn,
freely adapted by Arnold Schönberg

I think it has turned out a very brilliant piece. Anyway I went to *very* special trouble with the *sound* of it and am very pleased with the result. In certain respects the piece is less soloistic than a concerto of Monn's would be; for very often the 'cello's function is rather like a chamber-music soloist's, whose brilliant playing produces very beautiful and interesting sound. For the rest, I was mainly intent on removing the defects of the Handelian style (prevailing in the original work). Just as Mozart did with Handel's 'Messiah', I have got rid of whole handfuls of sequences (rosalias, '*Schusterflecke*'), replacing them with real *substance*. Then I also did my best to deal with the other main defect of Handelian style, which is that the theme is always best when it first appears and grows steadily more insignificant and trivial in the course of the piece. I think I've succeeded in making the whole thing approximate, say, to Haydn's style. In harmony I have sometimes gone a little (and sometimes rather more) beyond the limits of that style. But nowhere does it go much further than Brahms, anyway there are no dissonances other than those understood by the older theory of harmony; and: it is nowhere atonal.

What I now want to ask you is if you would like to be *the first person* to see the score. For if you like[d] it and felt inclined to play it, I would

[1] Webern was *not* elected a Member of the Academy.
[2] See Letter 148.

To Pau Casals FEBRUARY 1933

propose your giving the first performances, and also any others that were artistically and materially worth doing, with me conducting.

[..........]

ARNOLD SCHÖNBERG

151. TO WALTER EIDLITZ *Berlin, 15 March* 1933

Dear Herr Eidlitz,

Thank you very much indeed for both your books,[1] which I liked very much, even though being so personally involved with my own work to some extent prevents me from following your line of thought. Nevertheless, I was able to appreciate its beauty and significance.

The elements in this tremendous subject that I myself have placed in the foreground are: the idea of the inconceivable God, of the Chosen People, and of the leader of the people. My Aaron rather more resembles your Moses, although I have not portrayed him in so many aspects or shown him in terms of his human limitations, as you have. My Moses more resembles — of course only in outward aspect — Michelangelo's. He is not human at all. But what is interesting is that we come fairly close to each other in the introduction, formal presentation, and even in the evaluation of the scene with the golden calf. For me too this signifies a sacrifice made by the masses, trying to break loose from a 'soulless' belief. In the treatment of this scene, which actually represents the very core of my thought, I went pretty much to the limit, and this too is probably where my piece is most *operatic*; as indeed it must be.

My third act, which I am working over again, not to say re-writing, for at least the fourth time, is for the present still called: Aaron's Death. Here I have so far encountered great difficulties because of some almost incomprehensible contradictions in the Bible. For even if there are comparatively few points on which I adhere strictly to the Bible, still, it is precisely here that it is difficult to get over the divergence between: 'and thou shalt smite the rock' and: 'speak ye unto the rock'! You have worked on this material for so long: can you perhaps tell me where I could look up something on this question? Up to now I have been trying to find a solution for myself. As for my drama itself, I can manage even without solving this problem. Still, it does go on haunting me![2]

[..........]

ARNOLD SCHÖNBERG

[1] Walter Eidlitz had sent Schoenberg his book *Der Berg in der Wüste* ['The Mountain in the Wilderness'], the subject of which was the story of Moses.

[2] The passages are: *Exodus* 17, 6 and *Numbers* 20, 8.

AETAT 58   *To Dr. Lemberger*
152. TO DR. LEMBERGER   *Berlin*, 15 *March* 1933

My dear Dr. Lemberger,

Very many thanks indeed for your kind letter. I too am now at that advanced age of which you speak (for some time, after all, we have all been 'the same age'), and it is the same with me too: although I have acquired younger friends, my feelings of friendship for those who were young together with me have not perceptibly lessened even in cases where, for instance in professional matters, criticism or lack of faith has had a tendency to cause a rift. This I find — with joy — at every encounter of this kind: and this time with special joy! For I have often remembered that you were perhaps the only person who so often voluntarily came to my aid and helped me to endure the battle I was waging!

[..........]

ARNOLD SCHÖNBERG

Section IV
FRANCE — AMERICA
1933 – 1944

BIOGRAPHICAL NOTES

The events of 1933 caused a complete change in Schoenberg's life. He was deeply hurt and indignant at being driven out of the country to which he belonged, and the more so because his work was rooted in the world of German music. As though in protest he formally re-joined the Jewish community, which he had left as a young man (see Letter 156). Although it was more than ten years since he had intuitively known what was coming (see Letters 63 and 64), his letter of 23rd September 1932 to Alban Berg (Letter 145) reveals how difficult it was for him to find his bearings. In the given situation his loyalty was inevitably all on the Jewish side, yet as a composer he remained loyal to the German tradition.

1933: Left Berlin for France. Failure of endeavours to find new source of steady income (see Letters 153 and 154). In September dismissed from the Academy, in violation of terms of contract. Having no other prospects, accepted engagement at a conservatoire in Boston. On 25th October sailed for America, settling first in Boston.

1934: Conducted *Pelleas und Melisande* at a concert of the Boston Symphony Orchestra. At the University of Chicago gave a lecture on 'Composing with Twelve Notes'. Numerous receptions in his honour. His health suffered from the great variations of temperature in the Boston climate and the fatigue of weekly journeys to New York. He became ill, in March moved to New York, and finally gave up his appointment in Boston. Spent the summer recuperating in Chautauqua, in the South of New York State (see Letter 159). Was offered teaching appointments at the Juilliard School of Music, New York (see Letter 162) and also at Chicago, but for reasons of health did not consider it wise to accept. With no prospect of employment, that autumn went to Los Angeles for the warm climate and rented a house in Hollywood. He found a publisher for his new works in Carl Engel, president of the house of G. Schirmer, New York.

Biographical Notes

- 1935: In Hollywood began by giving private lessons. A number of film composers among his pupils. Lectured at the University of South California (U.S.C.). Marked improvement both in his health and in his financial situation.
- 1936: Composed the violin concerto and the Fourth String Quartet (see Letter 173). Appointed Professor of Music at the University of California, Los Angeles (U.C.L.A.). Moved to a new house in Brentwood Park, where he lived for the rest of his life.
- 1937: Teaching and travelling. In Denver, Colorado, a music festival was devoted to the works of Schoenberg and his school.
- 1938: Nazi-German annexation of Austria. Schoenberg endeavoured to help his friends and relatives arriving from Germany and Austria (see Letters 176 and 177).
- 1941: Became an American citizen on the 11th April.
- 1944: His seventieth birthday was celebrated by performances of his works. His state of health, which had been deteriorating for some years, took a turn for the worse. In a subsequent letter (of 6th January 1947) to Josef Rufer, he wrote: 'I haven't been able to get really well since February 1944. First I had diabetes, then my asthma got steadily worse. And later I began to have attacks of fainting and giddiness, as well as disturbances of vision. — All this said to be "only" nerves.' On completing his seventieth year he was compelled by statute to retire from the Chair of Music. For a time he considered emigrating (see Letter 194).

WORKS

- 1934: Suite in G major for string orchestra (without opus number).
- 1936: Fourth String Quartet, op. 37.
  Violin Concerto, op. 36.
- 1938: *Kol Nidre*, for speaker, chorus, and small orchestra, op. 39.
- 1939: Second Chamber Symphony, op. 38 (begun in 1906!).
- 1940: Variations on a Recitative for organ (in D minor), op. 40.
- 1942: *Ode to Napoleon Buonaparte* (after Byron), for reciter, piano and string quartet, op. 41a.
  The same with string orchestra, op. 41b.
  Piano Concerto, op. 42.

Biographical Notes

1944: Theme and Variations for wind band (in G minor), op. 43A.

The same for large orchestra, op. 43B.

1937/38: Brahms's Piano Quartet in G minor, op. 25, arranged for orchestra.

1942: *Models for Beginners in Composition* (textbook).

153. To Jakob Klatzkin[1] 26 *May* 1933[2]

Dear Herr Dr. Klatzkin,

Thank you very much for your friendly letter and your kind intention of helping me to find a publisher. Perhaps then I may say, without beating about the bush, that the main point for me in this respect is to be able to lay my hands on something like 5,000 Marks as soon as possible. For my asthma is again giving me a lot of trouble and I must get South in order to recuperate a bit.

I should very gladly empower you to act for me; possibly up to the stage where all that is necessary is to put the final terms before me. Here therefore is the necessary information in as much detail as possible. But I should like to say at once: if you happened to know someone who would advance me the above-mentioned sum until an agreement is concluded with a publisher, I should prefer that, because one is always at a great disadvantage with a publisher if he feels, or actually knows, that one needs money!!

I. Well then: the drama: 'Der biblische Weg' ['The Biblical Way'] is a very up-to-date treatment (written 1926–27) of the story of how the Jews became a people. Acquaintances of mine who have a thorough professional knowledge of this sort of thing, and to whom I showed it only recently, are very enthusiastic and agree with me that it would be a huge success in the theatre. Produced by someone such as Reinhardt, in London, it would probably have a very long run. It is very highly dramatic, stylistically the best thing I have written, and, although its profundities offer the superior mind plenty of food for thought, is vivid and theatrical enough to fascinate the simpler sort.

(You will forgive me for praising myself; but since it is now six years old, I am as objective about it as if it were not by me.)

II. The first two acts of the opera 'Moses and Aaron' you have read; the third I intend finishing in, at the outside, 6–8 weeks, as soon as I am on holiday. Its effectiveness can be judged only when I can show the music for it as well, the first two acts of course being performable now.

III. A concerto for violoncello and orchestra (a free adaptation of a concerto for harpsichord by Matthias Monn, a Viennese composer of

[1] A philosopher.   [2] Probably written from Paris.

To Jakob Klatzkin MAY 1933

Haydn's time). It is dedicated to Pablo Casals, with whom I shall give the first performance in October.[1] Here, instead of malodorous self-praise, I should like to quote what Casals has written to me about it: (I have just realised that I can't after all bring myself to deck myself out in the borrowed plumes of someone else's praise. I'd rather praise myself and be done with it. Anyway he is very enthusiastic.)

[..........]

I devoutly hope you will be successful on my behalf. I'm afraid I am myself the last person to undertake that sort of thing — for myself; for someone else I can do better.

In any case I do thank you very much for your good intentions, and if you should be able to fulfil them, the main thing is: quickly!![2]

[..........]

ARNOLD SCHÖNBERG

[Original in French, not traced; English translation from the German translation]
154. TO PAU CASALS *Arcachon, 22 September 1933*
M. Pau Casals,
Barcelona

Dear friend and great master,

Unhappily I am compelled to ask you whether it would be possible for you to give the first performance of the 'cello concerto I dedicated to you as early as the 29.xi.1933 with me for the B.B.C. in London. I say: Unhappily, and this is in this connection almost ridiculous; for in reality I should be happy if it were possible: to give a first performance with such an incomparable master as yourself. What is 'unhappy' is the cause that compels me to ask you to play the work at a time that may not suit you! The cause is, in brief, the following: Yesterday I received a letter from the Academy of Arts, at which, as you know, I was 'director of a course in musical composition'. I was; for since [receiving] this letter I no longer am so. They dismissed me, yesterday, on the 20.ix., ordaining that I shall receive my monthly salary for the last time on the 1st October!! Quite suddenly, without the least previous notification, my contract has been declared invalid, although without this violation it would have left me two years to build up a new life abroad. But now, as a result of this, I am compelled to do what I can to earn money. And I must say one of my greatest hopes was to get a certain

---
[1] See Letters 150 and 154.
[2] Dr. Klatzkin's endeavours proved fruitless.

AETAT 59 *To Winfried Zillig*

number of engagements as a conductor, in order to be able to give this concerto with you and — perhaps — if anyone wishes it, to perform some of my original works as well.

[..........]

Dear friend, I beg you to let me have your answer by return. Time presses, and it would be a great loss to me if the B.B.C. were to withdraw its invitation, because I should then lose a fairly large sum.

In a letter a fortnight ago my friend Robert[o] Gerhard told me that he had heard you play the concerto at a private concert in your house and that he was entranced by your rendering of it. He says he does not understand why you still hesitate to perform it in public.

To tell the truth, it is this fact that encourages me to ask you to accept this date.[1]

In the hope of soon receiving a favourable answer, I am, with many very cordial and most respectful regards,

Yours very sincerely,

ARNOLD SCHÖNBERG

155. TO WINFRIED ZILLIG[2] *Arcachon, 23 September* 1933

My dear fellow,

I'd rather write briefly but at once.

Your very nice letter gave me much pleasure; and nowadays, when so much disloyalty is surging to the top, encountering loyalty does one all the more good; and nowadays, when one doesn't know whether one isn't really less than the last scum, it does actually take some copious over-estimation (Bach-Schönberg) — to get one back on to a more or less middle line again, where one can hope: 'Well, so I can't be all that bad as a composer, no worse than poor old Graener anyway, if Zillig (he's a friend of course, but still...) says Bach-Schönberg (!).'[3] — Meanwhile however I have some new worries on top of those I had then. I have been sacked as from the 31st October, ... Perhaps something will eventuate in America: that remains to be seen in the next few weeks. Not that anyone is actually screaming for me. — It's pure fairy-tale that I have founded an orchestra; a very pretty fairy-tale, admittedly, and one can only wish it were as true as it's beautiful!...

ARNOLD SCHÖNBERG

[1] The performance was not given. The work was later played by Emmanuel Feuermann.
[2] Schoenberg's former pupil (see also Letter 229).
[3] Zillig had expressed his conviction that in future the history of German music would always have to be reckoned from Bach to Schoenberg. It was Alban Berg who first established this historical and artistic parallel (in 1930 in *Die Musik*, Berlin, vol. 24, No. 5).

To Alban Berg   OCTOBER 1933

156. TO ALBAN BERG   *Paris*, 16 *October* 1933

My dear fellow,

It was only on the 1st October that my going to America became definite enough for me to believe it myself. What was in the newspapers before that and since is fantasy, just like the alleged ceremonies and the presence of 'tout Paris' on the occasion of what is called my return to the Jewish religion. (Tout Paris consisted, apart from the rabbi and myself, of: my wife and a certain Dr. Marianoff, presumably the source of all these sensational stories.) As you have doubtless realised, my return to the Jewish religion took place long ago and is indeed demonstrated in some of my published work ('Thou shalt not . . . Thou shalt'[1]) and in 'Moses and Aaron', of which you have known since 1928, but which dates from at least five years earlier; but especially in my drama 'Der biblische Weg' which was also conceived in 1922 or '23 at the latest, though finished only in '26–'27. — In these last few days I have once more very often thought of writing a 'Schoenberg'-journal and sending a copy to each of my at least 25 to 30 nearest and dearest scattered in all four quarters of the world. It's difficult to write in detail about the same things to everyone, and also answer all the questions they ask. . . .

[. . . . .]

I'd like to know too if I can do anything for you in America: always supposing that I should have the power, of course. For there's no knowing how disregarded, slighted, and without influence I may be there. I only hope it won't be as in Holland, where I had the entire public against me from the moment I arrived, because everyone who feared me as a rival instantly mobilised the press and all the big battalions against me.

[. . . . .]   ARNOLD SCHÖNBERG

[*Written in English*]

157. TO SIR ADRIAN BOULT   *New York*, 14 *April* 1934

Sir Adrian Boult,*
The British Broadcasting Corporation,
Broadcasting House,
London, W.1.

My dear Mr. Boult [*sic*]:

I was so occupied all this time, that I did not find the possibility to answer your kind letter of the 1st of November 33.

---

[1] The second of the *Four Pieces* for mixed chorus, op. 27.

* Sir Adrian, however, was not knighted until 1937. [Trans.]

AETAT 59 — *To Sir Adrian Boult*

But now I have less to do: for not only having been occupied, but also sick whilst this bad winter, I am now forced to rest; and rest will say [i.e., 'means']: to write letters.

One of the first to you.

It was a great pity that the planned concerts of November 1933 could not be done.[1] I regret it very much, but if you will only consider the fact that I had not the money to order the wanted orchestra-material and the parts for the Kolisch Quartet etc.; and the other fact, that I waited in vain for your contract, granting the fee, wanted to pay costs of the copies, etc. — these two facts will convince you that I was unable to act otherwise than I did.

Now I learned you plan anew to perform the concertos. But I have not been told whether you have in view the Violoncello Concerto* or the String-Quartet Concerto with the Kolischs.† I should be very glad to conduct this performance, supposing I can come to Europe, which till now is not quite sure. But if you have the intention to ask me for conducting, I would like to know it at least by the end of May. As before mentioned, I was sick the whole winter and, my vacations beginning on 1st of June, I must fix in time the place for my recreation: the south of Europe or the south of America.

If possible I should prefer a date in June or one between the 15th of September and the 10th of October, for after this date I would like to go back to New York.

Remembering your performance of my 'Variations for Orchestra' which I heard by broadcast and which was remarkably beautiful, clear and vital, I could wish to get also these new works performed by you.

And to be sure, I would prefer to hear them, than to conduct, if I should not be forced to earn money by conducting.

Looking forward with great pleasure to your kind answer,

Yours very sincerely,

ARNOLD SCHOENBERG

---

[1] Schoenberg had cancelled the two concerts in London, the programmes of which included a new concerto for string quartet and orchestra, after Handel's Concerto Grosso, op. 6, no. 7. He left for America in October (see Biographical Notes, p. 177).

* with Feuermann. [S.]

† I.e., Schoenberg's adaptations of a harpsichord concerto by Monn and a Concerto Grosso, op. 6, no. 7, by Handel. [TRANS.]

To Walter E. Koons April 1934[?]
[*Written in English*]

158. To Walter E. Koons New York, 14 *April* 1934[?]
Walter E. Koons,
Music Supervisor,
National Broadcasting Company,
RCA Building,
30, Rockefeller Plaza,
New York City

Dear Mr. Koons;

Music is a simultaneous and a succesive-ness of tones and tone-combinations, which are so organized that its impression on the ear is agreeable, and its impression on the intelligence is comprehensible, and that these impressions have the power to influence occult parts of our soul and of our sentimental spheres and that this influence makes us live in a dreamland of fulfilled desires, or in a dreamed hell of ... etc., etc., ...

What is water?

H_2O; and we can drink it; and can wash us by it; and it is transparent; and has no Colour; and we can use it to swim and to ship; and it drives mills ... etc., etc.

I know a nice and touching story:

A blind man asked his guide:

'How looks milk?'

The Guide answered:

'Milk looks white.'

The Blind Man:

'What's that "white"? Mention a thing which is white!'

The Guide:

'A swan. It is perfect white, and it has a long white and bent neck.'

The Blind Man:

'... A bent neck? How is that?'

The Guide, imitating with his arm the form of a swan's neck, lets the blind man feel the form of his arm.

The Blind Man (flowing softly with his hand along the arm of the guide):

'Now I know how looks milk.'

Yours very sincerely,
Arnold Schoenberg

AETAT 59   *To Walter E. Koons*

No. 158 was Schoenberg's answer to a question put to him in the following letter:

> Mr. Arnold Schoenberg,   14 *April* 1934
> Hotel Ansonia,
> New York, N.Y.
>
> Dear Mr. Schoenberg,
>   Following our conversation in your dressing-room after the Cadillac Concert last Sunday night I would be greatly honored to receive your answer to the following question —
> > Will you please give me *your* definition of music — not just your appreciation of music-making nor your reactions to it, but *what music* (in the abstract) *means to you*?
>
>   As I tried to explain to you, I ask this question in all seriousness, not as a joke as some have thought, for I am earnestly trying to explain this mysterious 'thing' we call music. I have obtained 170 answers to this question from the foremost musicians of our generation — also from distinguished minds in other fields of mental activity, such as Dr. Albert Einstein, George Bernard Shaw, Premier Edouard Herriot, Aldous Huxley, professors of philosophy, psychology, psychiatry and physics at the world's leading universities — and these I am including in a book I have written on the subject. That work is completed but I have received so many additional answers that I am re-writing my last chapter in order to include these. I sent my question to you in Germany about a year ago but perhaps you did not receive it — or if you did it may have impressed you as a rather stupid sort of question.
>   Mr. Alexandre Siloti, who also lives at the Hotel Ansonia, is greatly interested in this work and can tell you more about it and me. He has answered my question — also Rachmaninoff, Ernst Toch, Alexandre Tcherepnine, Cyril Scott, Felix Weingartner, Josef Hofmann, Ossip Gabrilowitsch, etc., etc. and I am most anxious to include your thoughts in this work. As far as I know no similar attempt has ever been undertaken in this way — Grove's Musical Dictionary lists everything about music but does not attempt to define the word 'music' itself.
>   My answers range from one (very intelligent) word to nine typewritten pages. I make no limitations. From what I have already assembled I can assure you that this work will be most unusual and interesting — not only to professional musicians and to those who have the capacity to enjoy music but also to physicians, psychologists and scientists who have been conducting such interesting experiments with music in their respective professions. . . . You see, I have been trying to examine this 'thing' called music with the 'telescope' as well as with the 'microscope', from without and from within. I feel that my work would not be complete without including your thoughts and I am hoping that you will accord me that honor.

To Walter E. Koons April 1934(?)

 At the same time I hope that I may have the opportunity to become better acquainted with you while you are in the United States.
   Sincerely yours,
       (Signed)
      WALTER E. KOONS
      Music Supervisor

[*Handwritten at foot*]
 If you prefer to answer in German I can have accurate translation made. Please answer in the form of a letter addressed to me.

159. TO RUDOLF KOLISCH[1] *Chautauqua, 27 August* 1934
Herr Rudolf Kolisch,
Molveno, Italy.
 [. . . . .]
 We don't yet know whether we shall be in New York this winter. It's very expensive, and we can live on 2/5ths of the money in the South, and I can recuperate. In the South we can live for 5–6 months on the few dollars we have saved, even if I am not earning anything. But I dare say there will turn out to be some pupil or article or some other source of income, since everyone is perfectly delighted with me. There actually isn't any money to be had. I have now got to know Hutcheson and Stoessel of the Juilliard School here and have spent quite a lot of time with them, have the impression that they liked me very much, both of them being eager to meet me frequently . . . and I'm certain they would like to have me at the Juilliard School if there were the money for it. (True, they don't know how cheap I'd be.) Unfortunately we have had to decline an offer from Ganz's college in Chicago* at $4,000. Above all because it really is too little (I can't manage under 6,000) and because I'd have been tied to the bad Chicago climate for 8–9 months of the year.
 For all that, we aren't at all worried. Sooner or later there *will* be a publisher for the concertos, which are bound to be a great success, and then the whole year will be covered. Admittedly it is very difficult, for all the publishers (who've been publishing worthless rubbish, exclusively, for decades) are bankrupt, since all their stuff is fit for nothing but pulping! It serves them right, but it doesn't do me much good either.
 [. . . . .]
       ARNOLD SCHOENBERG

---

 [1] See note 2 to Letter 143.
 * Ganz's college, i.e., the Chicago Musical College, of which Rudolph Ganz, a distinguished pianist and conductor, was director from 1929–54. [TRANS.]

AETAT 60   *To Maurice Speiser*

160. DAS LANDESFINANZAMT, BERLIN

Chautauqua, 27 August 1934

Das Landesfinanzamt [a department of the Ministry of Finance], Berlin

In view of the fact that the Ministry of Education has terminated my contract (as teacher in charge of an advanced class in musical composition at the Academy of Arts), although the contract does not permit of such a termination, and has hitherto not met my justified claim for payment . . . nor paid me the removal expenses to which I am entitled, I herewith request that my last month's salary, together with the amount of income-tax paid in excess of the sum due, amounting to a total of:

M. 1,224, —

be paid into my account at the Deutsche Bank und Diskontogesellschaft, Berlin, in order that I may be enabled to pay debts that I otherwise have not the means to settle and which were incurred as a consequence of my removal abroad under duress.

I shall be obliged if you will inform the Deutsche Bank und Diskontogesellschaft, Department 3 (America) of the granting of my request and will authorise them to act on my instructions.

ARNOLD SCHOENBERG

PS. Enclosed: a letter from the firm of Schanker in Paris, stating their claims on me.

[*Written in English*]

161. TO MAURICE SPEISER   [*Chautauqua,*] 25 *September* 1934

Mr. Maurice Speiser,
1000, Girard Trust Building,
Philadelphia, Pa.

Dear Mr. Speiser:

At first I must apologize for my silence. You surely remember how sick I was in New York; and when I finally came here, the first part of the sojourn was dedicated to restore my health and to rest from this 'too much working' of my first American season. But the rest of this summer I was then as lazy as I had not yet been in my whole life.

This is one reason, but the second [reason for] my silence is that the contract of Universal Edition can give you no possibility of assault: it is all right. The question is only, they have violated the contract in permitting the recording of my Verklaerte Nacht, though the right to permit it belongs to myself.

To Maurice Speiser SEPTEMBER 1934

I think we shall not stay here more for a long time and I think it is better to speak about these matters in New York.

My letter today has one more goal: I know you were interested in modern painting and also in Oscar Kokoschka. A recent letter from Vienna informed me that the Nazis in their worldwide geniality had not only expelled Jews of outstanding importance, but also Aryans, if only the old fashioned artists, whose taste has now supreme command, desired it. And so Kokoschka's paintings, once bought with very much money, have been expelled from all German art galleries and (if I am well informed) burned! You will conceive that Kokoschka, as I learned, is in a very strong depression of mind; and I suppose his financial position may also not be the best.

I know your influence in society and artistic circles and therefore I think you are the man who can do something for Kokoschka. I think the best would be to arrange an exposition of his paintings and to try to interest buyers of paintings in his art. I am convinced it will be possible to procure him his right as one of the most important painters of our time: to have his paintings in every art gallery of any importance.

Looking forward to your kind answer with much interest, I am, with kind regards,

Yours truly,

ARNOLD SCHOENBERG

162. TO ERNEST HUTCHESON[1]   3 *October* 1934[2]

Dear Mr. Hutcheson,

First and foremost I want to tell you that your offer gives me very great pleasure indeed, for it shows me that I need not feel superfluous in America; and it confirms what I had already realised in Chautauqua: that we should be able to get on very well together both personally and artistically. This is something that I always value very much; and is the main reason why I have taken so long to reply.

But unfortunately there are too many strong arguments against it, and I cannot take the risk of thrusting these qualms aside.

Above all it is, I am afraid, quite certain that I shall have to spend at least this winter in a milder climate and that I shall not be able to stand up to the New York climate before spring (which I hope will be mild!) at the earliest.

[..........]

[1] Ernest Hutcheson, at that time director of the Juilliard School of Music in New York, had offered Schoenberg a teaching post at the School.
[2] Probably from Hollywood.

I am sure you will understand and appreciate my wish: that you should not regard this as a refusal. For it would be a great pleasure and honour for me to work at your school, collaborating with you and helping to develop your student material. And as I indicated in my telegram ('let me think it over'), I should like to make you a counter-suggestion:

Let us postpone the whole thing until next year, or at least until the spring and the summer (Chautauqua), and in this case I would give you an instant acceptance.

I would, then, candidly, have just one little request: that the agreement may be made with all possible speed so that I can make my arrangements in good time and not be hampered by expensive removals.

[. . . . .]

ARNOLD SCHOENBERG

163. THANKS FOR BIRTHDAY WISHES   *Hollywood, October* 1934
[*Schoenberg's thanks for good wishes received on the occasion of his 60th birthday*][1]

On my fiftieth birthday many people felt an urge or necessity to make a declaration of sympathy with me, and even of adherence to me; on my sixtieth many felt they were now free of this wearisome compulsion, while others, under the compulsion of Nordic ideology, attained the same freedom, even though against their will; on my seventieth — that is as far as I presume to envisage the future — the circle of those who do not regret my first birthday will perhaps be still smaller; but it is to be hoped that those who address me then will be only such as do it of their own free will, and of those only such as recognise some achievement in the few little things I have jotted down.

I have for a long time known that I cannot live to see widespread understanding of my works, and my far-famed resoluteness is a matter of dire necessity arising from the wish to see it for all that. I have set my goal far enough ahead to be sure that the reluctant and even the resistant will some day have to arrive there. For, after all, parallels — as mathematics assure us — do meet at such points, if one only has the patience to wait long enough.

It is perhaps expected that now that I am in a new world I should feel its amenities to be ample compensation for the loss I have sustained and which I had foreseen for more than a decade. Indeed, I parted from

[1] Mimeographed copies of this letter were sent to all who had conveyed their good wishes to Schoenberg. In October he had moved to Los Angeles, not with any prospect of an appointment there, but because the warm climate of South California was beneficial to his indifferent health.

Thanks for Birthday Wishes OCTOBER 1934

the old world not without feeling the wrench in my very bones, for I was not prepared for the fact that it would render me not only homeless but speechless, languageless, so that to all but my old friends I could now say it only in English: supposing they wished to hear it at all. On the other hand, here one does live like a fighting cock.* For here I am universally esteemed as one of the most important composers: alongside Stravinsky, Tansman, Sessions, Sibelius, Gershwin, Copland, etc., ... etc., ... etc., ... And so I can safely count on my seventieth birthday turning out just as I have prophesied.

I am nevertheless set on living to see it. For if, besides my domestic happiness, there then really remain these friends who give me so much joy and each single one of whom makes me proud of the force, courage, intelligence, originality, and knowledge with which he can express his reasons for saluting me: then I can congratulate myself on the occasion even now.

The fact that I can be proud of having such friends determines the measure of my gratitude. But how deeply from the heart it comes is something I could really express only in music.

ARNOLD SCHOENBERG

164. TO OTTO KLEMPERER *Hollywood, 8 November* 1934

Dear Herr Klemperer,

Yesterday I was under the necessity of refusing an invitation to a banquet in your honour.[1] You know I have no cause to show you greater respect than you show me. But that is not my motive in the case of this refusal. For you also know that I am thoroughly capable of expressing such things in a much less ambiguous manner. But the fact is: I consider it unspeakable that these people, who have been suppressing my works in this part of the world for the last 25 years, now want to use me as a decoration, to give me a walking-on part to play on this occasion, because I simply happen, entirely at my own pleasure, to be here: and I consider that if these people now have a bad conscience or even indeed want to make good their errors, it is up to them first of all to conciliate me by other means. In any case they will have to recognise that I cannot be fobbed off with a mere *douceur*.

Let me repeat it clearly: this refusal is not directed at you, for I esteem your talents sufficiently to adopt much sharper weapons against

* 'live like a fighting cock': the corresponding German phrase is 'live like the Lord God in France', and Schoenberg continues: 'where He would have even more difficulty in getting a labour-permit than here.' [TRANS.]

[1] Otto Klemperer had been appointed conductor of the symphony concerts in Los Angeles.

you. These are jests: please do not misunderstand. With, despite all, very kind regards to you.

ARNOLD SCHOENBERG

165. To ERNEST HUTCHESON[1]   *Hollywood, 28 March* 1935
[..........]

Regarding my sphere of activity, perhaps I may let my general and my specifically American experience speak. It is concerned first and foremost with the students' grounding. Although even in Europe I was almost unfailingly very dissatisfied, I did usually find that there was at least a certain fairly extensive knowledge of the works of the masters. This indispensable basis for teaching appears to be in the main lacking here. I attribute this to two circumstances: above all to the high price of printed music, which for most students makes it impossible to own the rudimentary little collection of something like 200 volumes that all but the very poorest had in Austria; and secondly to the excessively high price of tickets for concerts and opera, and the social style in which they are got up. It is not in my power to do anything about this (but a benefit fund might effect something).
[..........]

ARNOLD SCHOENBERG

166. To ALBAN BERG   *Hollywood, 4 May* 1935
My dear fellow,

In haste just one request: I have been told you are on the A.K.M. committee;[2] but even if not, perhaps you will have some other way of getting my request fulfilled through an intermediary. I should like to join the A.K.M. (I must, for otherwise there's only the Czech Assoc. open to me). You'll find the application enclosed. Please hand this in, and they can enter the works themselves from the *Festschrift*.* What I want to ask you is to see that my case is considered on its proper merits, including appreciation of the fact that I haven't received anything for the last two years and haven't had much luck with my royalties either, and that I would perhaps be entitled to some special form of consideration in view of what I have done for others.

[1] See Letter 162.
[2] The Austrian *Gesellschaft der Autoren, Komponisten und Musikverleger*, Vienna [Association of Authors, Composers, and Music Publishers].
* Presumably the collection of essays published in honour of Schoenberg's 60th birthday (Vienna, 1934). [TRANS.]

To Alban Berg MAY 1935

The G.D.T.[1] recently sent me a final statement of account and paid up the money for foreign performances, which they always do only a year after the statement, which is almost two years after the performance, so that is now completely done with.

With all this, I am hoping things in Austria aren't yet coming to the same pass as in Germany. Anyway I've included a clause protecting me against expropriation.[2]

[..........]

ARNOLD SCHOENBERG

167. TO ERNEST HUTCHESON *Hollywood*, 11 *June* 1935

My dear Mr. Hutcheson,[3]

Please do regard my not answering for so long as at least partly caused by the great struggle I had before fighting my way through to a decision fraught with such consequences. But partly too it was caused by the fact that Carl Engel,[4] who has been going to so much trouble to oblige me, did not answer for so long: I had asked him to act as he thought best, knew he would do so, and therefore could not intervene.

Well, I'm afraid your negative answer failed to help me over the grave qualms of which I told you. I tell you frankly that I would have been prepared to risk my health if even one of the two other qualms had been disposed of. Above all the question of the scope of activity. However little worldly sense I may otherwise have, I do know that I should have had to make a success of it if my appointment at your School were to become a permanent one. Considering the work allotted me and the improbability of my getting the best, most gifted student material, this seemed practically out of the question. Let me pass in silence over the fact that the salary could not be adequate to my needs, to say nothing of my wishes, and that I was offered no certainty of any future improvement.

Do believe me when I say I find it extremely hard to have to tell you that I shall, then, not be able to come after all. I had been looking forward very much to working with you and being pleasantly in contact with you, and was very grateful for the token of confidence and respect that you gave me in making this offer.

[..........]

ARNOLD SCHOENBERG

[1] *Genossenschaft deutscher Tonsetzer*, Berlin [Association of German Composers].
[2] The Austrian Association refused Schoenberg's application for membership.
[3] See Letters 162 and 165.
[4] Carl Engel, in charge of the music department of the Library of Congress, Washington, had become president of G. Schirmer, music publishers in New York, who published several of Schoenberg's works.

AETAT 61 *To Bessie Bartlett Fraenkel*

NB: Would you not consider Anton von Webern (Im Auhof 8, Maria-Enzersdorf, near Vienna) for the position[?] He is the most impassioned and intensive teacher imaginable and is at present not very satisfied with conditions in Vienna.[1]

[*Written in English*]
168. To BESSIE BARTLETT FRAENKEL
Hollywood, 26 November 1935

Mrs. Bessie Bartlett Fraenkel,
La Casa Sogno,
643, Palisades Beach Road,
Santa Monica, Calif.

My dear Mrs. Fraenkel,
I thank you very much for your very kind letter, and I acknowledge how busy you are, and how much of your best time is taken up by the social duties of your position as president of so many important clubs. And therefore I want to propose you to take one Monday evening at 6.30 dinner in my home and to come with us at 7.30 to the class of 'Musical Criticism' at the University of Southern California.

I would very much like to have you sometimes or at least once among the audience of this class, because I know what I am doing there is of the greatest importance for everybody who is interested in music. I know from my experience of nearly forty years that a real understanding for music has to be based on a sound capacity to distinguish between value and non-value. And I know, too, how new my attempt is, to bring not only the amateur, but also the musician, to a real knowledge of basic elements for appreciation. Among my audience you will find four or five professors of both the USC and the UCLA. And it is very astonishing that these professors are not musicians, but, what I appreciate very much, professors of philosophy. And these professors are not only the most steady frequenters, but they are also very enthusiastic about the manner in which I handle this difficult matter and about the results and the advantage for music lovers of my attempt.

Nevertheless, I am very disappointed. I expected to have a class of at least 50 to 60 listeners, and I hoped to find a great number of the music lovers and musicians of Los Angeles there. I know this city likes music. But you yourself know how difficult it is to make it accustomed to attend the concerts regularly. People in general, the world over, are

[1] Webern was not asked.

To Bessie Bartlett Fraenkel NOVEMBER 1935

more inclined to appreciate the performers than the works which they perform. But what you need indeed is a great number of people who do not look at first in the programme, asking 'Who plays, conducts, or sings?', but 'What will be played?' As long as not a remarkable part of the public is attracted by the *work* to be performed, as long you will always suffer from this difficulty, how to fill the concert-hall?

What I am striving for in my lectures is directed on the *work* and everybody who is listening to them will be a listener, who knows what he likes and why he likes it. And there will certainly be in perhaps twenty years a chapter in the musical history of Los Angeles: 'What Schoenberg has achieved in Los Angeles'; and perhaps there will be another chapter, asking: 'What have the people and the society of Los Angeles taken of the advantage offered by Schoenberg?'.

Would you not like to have some influence on the answer, which historians in times to come will give to this question? Frankly: I am very disappointed not to find the interest of the society in my doing, not to find appreciated what I am doing in favour of the future state of musical culture in this city, not to find the support which is owed to such a doing. I do not know how long I will be willing or able to continue such a work. And suddenly it will be past and there will only be a small number of men who used this opportunity.

I am sure you understand perfectly what I mean and you will certainly consider it so as I mean it: Yes, I want you and many other of society people among my audience and making propaganda for my work in favour of the musical culture of Los Angeles.

I would like to hear your opinion upon this matter and I am looking forward with great interest to it.

With kind regards,
     Yours very truly,
         ARNOLD SCHOENBERG

169. TO ALMA MAHLER-WERFEL   *Hollywood, 23 January 1936*
Dear lady, dear friend,

Many thanks for your letter and the cutting about our poor friend.[1] Almost the only information about him I have had so far has been from newspapers. Everyone in Vienna writes in extreme horror, but without giving details. And I so much want to know *something*.

[..........]

---
[1] Alban Berg, who had died of blood-poisoning, the consequence of an abscess, on 24th December 1935.

AETAT 61 *To K. Kulka*

Here we are constantly being offered the earth, which then in the end brings forth sour grapes: at least we are ever and again under the necessity of so regarding them. For a time it looked as though I would be teaching at both universities,[1] which would have brought me in pretty much my Berlin salary. Then I almost agreed to write music for a film, but fortunately asked $50,000, which, likewise fortunately, was much too much, for it would have been the end of me; and the only thing is that if I had somehow survived it we should have been able to live on it — even if modestly — for a number of years, which would have meant at last being able to finish in my lifetime at least those compositions and theoretical works that I have already begun, even if not beginning any more new things. And for that I should gladly have sacrificed my life and even my reputation, although I know that others, who have held their own in less strict regard than I mine, would not have failed to seize the chance of despising me for it.

[..........]
ARNOLD SCHOENBERG

170. To K. KULKA *Hollywood, 24 January* 1936
Dear Herr Kulka,

I expect to have a chance of building myself a house here, and you will realise how it grieves me that Loos is no longer alive or that I cannot have it built by one of his pupils, for instance yourself. But I want in any case to have a modern house and am therefore in touch with two modern architects. One is an American, but the other is Richard Neutra, who comes from Vienna and whom I dare say you know. He also appears to be of Loos' circle and does very nice houses, even if a bit more doctrinaire than Loos, more studied, and not uninfluenced by Bauhaus principles. Still, anyway, he has Viennese taste and knows what a scribe needs.

Now what I want to ask you is something he doesn't know. It's about the use of marble as a wall-covering. Loos told me 'marble is the cheapest wallpaper'. He said he had the marble cut in sheets only a millimetre thick and these were then cemented on to the wall. This method is totally unknown here, and what I should like to ask you is to let me know who does this here, and where one can get further information about it. Does it call for a special mechanical saw? Who manufactures and sells it? Does one need specially trained craftsmen? Is it done in Vienna, or where else? Could one, if necessary, get the sheets direct,

[1] For a short time Schoenberg taught at the University of South California (U.S.C.); from 1936 to 1944 he was Professor of Music at the much larger University of California, Los Angeles (U.C.L.A.).

To K. Kulka   JANUARY 1936

ready cut? Is some special glue or cement needed for sticking them on, and can any workman do that, if necessary after being instructed? — How far up the walls did Loos carry the marble, and how is the transition made to ceiling or wall?

I hope these questions of mine will not give you very much trouble. For all eventualities, very many thanks indeed.*

                                                 ARNOLD SCHOENBERG

171. To HERMANN SCHERCHEN   *Hollywood*, 16 *March* 1936
Dear Herr Scherchen,

Thank you very much for sending me the programme of your *Festival International*. It is obviously a very big affair indeed, and if there is anything I miss, it is Webern. I should be sorry if he, who, like myself of old, is always left out of things, should be given any further grounds for bitterness. He is, after all, one of the most original figures in the musical life of our time.

[..........]

Now a small plea: 'Erwartung' is not a '*mimodrame*', which would mean a pantomime, in which many characters appear but none either sings or speaks. It is a monodrama, a play in which only one single person appears, in this case one who sings. I know I don't have to tell you this, but the French, who say *mimodrame* every time I insist on monodrama. Please do tell them, once and for all.

Let me know how you get on and how rehearsals go. After numerous illnesses I am at the moment in good health. Artistically I am more dissatisfied than ever, and as for what I am doing here, well, this year I have been teaching at one and next year shall be teaching at the other of the two universities here. But unfortunately the material I get has had such an inadequate grounding that my work is as much a waste of time as if Einstein were having to teach mathematics at a secondary school.

                                                 ARNOLD SCHOENBERG

172. To CHARLOTTE DIETERLE[1]   *Los Angeles*, 30 *July* 1936
Dear Mrs. Dieterle,

We were extremely sorry that you had no time to spend the evening with us last week. Not only because we should have enjoyed showing you approximately what the house will be like when it is all finished, but also because I hoped to be of use to you in the matter of the Beethoven film: in so far as my capacities and circumstances permit. For I'm afraid: in this case I am somewhat hampered.

Perhaps you read my answer: 'I shall tell you whether I can do it or

---

* The house did not materialize. [TRANS.]
[1] The wife of the film-producer, Wilhelm Dieterle.

whom I consider suitable . . .' as meaning that I cannot do it myself. My position in musical life would compel me to maintain a certain attitude even if I did not myself feel that way. Nobody could help understanding if I were, say to form a poetic version of Beethoven's life out of my own imagination and my own feelings about him, and make a film of it. For the conception would from the very beginning be a musical one, and what I would then do with Beethoven's music would not be a mere use of it but a 'fantasy', a symphonic-dramatic fantasy that would necessarily have the same artistic justification as if I were to write variations on a theme of Beethoven's. But if I were to 'serve' by adapting Beethoven's music to a 'libretto', no matter how good (and I do not doubt that yours is good), written by someone else, it would not be in keeping with what people are entitled to demand of me, namely that I should create *out of my own being*.

But after giving much thought to the matter I was going to suggest you should decide on Klemperer. He does know and understand Beethoven to a really quite exceptional degree; has the ability to feel his heroic quality, himself having fire and spirit enough not to fail in the task: and though he is a tyrant, that would only be to the advantage of the undertaking as a whole; for a slave cannot portray a hero. In addition, however, he has a gift that is not often found at his level: he has a sense of the theatre, and experience. And what I was going to suggest was that I would gladly be prepared to advise him on problems of style and composition, in which I, for my part, may doubtless be considered a specialist.

ARNOLD SCHOENBERG

[*Written in English*]
173. To ELIZABETH SPRAGUE COOLIDGE[1]

Los Angeles, 3 August 1936

Mrs. Elizabeth Sprague Coolidge,
Library of Congress,
Washington, D.C.
or:
Hotel Lake Merritt,
Oakland, Calif.

Dear Mrs. Coolidge,

I finished the string quartet on July 26[2] and should have sent it to you if only I knew where you are now. I send this letter to two addresses and hope at least one of them will be correct.

[1] The American patron of the arts.
[2] Schoenberg's Fourth String Quartet, op. 37, was commissioned by Mrs. Coolidge and is dedicated to her.

To Elizabeth Sprague Coolidge　　　　　　　　　　　AUGUST 1936

You were probably astonished to hear nothing more from us. But you could not imagine how much work we had through the arrival of our furniture. I lost more than four weeks and still have my library and my manuscripts not arranged. Besides I had to teach. Private lessons and these terrible summer sessions at U.S.C.[1] But every quarter of an hour I was free I used for the continuation of the string quartet. When you will get the manuscript you will see the first three movements were finished in a rather short time. But the fourth movement which I began on June 18 took more time than the other three. But not for composing.

I am very content with the work and think it will be much more pleasant than the third. But — I believe always so.

I am very anxious to hear from you and hope this letter will reach you.

I am very sorry we could not come to San Francisco. The concerts in Pasadena were such a wonderful time and the whole spirit which dominated everybody who was present was a great experience.[2]

I am looking forward to your answer with much pleasure and send you kindest greetings and best regards from both Mrs. Schoenberg and myself.

　　　　　　　　　　Yours very truly,

　　　　　　　　　　　　　　ARNOLD SCHOENBERG

[*Written in English*]
174. TO ELIZABETH SPRAGUE COOLIDGE
　　　　　　　　　　　　　　Los Angeles, 5 *February* 1937

Mrs. Elizabeth Sprague Coolidge,
34, Coolidge Ave.,
Cambridge, Mass.

My dear Mrs. Coolidge,

I wrote and wired you several times, but don't know whether you got my messages. Now I found this address of yours and hope you get it this time.

I send you this information because I think it might interest you. The records sound wonderfully. I am so glad to own them.

I [have] wanted for a long time to write to you about the way in which these University people behaved on the occasion of the four concerts. Firstly: no publicity at all. A few days before the concerts the letters were mailed. I insisted that they mention that these concerts were given

---

[1] University of Southern California.

[2] A series of chamber-music concerts had been given in Pasadena under Mrs. Coolidge's aegis; the Kolisch Quartet had played Schoenberg's earlier string quartets.

through your generosity. They did it on small postcards, which informed the receivers that one concert will be given at one o'clock in the afternoon, because the Budapest quartet played the same evening in Mrs. Fraenkel's Club and they and Mr. Beheymer were afraid their box-office would suffer. Though it is very usual here on such occasions that an official person introduces the players and addresses the audience, and although they had to mention your activities on behalf of chamber music and what you do for Universities, and although I am a professor of this University, which is certainly more honor to them than to me: nothing was done to inform the public and to mention that this festival is an honour, and that, last but not least, the world-renowned Kolisch quartet was playing. But that is not all. I was told the president was at the first concert. I doubt it. At least he did not come to offer me a friendly word, which is very easy, because I do not expect too much. But also nobody else from [among] the officials came to me to congratulate or I don't know what.

I am very much disgusted by this behaviour. I find it quite unusual, because I have been honoured always in America and I am sure this was not a mere accident. You have certainly already realized that I am not ambitious and I do not expect people to understand my music at the first hearing. I am content if they do not dislike it when they hear it the fifteenth time. I had to get accustomed to such an attitude. But it seems to me this behaviour is extraordinary.

On the other hand the concerts were a great pleasure to me, and you will understand how much I appreciate what you have done through these concerts and how you have done it. May I thank you again cordially.

The Kolischs played marvellously. Everything seems so simple, so self-evident in their performance, that one would think it is easy. Their virtuosity, their sonority, their understanding, their style, are admirable. I confess they are the best string quartet I [have] ever heard. I am so enthusiastic about their performances that I asked Kolisch to play my new Concerto for Violin, which Klemperer wants to perform next year in Los Angeles, London, and Moscow. I am sure there is nobody today who could play it as well as he.

I am very, very busy the whole time and besides I was again sick for two weeks. I had to postpone a concert in which I ought to have conducted my 'Pelleas and Melisande'; now it will be given on February 17. I am very sorry you can not hear this work. It was written immediately after the 'Gurrelieder' but is already more mature and advanced. Besides, I have now seven private pupils, who give me much pleasure

To Elizabeth Sprague Coolidge FEBRUARY 1937

but also much work. But nevertheless I hope now to find the time to finish my opera 'Moses and Aron'.

Now this [is] a very long letter.

Today I am exceptionally free and used this occasion to write you.

I hope to hear sometimes from you, and send you the best greetings of Mrs. Schoenberg and myself.

Yours very faithfully,
ARNOLD SCHOENBERG

[*Written in English*]

175. To ROBERT G. SPROUL 2 *October* 1937

Dr. Robert G. Sproul, President,
University of California,
Los Angeles, California

My dear President Sproul:

When you asked me to send you a memorandum concerning my plans for the Music Department, we were hoping that the University would be granted additional funds. In view of the reduction, I have tried to find a way for moving in the right direction without unduly increasing the music department's budget during the present biennium.

The department's primary need is at least one additional teacher, who could take over the lower classes in counterpoint and analysis, and eventually the composition for prospective teachers. This would give me at once the opportunity to teach in advanced classes the more talented students, so that we should not lack some progress in the upbuilding of the Music Department during these 'seven meager years', and should be prepared to continue as soon as the budget allows.

At the present time we have 25 students in composition, and 45 in analysis, both of which classes are far too large. But in counterpoint, we have 60 students, which I find very embarrassing. We have figured that if we wish to correct the assignments not very carefully, but only superficially, twenty hours of work a week would be necessary, which is far too much, even without the papers from the other classes. Furthermore, we have no opportunity to work with these students at the blackboard, to help them and to find out what they know. As there are very differing abilities, from the lowest to the highest, the good students must suffer a great deal through such superficial teaching.

Allow me to make this following proposal: If you should find it possible to offer Mr. Strang, my present assistant, a contract as instructor for next year, we should be able to make some such adjustment as this: The counterpoint class could be divided into two or three sections of reasonable size, to be taught by Mr. Strang, or possibly one group of more talented students could be taken by me. Similarly, the composition class could be divided into two sections, the more talented and able students coming to me, and the more average students being taught by Mr. Strang. If, finally, the class in beginning analysis could be given to Mr. Strang, I would be free to announce a second year of composition and a second year of analysis, for which there are now a considerable number of prepared students.

Some such adjustment is almost imperative for next year, for we must expect further increases in the number of students again next year (as indicated by the fifty per cent increase in the lower division counterpoint class this year). And the University will sooner or later need to provide classes for the more advanced students, who are becoming ready in increasing numbers.

If such a program for next year could be agreed upon, Mr. Strang will be willing to do approximately as much work this year as he would have to do next. This would enable me to put part of this program (specifically, dividing certain classes into workable groups) into operation at once. Meanwhile, complete details could be worked out with Mr. Allen.

Finally, as I had occasion to tell you, I need at least $150 to $200 a year to build a library for the classes in analysis and composition. It would help me very much if such an amount could be devoted to this purpose.

I very much hope it will be possible to put these proposals into effect, both for the ultimate upbuilding of the department and for the benefit of the present students, whose training suffers from the handicaps described.

With sincere personal regards,
    Very truly yours,
        ARNOLD SCHOENBERG
        Professor of Music

176. TO ALFRED HERTZ[1]   *Los Angeles, 2 May* 1938

Dear Dr. Hertz,

An old friend of my youth, that admirable pianist and theoretician, Moriz Violin, has written asking me for an introduction to you. He tells me, incidentally, that you may remember him as having been one of Adalbert von Goldschmidt's circle in Vienna. Of course that is a long

---

[1] Alfred Hertz, a native of Frankfurt-am-Main, was one of the leading musicians in San Francisco, where he had for years been conductor of the San Francisco Symphony Orchestra.

To Alfred Hertz MAY 1938

time ago, but I think it probable that you will have a memory of his playing. For it was really remarkable. Since then he has held various distinguished appointments, among other things having been a professor at the Academy of Music in Vienna and in a similar position in Hamburg. But now things are going with him as they go with all unhappy members of our race: he has now been in Vienna since Hitler came to power in Germany. These people's fate moves me as though it were my own, which, after all, it almost is. And if there were any way I could help, I would do anything. Unfortunately the expectations aroused in me when I took on the job at U.C.L.A. have not been fulfilled. I was promised that I would be able to build up a large music department. But, as you know, the Governor has meanwhile reduced the budget by half a million. If that were not so, Herr Violin would be one of the first I should engage, and if you have a chance to get him for San Francisco, I frankly envy you — but I most devoutly hope you have. For it is so sad that all these people with the finest musical culture there was in Europe should be cast out and have to spend their old age in anxiety and hardship and grief.

I hope soon to have some good news.

ARNOLD SCHOENBERG

177. TO FELIX GREISSLE[1] *Los Angeles, 7 June* 1938
Mr. Felix Greissle,
New York.

[.........]

The first thing you must do now is instantly get yourself a quota visa.[2] For then if Schirmer really gives you a job, you are all out of the wood. People here expect very hard work, but they also give it its due. Only I do beg you: be very careful. Here they go in for much more politeness than we do. Above all, one never makes a scene; one never contradicts; one never says: 'to be quite honest', but if one does, one takes good care not really to be so. Differences of opinion are something one keeps entirely to oneself. Servility is superfluous, is indeed likely to annoy. But everything must be said amiably, smiling,* always with a smile.

In the next few days I shall be sending you an affidavit and in the meantime you can be finding out what you have to do. Engel's[3] idea

---

[1] Schoenberg's son-in-law, who had escaped from Austria with his family and had now arrived in New York.
[2] This was needed in order to get permission to work in America.
* In English in the original. [TRANS.]
[3] See note 4 to Letter 167.

that you should go to Hollywood is sheer nonsense. So far there has been absolutely no chance of anything here, otherwise I should obviously have seized it. On the contrary, many excellent musicians who have had to spend a year here because of the union, without being allowed to earn a cent, are now leaving Hollywood again, having used up all their savings. For instance there's my former pupil Adolphe Weiss, who happens to be one of the best bassoonists in America. At present he's playing in a Federal (unemployed musicians') orchestra. And if he can't get an engagement by September, he means to try New York again. I'm now earning two-fifths of what I was earning about 15 months ago, and see no hope of improvement. My pupils have stopped, all except one, because either their salaries have been reduced or they have lost their jobs.

So you see: if Engel gives you a job[1] or even enough work to do, it would be tremendous luck.

Something very important: Don't say anything you don't have to say about your experiences of the last few weeks. Especially not to newspapermen or to people who might pass it on to them. You know the Nazis take revenge on relatives and friends still in their power. So be very reserved and don't get mixed up in politics. I have kept to this strictly, always refusing to tell any stories, out of consideration for my friends and relatives in Germany. And people completely understand this.

ARNOLD SCHOENBERG

178. To JAKOB KLATZKIN[2] *Los Angeles*, 19 *July* 1938
Herr Dr. Jakob Klatzkin,
Vevey, Switzerland
[..........]
I am much better in health, but by no means free of troubles.

Composing is something I've not done for two years. I have had too much other work. And anyway: whom should one write for? The non-Jews are 'conservative', and the Jews have never shown any interest in my music. And now, into the bargain, in Palestine they are out to develop, artificially, an authentically Jewish kind of music, which rejects what I have achieved. I am now working — in so far as I'm not occupied with answering letters from unfortunate people in Germany and Austria, and in so far as I don't give way to unbearable depression — at a 'practical' handbook of composition. For more than 20 years I've been wanting to write a theoretical book, but now I must decant the

[1] Greissle was in fact given a job at Schirmer's.   [2] See Letter 153.

To Jakob Klatzkin JULY 1938

results of my work and all my knowledge and skill into a practical textbook. But: it will certainly turn out to be something quite out of the common.

Do write again some time soon and tell me what you're doing. . . .

ARNOLD SCHOENBERG

[*Written in English*]
179. To OLIN DOWNES[1]   *Los Angeles*, 8 [or 9?] *November* **1938**
Mr. Olin Downes,
New York Times,
New York City

My dear Mr. Downes:

I see in the New York Times of October 30, 1938, that you call my 'Variations for Orchestra' erroneously 'Variations upon the theme B-A-C-H.'

This error might have been provoked by the quotations of these four tones in several places. But I consider as the theme of these variations measures 34 to 57 incl. on pages 7 and 8.

If I should explain why I used these quotations [what I should say is]: I saw suddenly the possibility and did it (perhaps one will call it 'Sentimental') with pleasure as 'Hommage à Bach'; perhaps an excuse for such a procedure might be found in Beethoven's 'Diabelli Variations', when he quotes from Don Juan* 'Keine Ruh bei Tag und Nacht', or in Mozart's quotation of a contemporary opera melody in Don Juan (later replaced by a quotation from Figaro). Of course my quotation is not as humorous as both these before-mentioned. But again I have an excuse: I believe I have woven it in rather thoroughly.

I hope this might interest you.

I am, with sincere greetings,

Yours very truly,

ARNOLD SCHOENBERG

180. To HUGO LEICHTENTRITT   *Los Angeles, 3 December* **1938**
Dr. Hugo Leichtentritt,
Music Department,
Harvard University,
Cambridge, Mass.

In the university I had no time to give a detailed answer to your question about the German books that interest me.

---
[1] The music critic of the *New York Times*.
* Schoenberg refers to Mozart's *Don Giovanni*. [TRANS.]

AETAT 64 *To Alfred V. Frankenstein*

I am no 'reader' and therefore actually know the following books only very superficially, and in most cases only certain sections, out of context. Nevertheless I remember many a good idea. Presumably you yourself will know most of them, if not all.

Above all (although I disagree with almost everything):
All Heinrich Schenker's writings.
Wilhelm Weker: Über den Bau der Fugen.
Alois Hába: Neue Harmonielehre.
Fritz Cassirer: Beethoven und die Gestalt.
Mayrhofer: Der Kunstklang.
Walter Howard: Auf dem Wege zur Musik.
Lotte Kallenbach Greller: Grundlagen der neuen Musik.
Paul Stefan's books on Mahler.
Adler's biography of Mahler.
Bellermann: Kontrapunkt !!!!!!!!
Bernhard Marx: Kompositionslehre.
Hermann Erpf: Studien zur Harmonie.

Perhaps [the names of] some more of my opponents will occur to me, then I'll write again. I think many of these books ought to be brought to the Americans' attention. It might help to convert them away from their fossilised aesthetics: for, in spite of the generally pompous and affected style in which most of these works are written, they do put forward views of a quite different sort from those one finds in English and American books on theory.

ARNOLD SCHOENBERG

[*Written in English*]
181. To ALFRED V. FRANKENSTEIN   *Los Angeles*, 18 *March* 1939
Mr. Alfred V. Frankenstein
San Francisco Chronicle

Dear Mr Frankenstein:
Here [are] a few remarks about the 'Brahms'.[1]
My reasons:
1. I like this piece.
2. It is seldom played.
3. It is always very badly played, because the better the pianist, the louder he plays and you hear nothing from the strings. I wanted once to hear everything, and this I achieved.

[1] Schoenberg had arranged Brahms's piano quartet in G minor for orchestra. The first performance, conducted by Klemperer, was given in Los Angeles on the 7th May, 1938.

To Alfred V. Frankenstein   MARCH 1939

My intentions:

1. To remain strictly in the style of Brahms and not to go farther then he himself would have gone if he lived today.

2. To watch carefully all these laws which Brahms obeyed and not to violate [any of those] which are only known to musicians educated in his environment.

How I did it:

I am for almost 50 years very thoroughly acquainted with Brahms's style and his principles. I have analysed many of his works for myself and with my pupils. I have played as violist and cellist this work and many others numerous times: I therefore knew how it should sound. I had only to transpose this sound to the orchestra and this is in fact what I did.

Of course, there were heavy problems. Brahms likes very low basses, of which the orchestra possesses only a small number of instruments. He likes a full accompaniment with broken chord figures, often in different rhythms. And most of these figures can not easily be changed, because generally they have a structural meaning in his style. I think I resolved these problems, but this merit of mine will not mean very much to our present-day musicians because they do not know about them and if you tell them there are such, they do not care. But to me it means something.

I hope this satisfies you.

Many thanks for your kindly mentioning our meeting in my home and we really hope ourselves to see you once in your home: perhaps on the occasion of a visit to the world fair.

                     Yours very sincerely,

                             ARNOLD SCHOENBERG

182. TO PROFESSOR LEO KESTENBERG   *Los Angeles*, 16 *June* 1939

Dear Professor Kestenberg,

It was with pleasure that I read of the performance of my 'Pelleas' in Tel Aviv,[1] and I was delighted that it was Scherchen who conducted, for he was, after all, once a sort of pupil of mine and I'm sure still has a certain affection for me.

Well, I am delighted to hear that you have escaped the Nazis' clutches and are in a position where something really worth while can be achieved. I should much like to know if you have heard at all from Karl

---

[1] Leo Kestenberg had become director of the Palestine Orchestra in Tel Aviv.

AETAT 64   *To Professor Leo Kestenberg*

Rankl,[1] my former pupil. I last wrote on his behalf to Sir Adrian Boult[2] and Willem Mengelberg — unfortunately without success. That was several months ago and since then I have heard nothing from him. I hope he is safe!

The question in what order my music can best be introduced to the Palestinian public is one I should like to answer by saying: 'gradually, step by step.' What I have sought to achieve in my music has never been a 'style', but always content and the most precise possible reproduction of that content. Hence my early work paves the way for understanding of my musical ideas, and it is wiser first to become acquainted with the former, before my mode of expression becomes as concise as in my latest works.

So I think knowledge of my works from the first to the second string quartet will help to make comprehensible the language of the works between the Piano Pieces op. 11 and Serenade. And it seems to me that till then nothing of the third period should be served up, since even for most 'musicians' this period scarcely amounts to anything but its style.

[. . . . .]

Your writing of a Schoenberg Festival as a dream reminds me of the European times when such a thing would have been possible had not antisemitism (and particularly its Jewish brand) prevented it. To judge by the experience I had in Denver two years ago (when there was a four-day chamber-music festival of my works and [works of] some of my school), that would very much please and interest me. One positively sees how one grew and developed.

In conclusion I should like to ask you if there is any chance of saving valuable Jewish lives by getting people to Palestine with your help. I have so many people asking me, people in other professions too, but especially musicians. Here in America it has become almost impossible, at the moment, to get an affidavit. In many cases it's simply a matter of giving Jews who have been ordered to leave Germany or Italy the chance to stay in a neutral country while waiting for a visa. Is that possible in Palestine? I should like to know more about this.

[. . . . .]

                                          ARNOLD SCHOENBERG

---

[1] Karl Rankl, musical director of the German Theatre in Prague, had emigrated to England.
[2] Then conductor-in-chief of the B.B.C. Symphony Orchestra.

To Ernst Krenek   December 1939

183. To Ernst Krenek[1]   *Los Angeles*, 1 *December* 1939

Dear Herr Krenek,

Last night I put your letter of the 5th September on my desk, in order to answer it in the next 'rush', and now today your book has come.

So far I have only leafed through it, but I can see that it is highly interesting. I shall read it as fast as possible, but even that always takes me a very long time: I am a very bad reader, reading slowly, misunderstanding a great deal, and reading only at night. So you can easily imagine what it amounts to.

I share your opinion of American students of music. It's a great pity that the grounding is bad. Actually I was not very enthusiastic about German teaching either, because the mechanical methods. . . . .

12th December!!!

Until today I had no time to finish this letter (but now must do so quickly). Yes, those mechanical methods equipped people with a certain amount of knowledge and armed them with technique that one should get for oneself if one means to use it. Nevertheless, and because the bad teachers and methods here are no less mechanical, only covering a considerably smaller field, nevertheless, I repeat, I find that even the less admirable types of musician in Germany and Austria had a better grounding, a basis on which one could build.

But American young people's intelligence is certainly remarkable. I am endeavouring to direct this intelligence into the right channels. They are extremely good at getting hold of principles, but then want to apply them too much 'on principle'. And in art that's wrong. What distinguishes art from science is: that here there should not be principles of the kind one has to use on principle: that the one 'narrowly' defines what must be left 'wide open' [in the other?]; that musical logic does not answer to 'if —, then —', but enjoys making use of the possibilities excluded by if-then.

Well, enough for today. Write to me again soon and don't be offended if I don't answer until I have time.

Arnold Schoenberg

184. To Paul Dessau[2]   *Los Angeles*, 23 *September* 1940

Dear Herr Dessau,

I gladly agree to my name's being used in any way that can help to get Herr Leibowitz out of the enemy's hands. I am unfortunately too

[1] The composer Ernst Krenek was then on the music staff of Vassar College, New York.
[2] The composer.

AETAT 66   *To Louis Krasner*

busy to find out for myself what musical importance there may be in Herr Leibowitz's work.[1] However, I authorize you to say all that you consider I might say. The main thing, after all, is that it should be of some use, and I feel no sense of responsibility whatsoever towards the enemy, who are in any case destroying our values without examining them.

[..........]

ARNOLD SCHOENBERG

185. To OTTO KLEMPERER   *Los Angeles*, 25 *September* 1940

Dear Klemperer,

You have been misinformed. I did not say that you 'do not like some of my works'.

On the contrary:

I quoted verbatim what you said to me in a discussion that I am sure you have not forgotten:

'Your music has become alien to me.'

That is: not 'some' of my works, but *all* my works.

There should therefore be no need for any further explanation why I then consider that you should cease to conduct my works. For what can a performance be like if the music has become alien to one?

How it can possibly be insulting to you for me to quote your words requires elucidation.

The fact that you have become estranged from my music has not caused me to feel insulted, though it has certainly estranged me. I do not mean to say that I shall take no further interest in you; although I have no notion how the broken (artistic) bridge is ever to function again.

With best wishes for your health, Yours sincerely,

ARNOLD SCHOENBERG

[*Written in English*]

186. To LOUIS KRASNER   *Los Angeles*, 17 *December* 1940

Mr. Louis Krasner,
74, Fenway,
Boston, Mass.

Dear Mr. Krasner:

It is a great pleasure to me to thank you for your great achievement: to play my Violin Concerto in such a perfect and convincing manner so

[1] See Letters 204, 216, 222, etc.

To Louis Krasner DECEMBER 1940

shortly after it has been written and so shortly after it has been called unplayable. You must know yourself that you have achieved something which must be called 'a historical fact', whether my music will survive or not. Because these difficulties will survive in any case and you will be called their first conqueror.

Hearty congratulations.

Many thanks also for the very enlightening reports you made during the rehearsal and after the performance. Will you believe me that none of my friends and relatives, and also nobody from my publishers, wrote me one single word about this first performance of an important work of mine? Don't be too much disappointed: friends are [like that].

Let us hope that I might have also once the opportunity to play this work with you; or, at least, to hear it.

Many cordial greetings, also to Mrs. Krasner and also from Mrs. Schoenberg. And we hope to see you sometimes in Los Angeles.

Faithfully yours,
ARNOLD SCHOENBERG

187. TO PAUL DESSAU *Los Angeles*, 22 *November* 1941

Dear Herr Dessau,

I wrote 'Kol Nidre'[1] for Rabbi Dr. Jacob Sonderling [.........] He will certainly also be able to tell you about it.

At my request the text of the 'traditional' Kol Nidre was altered, but the introduction was an idea of Dr. Sonderling's.

When I first saw the traditional text I was horrified by the 'traditional' view that all the obligations that have been assumed during the year are supposed to be cancelled on the Day of Atonement. Since this view is truly immoral, I consider it false. It is diametrically opposed to the lofty morality of all the Jewish commandments.

From the very first moment I was convinced (as later proved correct, when I read that the Kol Nidre originated in Spain) that it merely meant that all who had either voluntarily or under pressure made believe to accept the Christian faith (and who were therefore to be excluded from the Jewish community) might, on this Day of Atonement, be reconciled with their God, and that all oaths (vows) were to be cancelled.

So this does not refer to business men's sharp practice.

The difficulty of using the traditional melody has two causes:

1. There actually isn't such a melody, only a number of flourishes

[1] *Kol Nidre* for speaker, choir and small orchestra, Schoenberg's op. 39, composed in 1938.

resembling each other to a certain degree, yet without being identical and also without always appearing in the same order.

2. This melody is monodic, that is, is not based on harmony in our sense, and perhaps not even on polyphony.

I chose the phrases that a number of versions had in common and put them into a reasonable order. One of my main tasks was vitriolising out the 'cello-sentimentality of the Bruchs, etc.[1] and giving this DECREE the dignity of a law, of an 'edict'. I believe I succeeded in doing so. Those bars 58 to 63 are at least no sentimental minor-key stuff.

I am very glad you like the piece. I am sure, too, that you see much of what I did for the main effect by means of laying a basis with the motives. It is such a pity that people like Saminski[*] decline to adopt the piece for use in the synagogue, on ritual and musical grounds. I believe it must be tremendously effective both in the synagogue and in the concert-hall [..........]

ARNOLD SCHOENBERG

[*Written in English*]
188. To H. H. BENEDICT   *Los Angeles*, 1 *June* 1942
Mr. H. H. Benedict,
Assistant Comptroller,
University of California,
Berkley, California

Dear Mr. Benedict,

Professor Leroy W. Allen, Chairman of the Department of Music at University of California at Los Angeles, advised me to get in touch with you about matters concerned with my retirement.

I was born on September 13, 1874, and was appointed Professor of Music in 1936.

On September 13, 1944, I will be seventy and it seems that under normal conditions I should then retire.

Frankly, I do not feel this way.

At first, it seems to me that as men below the age of 64 will probably be drafted for military service, only men of over 64 will be available for teaching.

But secondly, my career is not one which is ended by age. I was appointed on the basis of my merits as a composer and teacher and I do

---

[1] *Kol Nidre*, for 'cello and orchestra (or piano), by Max Bruch.
[*] Presumably Lazare Saminsky, the Russian-American composer, conductor and writer on music, with a conspicuous interest in Hebrew subjects and styles. [TRANS.]

To H. H. Benedict JUNE 1942

not feel I am an old man, because I am still improving my teaching methods; though, as the long list of excellent pupils of mine proves, my teaching has always been exceptionally good (excuse me for violating the laws of modesty).

Thirdly, I know of teachers of about my reputation (for instance at Columbia University) who at 80 and over still teach.

Anyhow, I want to ask you about the conditions of retirement and annuities as regards the normal regulations of the University of California. I hope you will be kind enough to tell me all that concerns me and my special case.

This is important to me, because knowing this in time would allow me to consider such offers of positions which reach me from time to time.

May I be allowed to bother you also with another problem? My sabbatical leave of absence.

Thanking you very kindly for your answers, I am,
    Most sincerely yours,
      ARNOLD SCHOENBERG

[*Written in English*]

189. To ROSE RESNICK *Los Angeles*, 19 *September* 1942

Miss Rose Resnick,
1395, Golden Gate Avenue,
San Francisco, Calif.

The composer of Pierrot Lunaire and other works which have changed the history of music thanks you for the honourable invitation of participating in the production of a Master Thesis.

But he thinks it is more important that he writes those works which candidates for a master degree will never know; and, if they know them, will never feel the distance which would forbid them to bother him with such questions.

[*Written in English*]

190. To ERWIN STEIN *Los Angeles*, 2 *October* 1942

Dear Erwin:

I found out that the very reason why I never offered you to drink hobnob over a glass of wine (thus Toussaint Langenscheid translates 'Bruderschaft trinken') was: You are no drinker. These things occur if, when and while one drinks.

AETAT 68 *To Erwin Stein*

I doubt that we two will ever take advantage of the 'Du', because when we meet we will probably both speak English. But anyhow, if we meet, we must celebrate it in a solemn manner.

I was very glad to hear of your performance of my Pierrot Lunaire. I regret that I could not hear it. Will you repeat it some time? Is there a chance to broadcast it? You know that under my conducting I have made records of this piece. Rudi, Steuermann and Erika Wagner participated. The other members of the ensemble were quite good, but not as good as our men. Have you heard these records? Are they on sale in England? I doubt it, because I was told that records can not be imported. Is that true? Could you find out about that? If it is allowed I would be glad to send you a set.

Now I want to make the suggestion that you record your performance. Mine is, unfortunately, in spite of my protest, in German, which is much in the way of a full success. Nevertheless there have been more than 2000 sets sold within a year. I am sure an English version would beat the American records and, according to the law, you can make them now. Could you perhaps ask Walter Goehr whether his company would do it?

If Pierrot could not be recorded I would gladly give you my permission to record another of my works, for instance Kammersymphony or Pelleas or Verklärte Nacht or the Five 'Orchesterstücke'.

Let me hear about the possibility of doing this.

You ask what I have written in these years. Not so much; I was always very busy with my teaching.

You might know about the concertos: String Quartet with Orchestra after Handel: Cello with orchestra after Monn; an original violin concerto; and at present I am finishing an original piano concerto. Besides I orchestrated Brahms's Piano Quartet in G minor.

You have probably also heard about the fourth string quartet; furthermore, the second chamber symphony, which was begun in 1906. I had a tremendous number of sketches. I could use most of them with slight alterations. Of this I made also an arrangement for two pianos. There are also a 'Kol Nidre' for Speaker, choir and small orchestra, 'Variations on a Recitative' for Organ and, written also this year, the 'Ode to Napoleon Buonoparte' by Lord Byron, for recitation, piano and string quartet.

I published also this year a syllabus, 'Models for Beginners in Composition'. Just a month ago Schirmer decided to publish this book and for this occasion I worked it over and extended it to about double size. It will not be printed before November.

To Erwin Stein OCTOBER 1942

You see it is very little for ten years. Besides teaching I spend much time on the Textbook on Composition, which is still far from being finished.

I have not always been well during this time. I should not smoke, and had given it up several times. Unfortunately I start always anew. My family is well. You know perhaps that Ronny, who is now $5\frac{1}{2}$ years old, had an operation for appendicitis in May. The poor boy had simultaneously measles and chicken pox. It was a terrific time for us — and, especially, for him. He is now well and looks very fine. Nuria is a big girl, now past ten, and the smallest is 20 months of age. He is a very intelligent child. Nuria is already a great help to her mother, who does alone all the house work — you can not get servants or if [so], you can not pay them. They ask now about $100 a month.

I am glad to hear that your wife and your daughter Marion do well. It is too bad that we have no chance of seeing all of you. Who knows how long this war might last!

At my 68th birthday we had a party and I got a great number of presents — only alcohol! Right now I do not drink — but if I give up smoking again, it will give me some pleasure.

Now you know much about me and I hope to learn soon also again from you.

Many cordial greetings to you, Mrs and 'Miss' Stein.

Faithfully yours,

ARNOLD SCHOENBERG

[*Written in English*]
191. To HELEN HEFFERNAN   *Los Angeles*, 19 *September* 1943
Miss Helen Heffernan, Chief,
Division of Elementary Education,
Department of Education,
Sacramento, California

Dear Miss Heffernan:

I would have answered earlier if I would have known a solution to one problem.

But let me at first thank you for your kind invitation to participate in your annual conference of California school supervisors and to contribute in presenting the subject of music.[1]

I accept gladly this invitation and the honorarium you offer, and I

---

[1] Schoenberg had been invited to represent music at a conference of Californian inspectors of schools, and to give a concert of his own works. The aim of those issuing the invitation was to demonstrate the educational and cultural importance of music.

am ready to speak about ways in which music can help in some of the problems of the post-war time — I wish we were also as far.

But what you call the major [part] of my presentation, a recital of my own compositions, embarrasses me to a certain degree. First, I am not an instrumentalist and could not play anything myself. But there might be a possibility that I find interpreters for one of my works. But if this should be a work through which I have interpreted problems of cultural integration confronting the people of the world, it would be difficult if I should be the one to decide which of my works possesses such high qualities.

However, it has always been my belief that a composer speaking of his own problems, speaks at once of the problems of mankind. But he does it in a symbolical way, without having been able, up to now, to develop definite vocables [a defined vocabulary], expressing matters of philosophy, economy or problems of labour, society or morals.

Thus the 'release of the creative spirit' is always the subject of music and, subconsciously perhaps, the motive of every composer, regardless of his standard. Whether his is a high or a low mind, whether his thinking is sublime or even vulgar, whether his style of expression is complex or simple — always will he present his share.

There is then, of course, only the possibility that one of my works is to be played and to let the audience find out for themselves what province of feeling and thinking has been touched by that which a composer can tell them.

Just when I wanted to write the last paragraph to this letter (which I had begun two days ago) your telephone call came, which makes it easier for me to finish this letter.

I am looking forward to your reply. In the meantime I am,
 Yours very sincerely,
 ARNOLD SCHOENBERG

[*Written in English*]
192. TO ANDREW J. TWA *Los Angeles*, 29 *July* 1944
Mr. Andrew J. Twa,
2605, Rosser Avenue,
Brandon, Manitoba,
Canada

Dear Mr. Twa:
 May I confess
 (1) that I resent your statements about 'atonalism' (a term which I never used);

To Andrew J. Twa

(2) that I am no physicist, but only a musician, and cannot entirely follow your deductions.

But I do not believe that a real composer can compose if you give him numbers instead of tones.

And I do not believe that a real composer can compose even if you give him these tones upon [at] which the numbers hint.

A real composer is not one who plays first on the piano and writes down what he has played.

A real composer conceives his ideas, his entire music, in his mind, in his imagination, and he does not need an instrument.

If our tempered scale were imperfect — which I doubt, as you could see from my Harmonielehre — it would still have an advantage over every scale consisting of small intervals: it lives in our minds, is very alive there, and very active.

There is no reason why 'music in its present scheme' should be without all these merits, but with all those shortcomings you mention in your script. Not only as a composer of such music but also as a theorist of musical composition I deny this strictly. In my Harmonielehre, by calling dissonances those relations which are more remote, I think I have made this concept one of an obsolete esthetic. And in my lecture 'Composition with Twelve Tones' I speak of the 'emancipation of the dissonance', which means that the comprehensibility of the dissonance is today tantamount to the comprehensibility of the consonance. With this statement, this problem has been shifted from esthetics to logic.

What do you mean by 'fundamentally new'? Besides character, mood, expression, illustration etc., there might be nothing else but form and structure wherein new rhythm, new melody, new harmony can manifest itself as being a new musical idea.

'Bizarre rhythms' are more frequently used in primitive music than in art music. In art music it might rather be a higher and more compound phrasing, which makes intelligibility more difficult. I would explain this as an approach towards what I used to call 'musical prose', which seems to me a higher form than versification: it can renounce the primitive makeshift to the memory of the unified rhythm and the rhyme.

As to instruments: you could also not use the Hammond Organ, nor another keyboard instrument, because you want to place four more keys in the space of an octave. Doing this would require making each a full third smaller — or else, your octave would be a third larger.

What do you mean by 'induced tones'? I can not find a convincing translation in my dictionary.

AETAT 70 *To Richard Hoffmann Senior*

I also disagree with your concept of tonality and therefore with your conclusions upon that.

I believe in *monotonality*, that is, there is only *one* tonality in one piece, and all that was called 'another key' is only 'a region carried out like a key' — a region of the one tonality of the piece. These regions . . .

[*The letter breaks off here.*]

[*Written in English*]

193. TO KURT LIST   Los Angeles, 17 October 1944

Mr. Kurt List, Editor,
Listen, The Guide to Good Music,
274, Madison Avenue,
New York, 16, N.Y.

Dear Mr. List:[1]

I hoped I might be able to send you a better picture of me than those two enclosed here. But they turned out worse.

After all, they are not impossible, even though the one is too sinister.

I want to tell you that I was very pleased with the two articles by you, the one about me in Modern Music and the one about Shostakovich — though I still think Shostakovich is a great talent. It is perhaps not his fault that he has allowed politics to influence his compositorial style. And even if it is a weakness in his character — he might be no hero, but a talented musician. In fact, there are heroes, and there are composers. Heroes can be composers and vice versa, but you cannot require it.

Tell me when your article will be published.

With kindest regards,
                 Sincerely yours,
                              ARNOLD SCHOENBERG

[*Written in English*]

194. TO RICHARD HOFFMANN SENIOR
                              Los Angeles, 17 October 1944

Mr. Richard Hoffmann sen.
785, Mt. Eden Road,
Ph. 62679,
Auckland Isl.
New Zealand

Dear Uncle Richard:[2]

Excuse me for calling you 'uncle' — the title which I have conferred myself.

[1] Founder of the magazine.
[2] Richard Hoffmann, uncle of Schoenberg's wife, was living in New Zealand.

To Richard Hoffmann Senior OCTOBER 1944

My wife will answer you as soon as her duties as a 'housewife' (to which she is forced by the impossibility of having servants at present) admit it.

In the meantime you must content yourself with me — but I have a special reason to write you:

Since my childhood I [have] had a great interest in islands and especially in the islands of New Zealand. This might have originated from stamp collecting, and I remember faintly that these stamps were extremely beautiful.

I have often, and especially in this last year, thought of New Zealand. Because I am, since September, retired from the University of California, and make plans to go to a country where the dollar is more effective than it is at present here and than it will probably be after the war.

I wonder whether you could give us information to this end.

(1) Is it difficult to enter this country? We are American citizens.

(2) What are the prices of houses, consisting of 3–4 bedrooms (we have 3 children, a girl 12, a boy 7, and another boy, $3\frac{1}{2}$; and your sister, Mrs. Henriette Kolisch, also lives with us) in one of the better districts?

(3) What are the rents for a house or apartment of this size, which must include a studio for me?

(4) What are the living expenses for a family like mine, with, if possible, one servant?

I read with interest that your younger son, Dick,[1] is a musician. Perhaps I could help him a little, if I am there.

I am very anxious to have your answer to my question, though I am afraid the war will not be over too soon and we will probably have to wait until then.

I am, with kindest regards,

Yours sincerely,

ARNOLD SCHOENBERG

---

[1] Dick Hoffmann later became Schoenberg's secretary and pupil in Los Angeles.

AETAT 70 *To Fritz Reiner*

[*Written in English*]

195. To FRITZ REINER[1] *Los Angeles*, 29 *October* 1944

Mr. Fritz Reiner, Conductor,
The Pittsburgh Symphony Orchestra,
Rambleside, Westport, Connecticut
forward to:
Hotel Webster Hall,
Fifth Avenue,
Pittsburgh, Penn.

Dear Mr. Reiner:

You are perfectly right in your criticism about Kussevitski's performance of my Variations, op. 43B.[2] Some of the shortcomings of this performance derive directly from his disregard of my metronomical indications. Why he did this is unimaginable to me. At least so far he need not have failed.

Another group of his 'shortcomings' derives from his general ignorance as a musician and as a man.

But a considerable part of it is caused by his perfect and constant ignoring of my music. See: he conducts 20 years in Boston and has even not conducted 'Verklärte Nacht', not to mention one of the more difficult of my works. One who is acquainted with my music, will know that it does not help to learn the upper main-voice by heart, but that one has to imagine the whole 'tissue' of voices and harmonies which makes up the texture of my music.

You are also right as regards the lack of differentiation of character. It is difficult to understand how he could fail in this respect, because there are seven distinctly contrasting characters [variations], and the finale consists also of many contrasts. It is the more astonishing because I selected the form of variations in order to respond to a demand made to me by Schirmers to compose a piece which fits to the desire of band authorities. They supposedly want as many different characters and moods in one piece as possible. That's what I did.

Yesterday I received a record of it and today I got the Boston reviews. The record is bad enough. One hears almost no strings, but an astonishing amount of brass and tuba. But the critics are the worst I ever saw. The stupidity of these poor men is unsurpassed, and approached only by

---

[1] Conductor of the Pittsburgh Orchestra.

[2] Schoenberg wrote the Variations for Wind Band, op. 43A, at the suggestion of his publisher, G. Schirmer Inc., in New York, because music for wind instruments is very popular in America, especially among amateurs. Op. 43B is Schoenberg's version of the same work for symphony orchestra.

To Fritz Reiner OCTOBER 1944

their arrogance and ignorance. To every man with a minimum of intelligence and knowledge I have proved to possess some knowledge and to have some ideas. Why is not such a man ashamed of forgetting about whom he writes? Well, this is not one of my main works, as everybody can see, because it is not a composition with twelve tones. It is one of those compositions which one writes in order to enjoy one's own virtuosity and, on the other hand, to give a certain group of music lovers — here it is the bands — something better to play. I can assure you — and I think I can prove it — technically this is a masterwork. And I believe it is also original, and I know it is also inspired. Not only can I not write 10 measures [bars] without inspiration, but I wrote this with really great pleasure.

I did not finish this letter yesterday. I was too angry about these idiotic reviews. You know I am not any more accustomed to that — I did not read criticisms, whether they were good or bad, for many years. Except sometimes when somebody sent them to me.

I even stopped subscribing to 2 magazines because the critics were strictly enemies of my music. Why should I pay attention to this nonsense?

Now enough of that.

I regret very much that your performance will not be broadcast. But perhaps you have a friend who can make a record of it. I am ready to pay for that. I am sure your performance will be really enjoyable for me. Let me know how the rehearsals proceed and if there is anything obscure or unclear in my score, please ask me. I will answer at once.

With cordial greetings, Yours,
ARNOLD SCHOENBERG

[*Written in English*]
196. TO ROGER SESSIONS[1]   *Los Angeles*, *3 December* 1944

Mr. Roger Sessions,
108, Dickinson Hall,
Princeton, New Jersey

Dear Mr. Sessions:

You would not believe how fast time passes when you are old. In a week — at the utmost — a month might have passed, and you cannot catch up with it any more. As long as you were young, you could, and did. But now you even do not try any more.

[1] The composer.

I see your article, which I have read at once and with the greatest pleasure, was sent to me — yesterday I would say — but I see it was October 30th —

— And today it is December 8th, because I interrupted this letter for two reasons: First, I wanted to re-read the article, secondly, I suddenly started with the long-postponed plan of scoring and finishing 'Jakobsleiter', which I had begun in 1917, 27 years ago.

Now I am afraid I would never finish this letter if I insisted on writing all I wanted to tell you. But I see I would have to write almost the whole article, if I wanted to quote everything which pleases me.

Therefore I will restrict myself to two things: I send you a little 'cadeau', (a)* the first page of the score of 'Die Jakobsleiter', (b) the two Birthday Canons for Carl Engel. And finally I want to mention what I consider of the greatest value for a possible appreciation of my music: that you say one must listen to it in the same manner as to every other kind of music, forget the theories, the twelve-tone method, the dissonances etc., and, I would add, if possible the author.

There are of course more and more profound ideas in this article, but I think this one is of the greatest assistance for a future understanding of my music. In a lecture 'Veraltete und Neue Musik, oder Stil und Gedanke', I expressed a similar idea, by saying 'A Chinese poet speaks Chinese, but what is it that he *says*?' And I used to say: 'That I write in this or that style or method is my private affair and is no concern to any listener — but I want my message to be understood and accepted.'

I am most cordially yours,

ARNOLD SCHOENBERG

* This one under separate cover. [S.]

197. TO FERDINAND CZERNIN   *Los Angeles*, 8 December 1944
Mr. Ferdinand Czernin,
Chairman, Austrian Action,
New York

Dear Sir,

I have very great pleasure in declaring my readiness to do all that is in my power to contribute to the rebuilding of intellectual life in Austria and I thank you very much for the gratifying manner in which you have invited me to do so.

Since the beginning of the war with Germany I have unfortunately been out of touch with my Austrian friends, and have indeed heard

To Ferdinand Czernin   DECEMBER 1944

nothing more even from my son, who still lives in Mödling. For this reason I lack all information as to the degree of destruction in the cultural realm. Although I hope that my pupils and those who were well disposed towards my music have not abandoned their ideals, I cannot help fearing that musical life must also have been affected by views similar to those affecting the visual arts — a matter of which I have heard somewhat.

So I shall have to put off drawing up a memorandum until I receive information as to the nature and extent of the destruction. Should either you or any of your co-workers be able to give me any help in that way, it would considerably speed up my work.

[..........]

                                                    ARNOLD SCHOENBERG

[*Written in English*]

198. TO LESTER TRIMBLE   [*Undated.*]

S/Sgt. Lester Trimble, Ward 10,
Base Hospital, Davis Monthan Field,
Tucson, Arizona[1]
and
202, Fisk Avenue,
Avalon, Pittsburgh, Pa.

Dear Mr. Trimble:

I am sorry I can only answer you today. I have been sick very long, could not work and found your letter only today, when I looked over the pile of mail gathered on my table.

But I had already looked through your music just the day I received it. It seemed talented to me and certainly promising. I see you are aiming at a contemporary American style in some of these compositions. This is of course perfectly all right. It is your task, all of you young American talents, to create a style of your own, and it is every single man's duty to contribute as much as possible to this goal.

On the other hand there are two points on account of which I would advocate that everybody should become perfectly acquainted with the achievements of the masters of the past, with the development of the musical language up to our times. Firstly: after some time most of these national characteristics fade and only the idea remains. Secondly: It would be too great a loss, if this technique, produced by centuries,

    [1] Schoenberg's correspondent was at that time in the Army; the letter was probably written during the war.

[were to] be abandoned and a new technique started at the point where the European started long, long ago.

This is why I recommend you to study the masterworks.

I return your music tomorrow, when I go to the post office. In order to compensate for the loss of time I enclose in this package a small book on composition which might interest you.

I just see I forgot to sign this book for you. So we must postpone this until the war is over and I see you. Good luck to you.

Yours sincerely,
Arnold Schoenberg

A copy of this letter goes to your home address.

[*Re-translated from the German translation of the English original*]
199. To Friends[1]   *Los Angeles, 3 October* 1944
Dear Friends,

For over a week I have been trying to compose a letter of thanks to all who have sent me good wishes for my seventieth birthday. I have not succeeded. It is frightfully difficult to produce something when one is conceited enough to think people expect something quite out of the ordinary on such an occasion as this.

But actually it may be just the other way round: everyone should regard it as in itself a satisfactory achievement for someone of my age to be still capable of giving a sign of life from time to time. I noticed this when my piano concerto was performed for the first time and to my astonishment many people were astonished that I still had anything to say. Or perhaps that I don't stop saying it — or that I am not yet wise enough to keep it to myself — or to learn, at long last, just to stay quiet?

Many people wish me: 'Many happy returns!'
Thank you, but how will that help?
Shall I really grow wiser that way?
I cannot promise, but let us hope for the best.

Arnold Schoenberg

---

[1] Printed letter of thanks to his friends.

Section V
LOS ANGELES
1945–1951

BIOGRAPHICAL NOTES

Schoenberg hoped that after retiring he would have the leisure to complete works he had begun long before. But the pension he received after eight years' work at the university was so small that he was compelled to continue giving private lessons.

1945: Schoenberg applied to the Guggenheim Foundation for a grant to enable him to devote himself exclusively to his creative work (see Letter 200). His application was rejected.

1946: Resumed contact with old friends in Germany and Austria (see Letters 205, 212, 213, 220). Gave lectures at the University of Chicago and suggested establishing a department of music there (see Letter 210). Was invited to Princeton to receive the honorary doctorate conferred on him in connection with the celebration of the university's second centenary. But on the 2nd August he suffered a severe, almost fatal attack and, after other attempts had failed, was revived from apparent death only by an injection into the heart.

1947: Schoenberg was elected a member of the American Academy of Arts and Letters. Being unable to make the journey to New York to deliver his inaugural address, he sent it by mail in the form of a gramophone record (see Letter 214). His health markedly improved. He composed *A Survivor from Warsaw*, op. 46, and worked on his textbook, *Structural Functions of Harmony*, and his volume of essays, *Style and Idea*.

1949: Schoenberg's 75th birthday (13th September). After considering accepting an invitation to lecture and to be present at birthday celebrations in Europe, finally had to decline on grounds of ill-health (see Letters 236 and 238).

1950: Illness prevented his undertaking major works. He

Biographical Notes

wrote words for a number of Modern Psalms (see Letter 256). The first (the only one for which he also wrote the music, op. 50c) is for speaker, chorus, and orchestra.

1951: Schoenberg continued working on the words of his Psalms. The last, uncompleted, was begun ten days before his death. He died on the 13th July, at the age of 76.

WORKS

1945: *Prelude* for chorus and orchestra, op. 44.
1946: Trio for violin, viola and 'cello, op. 45.
1947: *A Survivor from Warsaw*, for speaker, male-voice chorus, and orchestra, op. 46.
1948: Three Folksongs for mixed chorus *a cappella*.
1949: *Fantasia* for violin with piano accompaniment, op. 47.
Dreimal Tausend Jahre ['Thrice a Thousand Years'] for mixed chorus *a cappella*, op. 50A.
1950: *De Profundis* (Psalm 130), for mixed chorus *a cappella*, op. 50B.
Modern Psalm, for speaker, chorus, and orchestra (unfinished), op. 50c.
1950/51: Modern Psalms (texts).
1947/48: *Structural Functions of Harmony*.
1947/50: *Style and Idea*, essays.

[*Written in English*]
200. To HENRY ALLEN MOE   *Los Angeles, 22 January* 1945

Mr. Henry Allen Moe, Secretary General,
John-Simon-Guggenheim Memorial Foundation,
551, Fifth Avenue,
New York, 17, N.Y.

Dear Mr. Moe:

I have served the Guggenheim Foundation quite a number of times in writing opinions about potential candidates for Guggenheim awards — with more or less [only relative] success, because, seemingly, not everybody considered me an authority of the same magnitude as did the applicants who longed for a good opinion of mine [from me].

Today I am writing on my own behalf, and I hope the powers to whose decision I submit my application will grant better credit to my creative accomplishments than they did to my judgement.

You have perhaps heard that on December 13, 1944, I have become 70 years of age. At this date — according to regulations — I had to retire from my position as professor of music at the University of California at Los Angeles. As I was in this position only eight years, I will receive a 'pension' of $38.00 (thirty-eight) a month, on which I am supposed to support wife and three children (13, 8 and 4 years old).

At present I still have private pupils and there is a chance that their number might increase. But considering the fact, that I [have taught] now for almost fifty years; that, while in Austria and Germany I taught exclusively the most talented young composers, with the best background (think only of Alban Berg, Anton von Webern, Hanns Eisler, etc., etc.), here I teach generally beginners; and though many are very talented and promising, the chances are not very bright that I could teach them for the five to six years which I deem necessary for a real knowledge of an artist .

Can you understand that under these circumstances I am tired of teaching — at least temporarily?

I have done so much for my pupils, exhausted my powers, irrespective of my own interest, that I have neglected my own creative work.

To Henry Allen Moe JANUARY 1945

I feel, as long as I am living I must try to complete at least some of the works which for a number of years wait for that.

I feel: my life task would be fulfilled only fragmentarily if I failed to complete at least those two largest of my musical, and two, or perhaps three of my theoretical works.

The two musical works are:

(a) MOSES AND AARON, opera in three acts, whose second act I finished (in full orchestra score) in March 1932 — almost 13 years ago. (Performance time about 2 hours and 20'.)

(b) DIE JAKOBSLEITER, an oratorio for soli, large choruses and large orchestra (performance time about an hour and 45'). Half of this is composed already, much is outlined and sketched.

The completion of the opera might occupy me for about 6–9 months: but the oratorio would demand about one-and-a-half to two years.

The theoretical works include:

(1) A textbook on counterpoint in three volumes:
  I. Elementary Exercises*
  II. Contrapuntal Composition
  III. Counterpoint and Semi-Counterpoint in the Music of the masters after Bach.
    NB. Nothing has yet been written about the subject of Vol. III.

Of this textbook I have written only Vol. I, while the other vols. exist only in an outline and number of examples. The completion of these books might take two years, but much of it can be done besides composing.

(2) A textbook: STRUCTURAL FUNCTIONS OF HARMONY, something very essential for future composers. This I could write in a few months.

(3) Either a textbook, 'Fundamentals of Musical Composition',† of which I had started the third draft already 4 or 5 years ago:
  or
A textbook on orchestration, outlines of which go back to 1917!

I would like to apply for a Guggenheim Scholarship which enables me to devote all my time, or at least most of it, to the completion of my works, in order that I may renounce any income through teaching and other distracting activities as much as possible.

I wonder whether I have to write out a special application on pre-

---

* This first part of Schoenberg's project was published in 1963 (Faber), *Preliminary Exercises in Counterpoint* (edited by Leonard Stein). [TRANS.]

† In preparation (Faber). [TRANS.]

scribed forms or whether this letter might suffice. In case a special application is demanded, will you please send me the forms and give the necessary information.

I am looking forward to your kind answer with great apprehension.[1]

I am, most sincerely yours,

ARNOLD SCHOENBERG

[*Written in English*]
201. To HENRY ALLEN MOE   *Los Angeles*, 22 *February* 1945
Mr. Henry Allen Moe, Secretary General,
John-Simon-Guggenheim Memorial Foundation,
551, Fifth Avenue,
New York, 17, N.Y.

Will you, please, excuse the delay of my answer? I have been away for some time.

I have no reason to change my opinion of Mr. Anis Fuleihan's talent, though I have not had the opportunity of seeing his compositions recently.

It seems to me I can recommend the awarding of a Guggenheim Fellowship as warmly as I did the first time. And I am not surprised that he needs this support again. No serious composer in this country is capable of living from his *art*. Only popular composers earn enough to support oneself and one's family, and then it is *not art*.

I am, most sincerely yours,

ARNOLD SCHOENBERG

[*Written in English*]
202. To ROY HARRIS[2]   *Los Angeles*, 17 *May* 1945
Dr. Roy Harris, Chief, Music Section,
Radio Program Bureau,
Office of War Information,
224 West 57th Street,
New York, 19, N.Y.

Dear Dr. Harris:

It is only a very small amount of the music of American composers which I know from the score. And you may know, Brahms refused to judge a piece unless he had seen the score — with that I agree. Most

---

[1] Schoenberg's application was rejected. Of the works mentioned in this letter the only one that was completed was *Structural Functions of Harmony*.

[2] Roy Harris's letter was a circular sent to many musicians.

To Roy Harris MAY 1945

American music I have heard only over the radio, and only *once*. According to my long experience the impression of a work changes considerably with frequent listening.

This why I hesitate to give a list of the ten composers you want me to deliver. Besides there is the danger that I would just miss one or more who made a specially good impression upon me.

With this reservation I state that I used to name you, Mr. Harris, always among the first whom I considered characteristic for American music. Besides I have to mention:

Aaron Copland, Roger Sessions, William Schuman, David Diamond, Louis Gruenberg, Walter Piston, Anis Fuleihan, Henry Cowell, Adolphe Weiss, Gerald Strang. And among younger and lesser-known people I would like to mention Lou Harrison and Miss Dika Newlin.

In all these persons' compositions I have found talent and originality, though I could not deny that in many cases the technical performance was not on the same level as the talent.

I hope this gives you what you wanted.

I am,

      Sincerely yours,

         ARNOLD SCHOENBERG

[*Written in English*]
203. TO WILLIAM S. SCHLAMM   *Los Angeles*, 26 *June* 1945

Mr. William S. Schlamm,
Time, Inc.,
Time and Life Building,
Executive Offices,
Rockefeller Center,
New York, 20, N.Y.

Dear Mr. Schlamm:

That, and why, I am glad about your invitation: to become a charter contributor of the New Magazine: that, and why, I agree with almost everything in your exposé I can show with one basic principle of my thinking:

I believe in the right of the smallest minority.

Because democracy often acts in a manner resembling dangerously something like a 'dictatorship of the (very often extremely small) majority', it is impossible, in spite of the freedom of the press, to publish ideas which do not fit into the frame of one of the greater parties;

ideas whose truth might manifest itself only in five, ten, thirty, [one] hundred years; perhaps only at a time, when, to their author, they have become already obsolete!

I am very anxious to know the topics you expect to receive from me, to discuss these and my own, if possible, in a personal meeting.

As a composer, of course, I write ordinarily much about the theory, technique, aesthetics and ethics of composing. Thus, for example, I have recently started an extensive essay which I plan calling 'Theory of Performance' (Aufführungslehre). In many respects polemical, predominantly it will establish aesthetic (and ethical) categories, principles and yardsticks in a field which to my knowledge has not yet been tilled. It discusses, for instance, the problem whether, when and why a composition needs a performer; whether interpretation (rendition: Auffassung) is desirable or inevitable; I will explain theoretically and technically the way to produce various musical characters (dolce, grazioso, pathétique, scherzando, etc.); explain tempo and its modifications — and many other pertinent subjects. This might, I am afraid, grow to become a book — !

There is a smaller essay I have started, perhaps to be called 'Form in Music serves for Comprehensibility', denying Form the effect of beauty.

I have started a smaller essay explaining that, and why audiences, misled by critics, overestimate performers at the expense of the creators.

(continued 1 July 1945)

I plan rewriting an essay on Copyright, stating the injustice of this law,[1] which allows the theft of a creator's property, after a certain period: a period which in most cases deprives a creator of the right to bequeath his heirs his property; and which is especially cruel in cases when recognition has been denied to an author during his lifetime.

I intend writing on the question whether today's musicologists cultivate science as they do not much more but explore in a sterile manner the musical past. In contrast to that, the theory of musical composition is not only the grammar, syntax and philology of the musical language, but, most important, teaches functional organization.

If it is art, it is not for the masses.

'If it is for the masses it is not art' is a topic which is rather similar to a word of yourself on p. 7.

'Neuen Wein in alte Schläuche' (how can one translate this?)* is one of my 'favored dislikes'.

I hope I have now answered all your questions.

---

[1] I.e., American copyright law.   * 'New wine in old bottles.' [TRANS.]

To William S. Schlamm JULY 1945

I am looking forward to your kind reply, so that I might know your reaction to the subjects I could name.

I am,
>With kindest regards, yours sincerely,
>ARNOLD SCHOENBERG

[*Written in English*]
204. TO RENÉ LEIBOWITZ *Los Angeles*, 1 *October* 1945

Mr. R. Leibowitz,
16, rue de Condé, Paris, VI, France

Dear Mr. Leibowitz:

I am sorry you disagree with me, but I can not help you and I can not help anybody who does not like my music in the manner in which I am writing it. But I will give you a few explanations:

1. I do not compose principles, but music.
2. The method of composing with twelve tones was not introduced by me as a style to be used exclusively, but as an attempt at replacing the functional qualities of tonal harmony.
3. In my Harmonielehre, on page 505, I speak very cautiously about tonal harmonies and their use among dissonant harmonies. At this time I was of course eager (perhaps too eager) to have my new works different in every respect from the past. Nevertheless, you find in all the works between 1906 and 1921 occasional doubling in octaves. That is also quite correct. The fear that it might produce similarity to tonal treatment proved to be an exaggeration, because very soon it became evident that it had — as a mere device of instrumentation — no influence upon the purposes of construction.

This seems to answer all reasonable questions. I am of course not that much interested in historical considerations, leaving them gladly to musicologists.

I am, with cordial greetings, yours,
>ARNOLD SCHOENBERG

[*Handwritten addition to letter of* 1 *October* 1945]
Re-reading your letter, and mine, I see that it was not quite correct to say that you disagree with me. I changed my mind, indeed, in some respects; I would not consider the danger of resembling tonality [tonal resemblances] as tragically as formerly. But I am also convinced that even some consonant triads (I do not use them) would not necessarily be

a 'malheur'. The main purpose of the 'row' is to unify the motival [?] material and to enhance the logic of simultaneous sounding tones.

205. To HERMANN SCHERCHEN   *Los Angeles*, 12 *November* 1945

My dear Scherchen,

It is in the highest degree satisfactory to be able to talk to one another again at long last: and, moreover, about what is closest to our hearts: about music.

However gallant it was of you to stay in Europe, I do regret that you didn't come to America. It would be of the greatest importance — at least so far as European art-music is concerned — to have a man like you here, who dares to stand up for modern music. Among the many Europeans here it's only Mitropoulos who has the nerve to do so; since the war all the rest have been kowtowing to the nationalistic endeavours of American composers, and to some extent rightly. But since scarcely one of them (perhaps excepting Reiner) has enough musical education to distinguish between middling, not-so-good and downright bad, the chaos that prevails here makes the confounding of tongues at Babel seem a veritable (and desirable) Esperanto. — It's a pity, there is plenty of talent, but the teaching is superficial, and the outlook is focused on money-making.

[..........]

ARNOLD SCHOENBERG

Have you been able to find out anything about my poor Webern's death?[1]

[*Written in English*]

206. To KURT LIST   *Los Angeles*, 24 *January* 1946

Mr. Kurt List,
Listen Magazine,
274, Madison Avenue,
New York 16, N.Y.

Dear Mr. List:

I do not know whether you gave my manuscripts to Dr. Jalowetz. He himself had not asked for them, and if you gave them to him, he has not

[1] Anton Webern was accidentally killed during the post-war occupation of Austria: by an American rifle-shot on the 15th September 1945.

To Kurt List   JANUARY 1946

informed me. But in this case and also in the opposite: I would now like to get my manuscripts back.

I would prefer it if you yourself would demand them from Jalowetz and mail them *INSURED* to me.

Dr. Jalowetz is not very dependable in these matters. He is able to forget such duties for weeks and longer.

I agree with you about Furtwängler. I am sure he was never a nazi. He was one of these old-fashioned Deutschnationale from the time of Turnvater Jahn, when you were national because of those Western states who went with Napoleon. This is more an affair of Studentennationalismus, and it differs very much from that of Bismarck's time and later on, when Germany was not a defender, but a conqueror. Also I am sure that he was no anti-Semite — or at least not more so than every non-Jew. And he is certainly a better musician than all these Toscaninis, Ormandys, Kussevitzkis, and the whole rest. And he is a real talent, and he *loves* music.

I am, with cordial greetings,

                          Yours,

                                  ARNOLD SCHOENBERG

[Written in English]
207. TO THE EDITOR, THE JEWISH YEAR BOOK
                                          Los Angeles, 28 March 1946

To the Editor of
The Jewish Year Book,
88, Chancery Lane,
London, W.C.2.

I do not know how important I am in your opinion and how much space you plan to devote to me. Therefore I send you a copy of this list which I prepared for similar cases.

Select yourself what you find worthwhile.

According to my experience, Jews look at me rather from a racial standpoint than from an artistic. They accordingly give me a lower rating than they give to their Aryan idols.

This is why I underlined four of my works which even by Jews are considered outstanding. It is one of my greatest triumphs that I could create something that forces even Jews to look with a slight admiration upon another Jew.

                                              ARNOLD SCHOENBERG

AETAT 71   *To the Burgomaster of Vienna*
208. To Professor Julius Bauer   7 *April* 1946

Dear Doctor,

I had meant to ask you about the following problem, but did not want to keep you longer than necessary.

It seems to me people should be trained to describe their pains correctly, since these are, after all, symptoms of disease. I, for instance, as you may have noticed, cannot do this, and I am convinced that I am not the only person of the kind.

Is a stabbing pain like being stabbed? A burning one as when one gets burnt? A drawing pain like being drawn, pulled? Etc.

What is a referred pain? What are cramp, colic, asthma, etc? What is breathlessness?

It would perhaps be possible to establish a unified terminology and the relevant descriptions and definitions if one could begin by getting doctors to describe their own pains and then examined the general mode of sensation as reported in replies to questionnaires.

[..........]

Today I acted on your suggestion about having a glass of brandy and so far I have — at any rate — enjoyed it.

                                                 Arnold Schoenberg

209. To the Burgomaster of Vienna   5 *May* 1946

Dear Herr Bürgermeister,

Your magnanimity in calling upon me to return from exile, the flattering manner in which you convey the summons, and the honourable task you assign to me: that of helping in the work of reconstruction — all has moved me very deeply indeed.

Allow me to express my most profound gratitude to you and also the hope: that circumstances may make my return possible.[1]

With esteem and regard, I remain, yours faithfully,

                                                 Arnold Schoenberg

---

[1] Schoenberg never managed to get back to Vienna.

To Robert Maynard Hutchins   JUNE 1946

[*Written in English*]

210. To ROBERT MAYNARD HUTCHINS   *Los Angeles, 2 June* 1946

Robert Maynard Hutchins, Chancellor,
The University of Chicago,
Chicago 37, Illinois.

Dear Mr. Hutchins:

My talk with Mr. Hanns Eisler was very satisfactory. I knew that he would be a good teacher in the compositorial fields. But I did not know that he was also active in musicological subjects, among others lecturing in the New School for Social Research in New York.

Thus he might be the right man for you. He is progressive, very vital, and might last for at least 25 years, or more.

I would like to come back [to] answering the question about the Music Department of a University.

Putting aside the mere educational kind, there are three possibilities of organisation:

I. A clean-cut Musicological Department, admission to which can be obtained (best):

    (*a*) by a severe examination, written (in Klausur)* and verbal;
    (*b*) by graduation from preparatory classes;
    (*c*) by graduation from high school, if their curriculum conforms with the requirements of science.

This department should carry out research: (a) in the field of musical language, in the manner in which linguists work in their field: (b) in the field of structure corresponding to the matters of grammar and up to the higher requirements of the artistic forms. It should (c) remain in contact with the fields of esthetics, psychology, philosophy and history.

There should not be given another degree than that of Doctor. These middle dignitaries are worthless.

(On a separate sheet I mention a few such subjects with which classes could become busy.)

II. A real and complete conservatory-type School of Music. There should not be given doctor degrees. A good musician, though he has been taught his profession, and controls it, his knowledge is of a kind different from that of a researcher. He might be a 'gelehrter Musiker', but not an explorer ('Forscher').

History of music, acoustics and some languages should be required as secondary subjects.

If a Department of Musicology is retained, obligatory registration in

---

* I.e., under strict examination conditions. [TRANS.]

the history of forms, of harmony, of the development of instruments, etc., should be considered. Other subjects, like languages, philosophy, physics, esthetics, etc., could remain non-obligatory.

Admission to this institute should be based on an examination, requiring medium proficiency in an instrument and at least harmony and possibly counterpoint.

(I want to mention that several of my students and many from the Vienna Conservatory studied simultaneously in Guido Adler's Musikwissenschaftliches Institut and made their doctorates almost at the same time.)

III. There might be the possibility of adding to the Department of Musicology an *Academy of Music*, comprising only the main fields of practical musicianship in a number of *master classes*. If, later, preparatory classes were to be added, this would mean starting the school at the top and developing it gradually down to the bottom.

These master classes might gradually include all the main solo instruments and voice, musical composition, also the stage, the opera, the movies, churches and choirs. It should also offer classes in orchestration, conducting opera and concerts, stage-direction and education of 'soundmen'. Soundmen will be trained in music, acoustics, physics, mechanics and related fields to a degree enabling them to control and improve the sonority of recordings, radio broadcasting and of sound films.

I want to mention here only my program for their musical training:

The student should become able to produce an image in his mind of the manner in which music should sound when perfectly played. In order to produce this image he should not use the corrupting influence of an instrument. Merely reading the score must suffice. He will be trained to notice all the differences between his image and the real playing; he will be able to name these differences and to tell how to correct them if the fault results from the playing. His training in the mechanical fields should help him to correct acoustic shortcomings, as, for example, missing basses, unclear harmony, shrill high notes, etc.

This can be done and it would mean a great advantage over present methods where engineers have no idea of music and musicians have no idea of the technique of mechanics.

I have the feeling that this time I have submitted my ideas to the right man. And I hope they will now be used and developed.

I am looking forward with keen anticipation to what is now going to happen.

ARNOLD SCHOENBERG

S.S.L.

To Robert Maynard Hutchins   June 1946

Some Problems for the Department of Musicology

Modulatory movement in masterworks: comparison and evaluation.

Methods of subdivision in various types of larger and smaller compositions.

The historic development from the episode on V (or III in the minor) into the second theme or group of subordinate themes.

Methods of transition.

Methods of elaboration (development).

Structure of introductions.

The course of modulation in recitatives.

The technique of liquidation.

Systematic cataloguing of features of rhythm.

Methods of variations of motives, systematically arranged.

Methods of variation in theme and variations.

Developing variation.

Unvaried and varied recapitulations.

Grading and description of contrasts.

[*Written by hand*]

211. To Oskar Kokoschka[1]   *Los Angeles*, 3 *July* 1946

My dear Kokoschka,

I am so glad to hear from you again directly after so long. Though I had all the time been kept informed where you were. Somehow there was always someone among the many people I asked who knew something about you. We are living 'under the sign of Traffic' — 'the world is grown a small place' — one's no longer able to stay in *one* place where one would like to — one has to move on!

You complain of lack of culture in this amusement-arcade world. I wonder what you'd say to the world in which I nearly die of disgust. I don't only mean the 'movies'. Here is an advertisement by way of example: There's a picture of a man who has run over a child, which is lying dead in front of his car. He clutches his head in despair, but not to say anything like: 'My God, what have I done!' For there is a caption saying: 'Sorry, now it is too late to worry — take out your policy at the XX Insurance Company in time.' And these are the people I'm supposed to teach composition to!

[. . . . .]

What have you produced in these past years? — I once heard you were in New York, but couldn't find out if it was true. You had a great

[1] The painter.

friend here, who died some time ago: Frau Galka Scheyer. But I'm afraid it was a bit of a similar case to that of my adherents, who all rank Hindemith, Stravinsky, and Bartók if not above me at least as on a par with me: she had *too many gods*: Klee, Kandinsky, etc. But 'thou shalt have one God', and for all I care leave me out; I'm not a modern — don't you think the same way? — You asked for it, so on your own head be it: I am sending you a photograph, although I at least can't see in it any of the qualities you so flatteringly attribute to me. I can — honestly — only see that I have grown very old, although (this may be deceptive) I do perhaps look somewhat more intelligent than 25 years ago. But I shall gladly leave it to you to judge that, particularly so long as it turns out more favourable to me. [..........]

Once more: I'd like to hear something about your latest works: pictorial and literary.

    With most affectionate greetings,
      Yours,
        ARNOLD SCHOENBERG

212. To HANS ROSBAUD[1]   *Los Angeles*, 12 *May* 1947

My dear Rosbaud,

A few days ago I received the programme of your performance of my chamber symphony, and today I have your very nice letter. I had indeed been thinking that you would this time have used such an excellent piece of work as the analysis of my Variations in relation to the chamber symphony. This strikes me as an even more important contribution than the preceding, for understanding of my music *still* goes on suffering from the fact that the musicians do not regard me as a normal, common-or-garden composer who expresses his more or less good and new themes and melodies in a not entirely inadequate musical language — but as a modern dissonant twelve-note experimenter.

But there is nothing I long for more intensely (if for anything) than to be taken for a better sort of Tchaikovsky — for heaven's sake: a bit better, but really that's all. Or if anything more, then that people should know my tunes and whistle them.

I think if your experiment were repeated often enough my music's success would be considerably more 'satisfactory'! at least more satisfactory for me, who have no ambition to be interesting.

Perhaps this conveys to you how and why I esteem your achievement so highly.

I am particularly glad that so many young people take an interest in

[1] Hans Rosbaud (see Letter 126) was at the time *Generalmusikdirektor* in Munich.

To Hans Rosbaud MAY 1947

your concerts. This is extremely encouraging. Probably you did not make a record, and if so it could scarcely be sent anyway. I wish I could have heard it.

I can more or less imagine who the 'great' colleagues are who are beginning to attract attention again (to *themselves*). But it seems to me there are several degrees of 'greatness' even among the great of this sort. I came to be closer acquainted with some of them here and discovered that the differences in degree of greatness nevertheless do not matter any more than the great ones themselves.

[. . . . .]

ARNOLD SCHOENBERG

213. TO H. H. STUCKENSCHMIDT AND MARGOT HINNENBERG (FRAU STUCKENSCHMIDT)[1] *Los Angeles*, 21 *May* 1947

My dear friends,

I could scarcely fight back the tears on reading that you, dear Frau Hinnenberg

!!!! 26 *August* 1947

You see: in these *three* months I have literally not found time to finish this letter. And I was really deeply moved at reading that you, dear Frau Hinnenberg, had burdened yourself with the weight of a score, you for whom the notes were so easy.[2]

But here I have to work to earn a living and can only seldom indulge in the luxury of corresponding with old and true friends. Were it otherwise I should long ago have sent food parcels to you and other friends, but food is expensive and sending parcels almost more expensive.

Well, three days ago I finished a piece for orchestra, speaker, and male-voice chorus: 'A Survivor from Warsaw', and am just having a little time off before starting on other work. I mean to deal with at least 8–10 of 50 unanswered letters and have taken yours *first*. Next are Rufer and Rosbaud.

But I have to make this a short letter, else it will lie around for months again. So: I am delighted by your intention to write my biography.* I shall see that you are sent everything I can trace. Above all a

---

[1] H. H. Stuckenschmidt, of Berlin, the writer on music, and his wife, the singer Margot Hinnenberg. (In German, as in other Continental usage, a married woman who uses her own name professionally prefaces it with Mrs. [TRANS.])

[2] In flight from Prague after the war Miss Hinnenberg had taken Schoenberg's sheet-music with her, in a rucksack. (Schoenberg here turns a phrase in a way that cannot be rendered in English: in German there is one word (*leicht*) for both 'light' and 'easy'. [TRANS.])

* Stuckenschmidt's study of Schoenberg appeared in an English version in 1959 (John Calder), translated by Edith Temple Roberts and Humphrey Searle. [TRANS.]

book by René Leibowitz (in French) and one by Dika Newlin (in English); perhaps also one by Merle Armitage, if it contains enough material. I am sending you, besides, a little notebook containing a short biography and a list of works, to which I am making additions.

ARNOLD SCHOENBERG

[*Written in English*]
214. TO THE NATIONAL INSTITUTE OF ARTS AND LETTERS[1]
Los Angeles, 22 *May* 1947

Mr. President, ladies and gentlemen,

I am proud about the formulation under which this award has been given to me. That all I have endeavoured to accomplish during this fifty years is now evaluated as an achievement, seems in some respects to be an overestimation.

At least not before I could sum up — that is: while it still looked like a pell-mell of incoherent details — at least then did I fail to understand it as a direction leading towards an accomplishment. Personally I had the feeling as if I had fallen into an ocean of boiling water, and not knowing how to swim or to get out in another manner, I tried with my legs and arms as best as I could.

I did not know what saved me; why I was not drowned or cooked alive . . .

I have perhaps only one merit: I never gave up.

But how could I give up in the middle of an ocean?

Whether my wriggling was very economical or entirely senseless, whether it helped me to survive or counteracted it — there was nobody to help me, nor were there many who would not have liked to see me succumb.

I do not contend it was envy — of what was there to be envious?

I doubt also that it was absence of goodwill — or worse — presence of ill-wishing.

It might have been the desire to get rid of this nightmare, of this unharmonious torture, of these unintelligible ideas, of this methodical madness — and I must admit: these were not bad men who felt this way — though, of course I never understood what I had done to them to make them as malicious, as furious, as cursing, as aggressive; — I am

[1] Schoenberg recorded this message, which is something midway between a letter and a speech, and sent it to the National Institute of Arts and Letters, of which he had been elected a member.

still certain that I had never taken away from something they owned; I never interfered with their prerogatives; I never did trespass on their property; I even did not know where it was located, which were the boundaries of their lots, and who had given them the title to these possessions.

Maybe I did not care enough about such problems; maybe I myself failed to understand their viewpoints, was not considerate enough, was rough when I should have been soft, was impatient when they were worried by time-pressure, was ridiculing them, when indulgence was advisable, laughed when they were distressed . . .

I see only that I was always in the red —

But I have one excuse: I had fallen into an ocean, into an ocean of overheated water, and it burned not only my skin, it burned also internally.

And I could not swim.

At least I could not swim with the tide. All I could do was swim against the tide — whether it saved me or not!

I see that I was always in the red. And when you call this an achievement, so — forgive me — I do not understand of what it might consist.

That I never gave up?

I could not — I would have liked to.

I am proud to receive this award under the assumption that I have achieved something.

Please do not call it false modesty if I say:

Maybe something has been achieved but it was not I who deserves the credit for that.

The credit must be given to my opponents.

They were the ones who really helped me.

Thank you.

ARNOLD SCHOENBERG

[*Written in English*]
215. To PERRY T. JONES[1]　　　　　　*Los Angeles*, 6 *June* 1947

Dear Dr. Jones:

I hope you remember me: we met at a dinner in Dr. Knudsen's house. At this time I was still Prof. of Music at UCLA. And I played also some tennis. But since five years I gave it up, and in 1944 I retired from teaching. Today I would like to have your advice about two of my problems. It

---

[1] Dr. Perry Jones was President of the Los Angeles Tennis Organization.

concerns the younger generation, my daughter Nuria, 15, and my son, 10. Neither of them is a problem child in school; they offer a problem to me with their tennis.

The girl, Nuria, started a little late, but I saw children of her age playing better tennis than hers. But the boy, Ronald, is always called a 'natural' tennis player. He started alone practising against our *windows*, at $6.00 a glass, and it was perhaps this that developed him technically. But he possesses also the mind of a fighter and — what I call the 'field sense'. Many people who saw him find him very promising — I of course am as incompetent as a father can be.

I would like to have your advice. What shall we do? He had some tennis lessons which did him much good. But he can not find often enough a good partner. Shall we try a club? Which would you recommend? It should not be too far from our house, because I do not drive and bringing the children to school is just enough for Mrs. Schoenberg.

I would appreciate your advice greatly.

In anticipation of your kind reply, I am, most sincerely yours,

ARNOLD SCHOENBERG

[*Written in English*]

216. To RENÉ LEIBOWITZ[1]   *Los Angeles*, 4 *July* 1947

Mr. René Leibowitz,
16, rue de Condé,
Paris VI, France

Dear Mr. Leibowitz,

I want to answer some of your questions to Mr. Stein myself. But at first I would like you to inform Dynamo Edition that I have not yet concluded an American contract and therefore I am free to give Mr. Aelberts [?] the rights for a French edition. If he wants a copy of The Structural Functions I will send it.

Under the term of loosening the 'rigour' of the treatment of the twelve tones you mean probably the occasional doubling of octaves, occurrence of tonal triads and hints of tonalities. Many of the restrictions observable in my first works in this style, and what you call 'pure', derived more theoretically than spontaneously from a probably instinctive desire to bring out sharply the difference of this style with preceding music.

Avoiding doubling of octaves was certainly a kind of exaggeration

---

[1] The conductor and composer René Leibowitz (see Letter 184).

To René Leibowitz JULY 1947

because if the composer did it, nature denied it. Every single tone contains octave doubling. Curiously I still do it not all too frequently, though I am today conscious that it is a question merely of dynamics: to emphasize one part more distinctly.

As regards hints of a tonality and intermixing of consonant triads one must remember that the main purpose of 12-tone composition is: production of coherence through the use of a unifying succession of tones which should function at least like a motive. Thus the organizatorial efficiency of the harmony should be replaced.

It was not my purpose to write dissonant music, but to include dissonance in a logical manner without reference to the treatment of the classics: because such a treatment is impossible. I do not know where in the Piano Concerto a tonality is expressed.

It is true that the Ode[1] at the end sounds like E flat. I don't know why I did it. Maybe I was wrong, but at present you cannot make me feel this.

The Organ Piece[2] represents my 'French and English Suites', or, if you want, my Meistersinger-Quintet, my Tristan-Duet, my Beethoven and Mozart Fugues (who were homophonic-melodic composers): my pieces in Old Style, like the Hungarian influence in Brahms. In other words, as I have stated often, almost every composer in a new style has a longing back to the old style (with Beethoven, Fugues). The harmony of the Organ Variations fills out the gap between my Kammersymphonies and the 'dissonant' music. There are many unused possibilities to be found therein.

With many cordial greetings, hoping to hear soon from you.

Sincerely yours,

ARNOLD SCHOENBERG

[*Written in English*]
217. TO VISCOUNT TAKATOSHI[?] KYOGOKU

Los Angeles, 19 *October* 1947

Viscount Takatoshi[?] Kyogoku,
36, Otsuka-Nakamachi, Bunkyoku,
Tokyo, Japan

Dear Viscount Kyogoku:

I am very glad to hear again from you. And what you tell me about the interest of Japanese music-lovers in our Western music is very much appreciated.

---

[1] *Ode to Napoleon Buonaparte.*
[2] *Variations on a Recitative for Organ* (in D minor).

AETAT 73 — *To K. Aram*

I am ready to send a message to you and your friends on this subject, if only you tell me exactly upon which part of our problem I should concentrate.

There is one thing which I want to say already at this time:

If it is the task to speak to music lovers, I am not so much concerned about the style of music they love. To me, a music lover is one who loves things which I love myself; it is music, not style. Whether it is Bach or Mozart, Beethoven or Brahms, Wagner or Mahler, Richard Strauss and modern music, and even Offenbach and Johann Strauss; all this is music, and all this deserves Love.

The idea that we Western musicians can never forget the centuries of tradition upon which our culture is founded — this idea will probably find an echo in your own heart. Though we are modern, though we know our duty to conform adequately to the requirements of to-day's ways of thinking, we never forget what we owe to our predecessors. Thus if we expect appreciation of what we have achieved, we know our debt to our predecessors and want them to be included in our successes.

[..........]

Yours very sincerely,

ARNOLD SCHOENBERG

[*Written in English*]

218. To K. ARAM[1]　　　　*Los Angeles*, 15 *November* 1947

Dear Mr. Aram:

In answer to your question: 'What can Mr. Reichold do for you?', I want to tell you:

I. The most natural thing is to see that my music is played. All non-partisan history books call me the father of modern music. Everybody knows what this generation of composers is owing to me. Mr. Sessions wrote that none of the composers of this generation is without my influence.

Besides: a great number of my works has found general appreciation.

Almost all of the works of my first period (up to 1908) will be liked by every musical audience. Many of the works of my second period (1908 to 1923) would not be disliked, and some, as for instance Pierrot Lunaire, are absolutely a success. But even works of my third period, e.g., the piano concerto or the Ode to Napoleon Buonaparte, have been quite successful.

---

[1] Who intended trying to interest an American patron, Mr. Reichold, in Schoenberg. Nothing came of the matter.

To K. Aram NOVEMBER 1947

I am quite conscious of the fact that a full understanding of my works can not be expected before some decades. The minds of the musicians and of the audiences have to mature ere they can comprehend my music. I know this, I have personally renounced an early success, and I know, that — success or not — it is my historic duty to write what my destiny orders me to write.

But this does not excuse those parasites who live from music, but ignore their duty toward the artist and the audiences.

II. Just like the racket of the concert agents, there is now a racket in the making which intends to suppress gradually all European composers. Though I was probably the first European composer to speak and write publicly in favor of American composers, establishing their rightful claim to a place in American concert programs, the thanks for my attitude seems to be that I have been elected to be the first victim of the nationalistic movement — with others to follow. I think Mr. Reichold should be able to prevent this racket from attaining such an overwhelming power in order to do wrong and act in an unfair manner against musicians whose generosity and artistic achievements deserve recognition and thanks.

It seems to me that Mr. Reichold might find ways to convince American authorities, that living composers, American or European, should not fight each other, because unity might be more helpful to both groups and it is questionable whether experimental music would not drive audiences out of the concert halls if they have not the support of some successful Europeans.

[..........]

ARNOLD SCHOENBERG

219. TO SERGE FRANK[1] *Los Angeles, 3 December* 1947

Dear Herr Frank,

I am in despair at having no choice but to write you a letter like this: but I really could not foresee that you, a civilized European, would have so little respect for another man's intellectual work as to expect him to permit changes such as those you are making in my articles.

You put bits in, leave things out, make something long-winded out of what was said clearly and concisely, choose uncharacteristic expressions to replace pertinent ones, and even go so far as to change the structure of paragraphs and [make alterations] in articles that I myself have rewritten. — I really can't understand you.

[1] A pupil of Schoenberg's, who was translating a collection of Schoenberg's essays, published in 1950 under the title *Style and Idea*.

AETAT 73   *To Serge Frank*

After what you have done with the beginning of 'New Music . . .' I don't feel like looking any further. There is only one thing for it:

I. Put all the published essays back into precisely their original form. That means: removing *every one* of your alterations, without exception. If the essays were good enough to be printed then, they'll be good enough now too.

II. Similarly clean up the articles that I myself wrote in English with the aid of American friends, such as: 'Style and Idea', 'Composition with Twelve Tones', 'On Collaborators', 'Eartraining through Composing', 'Heart and Brain in Music', 'Folkloristic Symphonies'.*

III. Your translations of the rest of the articles, such as 'Mahler', 'Verhältnis zum Text' ['The Composer's Relation to his Libretto'], and 'Rondo Form' are here being examined by an Englishman and Mr. Leibowitz with special reference to their *'faithfulness to the original'*, and will then be sent back to you.

I am sorry to have to be so firm and to have to ask you not to change anything in 'Brahms' and the still missing 'Criteria' unless it is wrong. If 'Rights of Man' should present too many difficulties, I shall try to make a translation myself.

Understand me rightly: I can only publish under my name what I have done myself or at least have subsequently approved. I should not hesitate to admit a real mistake and correct it. But your changes go beyond the limit of what even my Americanised conscience can permit. — I must not fail to mention that Mr. Hoffmann and Mr. Leibowitz find your translation of 'Mahler' very good. But I cannot permit alterations. I also found 'Relation to Libretto' good.

I should really like you to continue your work on my book, for I appreciate the self-sacrificing spirit you show in devoting yourself so intensively to someone else's work. Besides, I am sure you did all these things with the *very* best of intentions, and I assume that you have been given entirely improper information as to the rights and duties of an editor† in America. I also appreciate the fact that you are among the few people who can follow my ideas. Only in spite of various inadequacies I do happen to be a better writer than you have assumed; and such a writer's style only suffers by being corrected and improved.

Whatever the Philosophicals[1] may expect of an editor, whatever the extent to which he may be compelled to make the original worse in

---

* The English of the titles in this paragraph is Schoenberg's own. [TRANS.]
† Here, and again below, Schoenberg uses the English word 'editor'. [TRANS.]
[1] The Philosophical Library, publishers of *Style and Idea*.

To Serge Frank   December 1947

order to prove he has worked hard enough 'for the little money'* — you can prove it to these sages by showing them the alterations that I reject. Work enough.

Write soon, and don't be offended about this letter. It is probably neither my fault nor yours.

                       With very best wishes, Yours,

                                               Arnold Schoenberg

220. To Josef Rufer[1]   *Los Angeles*, 18 *December* 1947

Herr Josef Rufer,
Berlin

[..........]

It's frightful that the Russians should be causing such difficulties. They would do better to put their own house in order, instead of disturbing world peace, in so far as there is such a thing. I am no Communist, as you know, and have never hoped for any good from Communism. But I did think the leaders of that party had more common sense,† more political sense, than to throw their weight about like this. — Have you read anything about Eisler and his brother? Do you know anything about the views he had in his Berlin days? I shouldn't like to damage him any more than he has already damaged himself here. But it's really too stupid of grown-up men, musicians, artists, who honestly ought to have something better to do, to go in for theories about reforming the world, especially when one can see from history where it all leads. I hope that all in all they won't take him too seriously here. Certainly I never took him seriously, I always regarded those tirades as a form of showing off. If I had any say in the matter I'd turn him over my knee like a silly boy and give him 25 of the best and make him promise never to open his mouth again but to stick to scribbling music. That he has a gift for, and the rest he should leave to others. If he wants to appear 'important', let him compose important music.

[..........]

                                                 Arnold Schoenberg

221. To Karl Amadeus Hartmann[2]   *Los Angeles*, 6 *March* 1948

Dear Hartmann,

I was delighted to get your news. The programmes you have planned, if not already performed, are, I am sure, very important at the present

---

* The phrase in quotation marks is in Schoenberg's English. [trans.]
[1] See Letter 69.
† The English words 'common sense' are used in the original. [trans.]
[2] The composer, in Munich, who died in 1963.

juncture because they are so all-embracing. Today it seems more important to make things known; there'll be plenty of time for sifting later. One must simply start by showing what has been missed and how many composers there have been who have the power to make their contemporaries listen. It is an astonishing list: twenty-five composers and perhaps equally many different ways of creating new music. And that's without including Webern and Berg, or Zillig, Apostel and Einem, all Austrians except Zillig.

I don't know if I'll be able to send you the score and parts of the string trio. It isn't published yet [..........]

ARNOLD SCHOENBERG

[*Written by hand*]
222. To RENÉ LEIBOWITZ   *Los Angeles*, 15 *March* 1948
My dear Leibowitz,

I have just read your extremely pertinent article in 'Partisan Review'. The difference is certainly pretty crass, but one can't do anything about Str., although I find his present attitude a dignified one.

Just one thing: I always thought it was I who originated the term 'emancipation of the dissonance'. Am I mistaken? Did it exist before me? This X. is a brainless buffoon. What a trivial way of arguing. There are a 1000 ways in which something right can be wrong and vice versa.

I'm afraid List isn't quite right about 'atonal' polyphony, which would in itself be worthless. You know what I think of *contrapuntal* combinations and that they can scarcely amount to anything of any real merit in dissonant non-tonal harmony. Apart [from that] — it's an experiment I never tried — Berg has, I believe, also composed twelve-note movements with key-feeling. It goes without saying that this can be done, since after all the 5 'black notes' can appear even in the simplest secondary dominants:

Further, a follower of my music should not say 'atonal'. But otherwise List is perfectly right.

[..........]

To René Leibowitz   MARCH 1948

What a pity you're leaving! There's no knowing whether we'll meet again — I at least much enjoyed your visits, and it has been a great satisfaction to me knowing that such an excellent and thoroughly educated musician is in sympathy with my music. Very best wishes for your future welfare. I hope it's only *au revoir*.

                                                 ARNOLD SCHOENBERG

[*Written in English*]

223. To PROFESSOR PAUL A. DODD   *Los Angeles*, 12 *May* 1948

Professor Paul A. Dodd,
U.C.L.A.

Dear Professor Dodd,

Thank you very much for inviting me to give you information about my case.

At (1) After 8 years of service, during which I charged myself voluntarily with a double teaching lot — for the sake of my students — I retired in 1944 with a pension of $29.60 monthly.

At (2) I did not receive supplemental grants.

At (3) Unless I succeed in forcing exploiters of my works, publishers, performers etc., to pay what they owe me, I would have to live on $29.60 with a wife and 3 small children (16, 11, 7). It has often enough occurred that I had for months no other income. There remains still the hope that my works might provide for us; but this would not be a merit of the University Retirement System.

If you want more information, I am ready to supply it.

                     Very cordially yours,

                                         ARNOLD SCHOENBERG

224. To JOSEF RUFER, BERLIN   *Los Angeles*, 25 *May* 1948

My very dear Rufer,

Your letter of the 17th April 1948 came today. — So you see it still takes quite a time! You're right to complain about my long silence. But you have no idea what a pile of unanswered and also unanswerable letters keeps mounting up on all my tables. I've often thought of entirely giving up letters. But then again there are always some good friends one *wants* to write to at least now and then, and although I often neglect a lot of professional stuff and financially important things, on the other hand there is ever and again so much that simply has to be done.

I'm sorry to gather from your letter that you are very perturbed about the likelihood of political changes.[1] But, having a general view of it all as I now have, I should really like to say this to you: It is absolutely pointless associating oneself with the political ideals of any of the existing parties. None of these ideals, of whatever colour, will stand up to a closer examination. Suitable though they may be for publicity purposes, as a pretext, a masquerade, ideals have no vital force of their own, for they are non-material. I am convinced that every adept politician knows this and turns it to his own account. We who live in *music* have no place in politics and must regard them as something essentially alien to us. We are a-political and the most we can do is endeavour to stay quietly in the background.

[..........]

I didn't read 'Dr. Faustus'[2] myself, owing to my nervous eye-affliction. But from my wife and also from other quarters I heard that he had attributed my 12-note method to his hero, without mentioning my name. I drew his attention to the fact that historians might make use of this in order to do me an injustice. After prolonged reluctance he declared himself prepared to insert, in all subsequent copies in all languages, a statement concerning my being the originator of this method. Whether this has been done, I don't know.

[..........]

[added by hand]

Here is the answer to your question about my non-'puritan' compositions. I have found that a yearning for the contrapuntal style occasionally wells up in all composers since Bach, whereupon they set to writing fugues and the like. I myself often feel an upsurge of desire for tonality, and then I have to yield to the urge. After all, composing means: obeying an inner urge.

[..........]

ARNOLD SCHOENBERG

225. TO RENÉ LEIBOWITZ   *Los Angeles, 5 November* 1948
M. René Leibowitz,
Paris

[..........]

There is very little immediate likelihood of my being able to write anything you could perform. I did once begin writing a symphony:

[1] Relations between Russia and the Western powers had become tense. In May the Russians had begun the Berlin blockade, which was relieved by the Allied 'air-lift' maintaining communications with the city.

[2] Thomas Mann's novel. The correspondence about this matter has been published elsewhere. See also Letter 249.

To René Leibowitz NOVEMBER 1948

whether it will ever be finished, I don't know.[1] If I can work I should really best like to [finish] 'Die Jakobsleiter' and 'Moses and Aaron'.

But the way my eyes are there really isn't much chance of it at present. Besides, I have promised to finish the counterpoint [book], and I am also supposed to be going on with the theory of form. So you see it's all pretty bad.

[..........]

ARNOLD SCHOENBERG

[*Written in English*]

226. To HENRY COWELL[2] *Los Angeles, 6 November* 1948

Mr. Henry Cowell,
310, Riverside Drive,
New York, 25, N.Y.

Dear Mr. Cowell:

At first, I want to thank you for sending me reports about the performance of my Five Orchestral Pieces by Mitropoulos in New York.

Curiously, all my other friends came much later. This is why I thank you especially cordially for doing this.

The reports were really good. I was very astonished because, besides Virgil Thompson, who always writes well of me, I did not expect Olin Downes[3] to give me some credit for my former works.

It seems as if I have to celebrate a come-back in New York. It is time. It's a come-back because I have never been there, you know. I was so seldom performed in New York, that nobody knows whether my music is worth something or not.

It is worse here in Los Angeles. Mr. Wallenstein is 6 years here in Los Angeles and has not yet played one piece of mine.

You want to protest really against this man who wrote this stupid review? He simply wanted to write the contrary of everything, because one thing is clear: these Five Orchestral Pieces, however bad they might be, nothing could be more wrong than to associate them with imitation — because the one merit is that they were really new, and still are not obsolete.

I hope to see you then, and your wife.

Thank you very much, again. With cordial greetings,

Yours,

ARNOLD SCHOENBERG

[1] Schoenberg did not resume work on this composition.
[2] The American composer.
[3] See Letters 179, 230 and 231.

AETAT 74   *To Ingeborg Ruvina*

[*Written in English*]
227. To RENÉ LEIBOWITZ   *Los Angeles*, 12 *November* 1948
Mr. René Leibowitz,
Paris

Dear Mr. Leibowitz:

I am sorry you cannot read the letters of Mann, but if Mr. Rufer does not send you his copy, I will make new copies for you.

I have not yet read the translation of the Survivor text, but I am not afraid that it might not fit very well. But of one thing it is very necessary to warn you — this must never be made so musical as other strict compositions of mine. This never has to be sung, never should there be a real pitch. This means only the way of accentuation. As I said — never sing. This is very important, because singing produces motives and motives must be carried out, motives produce obligations which I do not fulfil — because I do not know what a singer will bring to my compositions.

If I have promised you the world premiere of the Survivor, I am very sorry, I have entirely forgotten it, and I also did not know that Mr. Frederick will come before you. It was a surprise to me and I did not know whether you had not already performed it in Darmstadt. But what is the advantage of a world premiere? I am sure you will make a premiere which will compare better than the very best world premiere which would be possible.

As regards Gallimar: I have not received a letter of his. Perhaps he can repeat it if it has been lost.

Excuse me for being so short, but I have so many letters.

             Cordial greetings,
                Yours,
                           ARNOLD SCHOENBERG

228. To INGEBORG RUVINA   *Los Angeles*, 22 *November* 1948
Frau Ingeborg Ruvina,
Geneva

Dear Frau Ruvina,

I received your letter today, 19th November.[1] It interested me very much, and your suggestions are definitely something one can discuss, perhaps indeed must discuss, although there are a good many preliminary points to clear up. There is much to be said in favour of your idea

[1] Cf. the date at the head of the letter. Obviously a slip.

To Ingeborg Ruvina NOVEMBER 1948

about 'Erwartung', since the music is in fact so difficult that it takes a quite outstanding actress, such as Marie Gutheil-Schoder,[1] to perform it so effectively that the high points of the drama, and the intermediate moods, do not get lost.

Frau Gutheil-Schoder did in fact have very great difficulty with the music; but the way you suggest having it spoken is something that I, as the composer, cannot possibly agree to.

It would perhaps be thinkable to make a division of labour: one actress merely miming the play, another, invisible, doing all the singing. But the question is whether such exact synchronisation can be achieved that there isn't some miming going on when there should not be, or something different being mimed from what the music is expressing. This strikes me as hardly possible.

Regarding the other suggestion, of doing a stage performance of the 'Gurre-Lieder', about this I have repeatedly expressed qualms on the grounds that the 'Gurre-Lieder' are epic music, tending to the lyrical rather than to the theatrical. When writing for the theatre I write quite a different sort of music from what I write with a concert performance in mind. Also, the poems would have to be adapted to suit quite a different kind of dialogue. It would after all really be impossible always to have one person singing his or her aria right through, with the other one standing by, staring into space. I simply wouldn't know how it could be done. Besides, the music in no way expresses anything of that kind.

I am very much afraid it would turn out to be boring and then even the music would not [succeed in] bringing out a tenth part of the effect it always has otherwise.

However, I do not want to discourage you from perhaps working out your suggestion in detail. Perhaps it is such that it can really be carried out. Perhaps you will let me know more about it.

[..........]

ARNOLD SCHOENBERG

229. TO WINFRIED ZILLIG[2]   *Los Angeles*, 1 *December* 1948
My dear Zillig,

Your letter was a great delight to me, and I simply don't know how to explain just what gave me such pleasure. You wrote a letter with so much *in* it, and actually almost all of it is something that particularly

---

[1] See note 1 to Letter 14.
[2] Winfried Zillig (see Letter 155) was at this time conductor at the Hessischer Rundfunk [Radio Hessia], Frankfurt-am-Main.

pleases me. Not least the many performances and in particular what is connected with that, your great and active interest in my art — for which I am really very grateful to you.

[..........]

The orchestra's liking my Five Pieces for Orchestra is a very great piece of progress, and the fact that they went along with Mahler, even though very reluctantly, is also very important as a step towards establishing Mahler's art. What most seems to set Mahler back is that faint reminiscence of popular tunes. I am quite convinced, though, that in 50 years' time these popular tunes would, in the nature of things, be entirely unknown or long forgotten, if [ever known?] at all and only then will people see the greatness of the experience behind them.

Your performance of my Variations op. 43 B, which you wrote you were conducting in Munich on the 26th October, is also over now. I should be very interested to hear more about the performance. Is it hard to play? It would be very interesting if you could send a tape or a record of the concert at which you also perform *your piece* and also [that] of the dodecaphonist Liebermann. Who is he?

Well, these are certainly tremendous plans you are making for my 75th birthday, if I live to see it. I should very much like to come over, but frankly I am a bit afraid that the change of climate is rather a risk. True, it's summer, but still, the climate isn't always so good even here either.

[..........]

You also remind me of how we first got to know each other, when you came to me as a pupil. It was very odd at first. For in those days one couldn't help being afraid that each new person might be a Nazi, and that was why I was a bit reserved the first time; but then I very rapidly became fond of you. I particularly enjoy recalling our trip to Paris, when you gave me such really great help with rehearsing the Suite. You remember, I spent most of the time going to restaurants with dear old Adolf Loos; he insisting on taking me to all the amusement-places and eating-places and showing me how good the food was. For all that, I ate the same chicken everywhere and was always very late getting to bed. So I was so tired I couldn't study my score. Without you I'd never have managed that concert. Do write again soon, particularly if it is as delightful as this last letter.

[..........]

ARNOLD SCHOENBERG

To Olin Downes   UNDATED

[*Written in English*]

230. TO OLIN DOWNES

[*Undated, presumably middle of December*, 1948]

Mr. Olin Downes,
Music Editor,
The New York Times,
New York, N.Y.

Dear Mr. Downes,

You end your review of Mitropolous's performance of Gustav Mahler's Seventh Symphony with the words: 'Chacun à son goût'.

This seems to me a great mistake, because if once for instance all of you 'chacuns' who are so proud of your personal 'goût' would vote for or against a work, one could perhaps make an advance poll, predicting the result of this voting. This might be very democratic and there is a slight hope that the true opinion of the majority might decide the destiny of the work of a master, right or wrong; it would include at least, instead of the 'goût' of only one single 'chacun', various opinions, and everybody would understand that in the average which it presents there are included positives and negatives, pros and cons of various grades.

Unfortunately you are so few in whose hands the destiny of a work is laid and your authority has been bestowed upon you by people who are too modest to do this job themselves. They deem that you understand much more music than they. But they do not expect that you are so much at variance with other, and even important musicians, who possess greater authority, one which is based upon their personal achievements, upon studies, and upon being recognized by a multitude of other even greater authorities.

If I who would not dare always to depend on my personal gusto, if I would look around for support of my judgement, I would in the first instance think of Richard Strauss who spoke once to me about Mahler with great appreciation and with a respect derived from his own self-respect. 'Only one who deserves respect himself is capable of respecting another man', I have once written. But nothing can surpass the enthusiasm of Anton von Webern, Alban Berg, Franz Schmidt and many other Viennese composers about Mahler's Symphonies. And why do you forget Mitropolous's enthusiasm?

One who is able to study a score need not depend upon his personal taste. He would see all those strokes of genius, which never are to be found in lesser masters. He would discover them on every page of this work, in every measure, in every succession of tones and harmonies.

AETAT 74 *To Olin Downes*

But all of you have the habit of criticizing a work only when it was performed; and then, after one single hearing, you pronounce your sentence of life or death, regardless of all the experience your trade has gone through when history turned to the absolute contrary of your judgement.

I assume you have for two or more decades written in an unfriendly manner about Mahler and now are afraid to deviate from your primary judgement. Why? You are not so old that you should not dare changing your mind. I am at least ten to twenty years older than you. I can assure you that I am still ready to change my opinions, to learn something new, to accept the contrary and to digest it, the contrary of all I have believed in my whole life — if it is capable of convincing me. If it is truly great it is capable. No courageous man would hesitate to do this.

I ascribe your favorable review of my Five Orchestral Pieces to the same resistance against a revision of your former attitude towards a composition. I assume, as in the case of Mahler, that you have two or more decades ago already written about these pieces, but in a favorable manner — as it was the tendency among young men at that time. Tell me: Why should an honourable man be afraid of changing his mind at the time of greater maturity? Must he remain forever the slave of his time of immaturity?

I am afraid many people, who read both these reviews about Mahler and me, will say: One who writes as unfoundedly about Mahler, will certainly also be wrong about Schoenberg. Accordingly I must either be ashamed to please you, or it will cease to be favorable to me.

As I have said before: If you would study the orchestral score you could not overlook the beauty of this writing. Such beauty is only given to men who deserve it because of all their other merits. You should not call me a mystic — though I am proud to be one — because this statement is based on experience: I have seen so many scores and I could tell at one glance how good the composition is. Even the piano score of Mahler's Symphony would have revealed much of its beauty.

In the piano concerto of a French composer you were able to discover a charming popular French folksong. Why would you not discover such qualities in Mahler's Symphonies? You seem to consider the use of a popular melody as an asset. I say it is a liability. It is a sign that he was not able to contribute one of his own; therefore he must borrow from other people's property.

If you only had noticed a few of these wonderful melodies. I do not know whether your enthusiasm would have matched Webern's (my dear

To Olin Downes UNDATED

old friend), who could play and sing it many times and would never stop admiring it.

First this accompanying figure of the Clarinet:

Then Horn, and Oboe:

Then this continuation:

Or this melody in the last movement:

In these melodies the creative power cannot be ignored. A master of this degree need not borrow from other people — he splendidly spends from his own riches.

ARNOLD SCHOENBERG

Aetat 74   *To Olin Downes*

[*Written in English*]

231. To Olin Downes[1]   *Los Angeles*, 21 *December* 1948

Mr. Olin Downes, Music Editor,
The New York Times,
New York, N.Y.

Dear Mr. Downes:

Before responding to some of the points of your very interesting letter, I must mention that I did not expect that in its imperfect form of a private letter it would be published. I was in a fighting mood, caused by your criticism of Mahler. I felt this can be a fight for death or life, in which case one is not obliged to worry about the correctness of the blows one deals out. If they only hurt.

Nevertheless, I should not have pretended that you do not study scores and that you are prejudiced by your own previous judgements. This, however, can not have hurt you as much as I am hurt by your reproach of illogicality — there is nothing worse to me than that. Fortunately you can not prove Mahler's vulgarity and neither can I prove my attack on your musicianship. It seems to me that the scale goes down on your side and that a true equilibrium requires some additional weight in favor of my logic.

In your letter to Mr. Mitropoulos* you say that music is to you like a religion and you reserve for yourself the right to be intolerant against a believer of a different faith. I should call this the claim of a fighter. But I will rather tell you a story:

Several years ago an announcer over a nation-wide network broadcast attacks on my music to a crowd of two and a half million listeners. I thought: This man is an. . . . Oh, perhaps it is better even now not to tell you what I thought. But at this time I was belligerently desiring to tell all the audience what I was thinking.

You write? 'Chacun à son goût,' and you are fortunate enough to be able to tell hundreds of thousands of your readers which is your taste. But how can I inform those two and a half millions of radio listeners that their announcer is wrong? One who possesses such an unlimited power must have a sense of responsibility.

You claim the right of a fighter, the right to be intolerant. Is it logical to deny the opponent the same rights if he is infuriated to a degree

---

[1] Olin Downes had published Schoenberg's previous letter (Letter 230), together with his own reply to it, in the *New York Times* of December 12th, 1948. This letter continues the correspondence.

* Only at the very end of this letter I discovered that it had been delivered to me by mistake. [S.]

To Olin Downes　　　　　　　　　　　　　　　　　　December 1948

which makes him refuse to see the forest as long as he has to conquer individual trees?

It is the word 'taste' which excites me.

In my vocabulary it stands for 'arrogance and superiority-complex of the mediocrity', and: Taste is sterile — it can not produce. And: Taste is applicable only to the lower zones of human feelings, to the material ones. It is no yardstick in spiritual matters. And: Taste functions mainly as a restricting factor, as a negation of every problem, as a minus to every number.

'Chacun à son goût' would have us believe that there exists an enormous number of ways to be extremely personal—but there is not enough caviare, or gold or good luck in the world for everybody. And those 'chacuns' must share the little 'goût' which exists, which of course is a commonplace mass product, with very few marks of personal distinction.

You write that your reference to your taste means simply that you express your personal opinion and that everybody is entitled to his own. 'Entitled' is the right word. Has he who disagrees with you a chance of telling this to the same audience as often as he disagrees?

Furthermore: You do not pretend 'that your ideas of music are conclusive'. Contrast this lighthearted standpoint to the standpoint of an artist like Mahler, who would have preferred to die a thousand times than be forced to believe he was wrong.

I hope you will now understand why your condemnation of a great man and composer on the basis of personal taste enraged me. Then I will gladly admit that another cause of this fury derived from the fact that between 1898 and 1908 I had spoken about Mahler in the same manner as you do today. For that I made good subsequently by adoration.

And, frankly, this is what I resent most: Why should you not also have experienced such transformations of your mind, from Saulus to Paulus, with many of the great ones in the arts, including, besides, Brahms and Wagner, Strauss and Mahler, even Mozart and Beethoven?

Still, I am not a windbag of an unsolid fixation, who gamingly changes his position for no intelligible reason. Also, these changes corresponded to my progressive development in various phases of my life, before maturity was reached. A very characteristic experience of mine may serve as an illustration. Between 1925 and 1935 I did not dare to read or to listen to Mahler's music. I was afraid that my aversion to it in a preceding period might return. Fortunately, when I heard in Los Angeles a moderately satisfactory performance of the Second, I was just as enchanted as ever before: it had lost none of its persuasiveness.

AETAT 74 *To Max Deutsch*

Now finally to your question whether I believe composers are as a rule fair or unbiased critics of other composers: I think they are in the first instance fighters for their own musical ideas. The ideas of other composers are their enemies. You can not restrict a fighter. His blows are correct when they hit hard, and only then is he fair. Thus I do not resent what Schumann said about Wagner, or Hugo Wolf about Brahms. But I resent what Hanslick said against Wagner and Bruckner. Wagner, Wolf, Mahler and Strauss fought for life or death of their ideas.

But you fight only for principles, or rather for the application of principles.

At the end I can tell you that I agree with the last of your points: '.... that this is merely another case of critics and their readers, disagreeing as, thank God, they will always disagree, and in the expression of their convictions greatly contribute to the development of an art' — negatively or positively.

[..........]

ARNOLD SCHOENBERG

232. TO MAX DEUTSCH[1] *Los Angeles, 3 January* 1949

My dear Deutsch,

Your letter of the 29.xii. came today, and in spite of having far too much to do I want to answer it at once. The fact is it contained so much that was delightful that I wouldn't want it all to grow cold; and in a few days, when I have finished with all that has to be done, my enthusiasm will necessarily have been dispersed over those various necessary matters.

I am really enthusiastic about your account of your activities and experiences in Switzerland. Apparently you 'broke' the glacial 'ice' piled up by ———'s[2] presence. In Geneva, it's taken them, strictly speaking, nearly 50 years to get to the point of even trying to discover anything about my music — apart from one single Pierrot concert.

I always knew this fellow Ansermet was antagonistic to me, but I thought he was a Stravinskyite. And so now he's even turned his back on that, has he? I'm afraid my new publishers, Bomart Music Publications, are going to let him do the New York performance of my 'Survivor', because that's the only way it'll be broadcast. — It's very sad.

In normal circumstances I should have been surprised to hear that any public still had difficulties with the first chamber symphony and the Five Pieces for Orchestra. But for an orchestra to get worked up about

[1] A pupil of Schoenberg's.   [2] A Swiss conductor.

To Max Deutsch January 1949

them, instead of feeling the self-evident nature of this music, is something that can be explained only by the existence of Ansermet and his like.

I wish I could have been there, unnoticed, to hear your lectures and elucidations. I know you have the ability to arouse enthusiasm in gatherings of musicians. And I always enjoy recalling that it was you who made possible the Viennese operatic performance of the Gurre-Lieder by rehearsing the choruses.

I am glad your career is now definitely on the upgrade at long last. I always expected it would be so and was only somewhat nonplussed by your not having reached the top long ago. But now let's hope you will soon get the summons to America.

And then I hope to see you again! [..........]

ARNOLD SCHOENBERG

[*Written in English*]

233. To G. F. STEGMANN[1]   *Los Angeles, 26 January* 1949

Mr. G. F. Stegmann,
Dept. of Chemistry,
University Stellenbosch,
South Africa.

Dear Mr. Stegmann:

The situation of music resembles in some respects the situation after the first World War. At present, as then, some nations have been excluded from competition and even the younger people who were in the army and in the war have not found the time to practise, to learn something and to compose.

After the first World War it was especially the Germans who were much behind, and the French, Americans, and Italians had used the opportunity to propagandize their music, while the Germans were restricted to Germany and Austria.

This time also France and Italy have suffered, besides Germany, in this same manner, so that only America was relatively free. America now thinks her time has come to achieve hegemony in music. The mentality of Americans goes always for mass-production and they try now to do the same in music — to produce music on the 'running band' [conveyor-belt]. One is astonished if one sees lists of American composers, and one is astonished by the production. There are many composers who have already written many symphonies and sometimes

[1] A music-lover who, it seems, felt confused by the different modern tendencies and had written to Schoenberg for enlightenment.

AETAT 74 *To G. F. Stegmann*

one is doubtful if a composer who announces his 5th Symphony has already written the first, second, third and fourth.

Technically, they all suffer from a lack of education. We in Europe had to study at least one year of harmony, two years of counterpoint, at least three years of a thorough formal study — if not longer. Here, they believe they can do it in three years, which is untrue. There are great talents among them and much skill, and they learn fast. They learn more from theories and from lectures than from master models.

One of the influences which is a great obstacle to richer development is the models which they imitate. It would not be so bad to imitate Stravinsky, or Bartok, or Hindemith, but worse is that they have been taught by a woman of Russian-French descent, who is a reactionary and has had much influence on many composers. One can only wish that this influence might be broken and the real talents of the Americans be allowed to develop freely.

With respect to my personal situation, I can admit gladly that the tendency of the method of composing with 12 tones has spread considerably. There are many composers in South America and in Europe and in other countries who try this method, and it seems they become more and more successful.

Mr. Humphrey Searle, an Englishman, considers the founding of an international society of composers with twelve tones. I have no idea whether this will succeed and whether it's a good idea, but after all it is significant of the spreading-out of this way of creating coherence in a piece of music. This seems the most attractive feature of the method of composing with 12 tones: that, from the very beginning, to a certain degree, coherence is assured. In no other method such an advantage is offered. The kind of tonality which is preferred today, which uses all kind of incoherent dissonances and returns without any reason to a major triad or to a minor triad, and rests then for a time and considers this the tonality of the piece, seems to me doomed. I cannot believe that this will last very long.

I hope this satisfies your question about my opinion on the present state of music.

May I add that I believe, when the movement of the reactionaries has died away, that music will return to composing with 12 tones. There will probably be various attempts at promoting coherence through this method, but I hope successors will not forget that it is not only 12 tone, but that the accent is on 'composing'.

I wish you good success.

ARNOLD SCHOENBERG

To Bud Behrens JANUARY 1949

[*Written in English*]

234. TO BUD BEHRENS *Los Angeles*, 31 *January* 1949

Mr Bud Behrens,
429, East Monterey Ave.,
Stockton, California

Dear Mr Behrens:
Generalization produces too often the ridiculous.

Whether music should arouse emotions or whether it does arouse emotion, whether it derives from emotion or not — all this depends on the two factors: the sender and the receiver.

No doubt composers like Beethoven and Schubert and Schumann were emotionally moved when they composed. No doubt, also, that their music arouses emotion, or at least in those people who are the proper receivers of this kind of music. Of course there are also people who are not receivers of emotional music. In them, there is not the ability to arouse emotional reaction.

[..........]

ARNOLD SCHOENBERG

235. TO EUGEN LEHNER[1] *Los Angeles*, 10 *February* 1949[2]

Dear Lehner,

My music is almost totally unknown in America and also in present-day Europe. My sole interest must therefore necessarily be to take every chance of enabling people to hear some of it. And so even if the records were really as bad as you say, I cannot help being very glad if even one small company sees to it that the largest possible number of people get to know at least that part of my work. But it is not only that I do not at all agree with you that these recordings are bad. I have often played them to friends and, on the contrary, everyone is immensely enthusiastic about them. One can always somewhat improve everything. But: can you guarantee it ???? After ten years' estrangement ????

Incidentally, I find the first quartet by far the most mature, and better than the second. The others will give adequate guidance to my

---

[1] The viola player, formerly a member of the Kolisch Quartet. The recordings under discussion are those of Schoenberg's four string quartets and were made before the Kolisch Quartet disbanded in 1939. The Alco Company now intended issuing them.

[2] Schoenberg's carbon copy bears the date '1940', but the contents of the letter itself indicate that this was a typing error, a nought for a nine.

chamber-musical ideas, at any rate for the first ten years that any owner will use them.

But even if they were much further removed from perfection (which after all can't be achieved in material things) than they actually are, they are certainly better than any real, under-rehearsed performance by any of the quartets giving concerts nowadays would be. In so many of my concerts I have had to put up with the minimum that Herr Klemperer or the like of him can provide, and these quartets were always the only thing I could point to as being *good*.

Once again: And if they were really so bad, still I must take the opportunity of making my music known by this means. Do you believe a performance conducted by Koussevitzky would have done me better service? Would you like me to mention more names?

No! I must ask you to give your unqualified agreement to this publication. I know you are artist enough to place the interests of a composer of my age and misfortunes above your artistic interest. And surely you would not want to be responsible for my having to go on waiting, longer than I need, for my — moral and material — success at long last. So if Alco ask you, do, please, say 'Yes'.

[..........]

ARNOLD SCHOENBERG

236. TO RENÉ LEIBOWITZ   *Los Angeles*, 15 *March* 1949
M. René Leibowitz,
Paris

[..........]

About the plan for my trip to Europe, I'm afraid I can't say anything definitive.[1] I agreed on the condition that my health permitted of my travelling and I may as well say that it will also depend on whether the American government grants me sufficient funds. I am not in a position to fling money about myself. I cannot imagine that I shall be in a position to get a definitive answer on the financial side for at least a month. As for the problem of health, *that* depends on minutes. A week ago I was fairly well, but nearly all the time since then I have been ill again. I am better now, but not yet quite all right. So in any case it would be a good thing if you could come here, although we should then miss each other in Paris, for that is certainly fixed: if I can get to Europe and if funds permit I mean to have a few days in Paris without fail, for we want our children at least to have a glimpse of it.

[..........]

ARNOLD SCHOENBERG

[1] See Letter 238.

To Rudolf Kolisch APRIL 1949
237. To RUDOLF KOLISCH *Los Angeles*, 12 *April* 1949

Dear Rudi,

Thank you very much for your last letter. It was a real joy to me. I need such encouragement, for, as you can imagine, I am often very depressed.

Fundamentally I agree with your analysis of musical life here. It really is a fact that the public lets its leaders drive it unresistingly into their commercial racket and doesn't do a thing to take the leadership out of their hands and force them to do their job on other principles. But over against this apathy there is great activity on the part of American composers, la Boulanger's pupils, the imitators of Stravinsky, Hindemith, and now Bartók as well. These people regard musical life as a market they mean to conquer, and they are sure they will do it with ease in the colony that Europe amounts to for them. [..........] They have taken over American musical life lock, stock and barrel, at least in the schools of music. The only person who can get an appointment in a university music department is one who has taken his degree at one of them, and even the pupils are recruited and scholarships awarded to them in order to have the next generation in the bag. The tendency is to suppress European influences and encourage nationalistic methods of composition constructed on the pattern adopted in Russia and other such places.

This is what they now mean to flood Europe with, treating it as a colony. This is a great danger; but I am firmly convinced that they will not succeed. True, one doesn't know what tightening the purse-strings may do — if no more food-parcels come from America, no more fuel, no more raw materials.

I have also observed that the public is at the moment more inclined to accept my music, and actually I did foresee that these people, so chaotically writing dissonances and that rough, illiterate stuff of theirs, would actually open the public's eyes, or rather ears, to the fact that there happen to be more organized ways of writing a piece, and that thus the public would come to feel that what is in my music is after all a different sort of thing.

I am very glad you stress this so emphatically and with such great conviction — if you can convince even me, then you will certainly also convince the rest of your public.

[..........]

A week ago I finished a piece for violin solo with piano accompaniment. Your cousin Richard Hoffmann, who is here, as you know, has

AETAT 74   *To Amadeo de Filippi*

already played it with Stein.[1] It is very difficult, but it is all technically very playable indeed and is said to sound very well. I haven't heard it yet. Do you want to see it? If so, I could have a copy made for you too.

                                        ARNOLD SCHOENBERG

238. TO JOSEF RUFER   *Los Angeles*, 8 *May* 1949

My dear fellow,

Perhaps you will be very much disappointed by what I have to tell you — I can't come after all.

Last week I was very much encouraged when both my doctors came to the objective conclusion that, so far as they were concerned, I could travel. But subjectively things are at such a pass that I really cannot. It may not be dangerous but it is tormenting beyond belief. I dare say what I am suffering from is something of no interest to a doctor because it can't either be operated on or alleviated by taking medicine. But for me it is really awful. I suffer from asthma, I suffer from giddiness, and I also have stomach troubles: cramps of all sorts, and pretty violent ones at that. Today it struck me that for severe maladies they give injections and analgesics. But for lesser maladies they do nothing at all, and that is what I have to endure. I don't think I can risk it.

[..........]

Well, for today all very best wishes, and I am very sad that I can't come over.

                                        ARNOLD SCHOENBERG

                    [*Written in English*]
239. TO AMADEO DE FILIPPI   *Los Angeles*, 13 *May* 1949
Mr Amadeo de Filippi,
4405, Waldo Avenue,
New York, 63, N.Y.

Dear Mr de Filippi:

It is very interesting to me that you like these Three Satires and especially that you find that the technique is similar to the Third String Quartet and the Wind Quintet. It is true — they must have been written about the same time. I think it was 1926. I wrote them when I was very

[1] Leonard Stein, an American pupil of Schoenberg's and for a time his assistant at the university. The work is the *Fantasia*, op. 47.

271

To Amadeo de Filippi   MAY 1949

much angered by attacks of some of my younger contemporaries at this time and I wanted to give them a warning that it is not good to attack me.[1]

The title 'Manysided' ['Versatility'], means only that it can be used by turning around the paper and reading it from the end to the beginning and the same music (if you call it music) would come out. This piece was never intended by myself to be sung or performed. It is merely on paper. But if one would try to perform it I think about 60 to the quarter-note would be a good tempo.

The Cantata is the piece which could and should be performed and I am ready to do as much as I can, if you send me your copy with your remarks. It will interest me very much.

The Canon for Bernard Shaw was made on the occasion of his 70th birthday when his German admirers, amongst whom I counted myself, sent him a birthday present with such contributions. Bernard Shaw was much too original to answer to such a present.

I not only forgive you for asking me these questions, but I am glad to see people being interested in so intricate details of my works and I am always ready, as much as my time allows, to answer such questions.

ARNOLD SCHOENBERG

240. TO LUDWIG GROTE   *Los Angeles*, 10 *June* 1949
Herr Dr. Ludwig Grote,
Der Blaue Reiter,[2]
Munich

Dear Herr Dr. Grote,

First of all I must apologize for my delay in answering, which was caused by my being frequently unwell.

I feel very honoured by your invitation to take part in an exhibition such as the Blaue Reiter is and would have the greatest pleasure in complying with your wishes if it were not for two points that appear to constitute an insurmountable obstacle.

---

[1] The *Three Satires*, op. 28, are choral pieces, with words by Schoenberg: 1. 'Am Scheideweg' [At the Crossroads], 2. 'Vielseitigkeit' [Versatility], 3. 'Der neue Klassizismus' [The New Classicism], a little cantata. The appendix includes the canon, mentioned below, for Bernard Shaw's birthday.

[2] *Der Blaue Reiter* [The Blue Horseman] was an art periodical, the first (and only) volume of which appeared in 1912, with reproductions of works by and contributions from Franz Marc, Kandinsky, Schoenberg, and others. The name was taken from a painting of Marc's and became the symbol of Expressionism. The *Blaue Reiter* exhibition that was being planned was evidently to include portraits of leading figures in the Expressionist movement.

AETAT 74   *To the Hessischer Rundfunk*

First of all, sending the pictures from here to Munich would be very expensive; even by sea, which would take immensely long, it would cost a comparatively large sum, but the air-freight charge would be utterly beyond my means. Secondly, however, you must bear in mind that the risk of losing the pictures is graver for me than for a museum. For a museum it is just one of the pieces that they have; for me it is — let us be quite frank about it — what I intend leaving to my heirs, hoping that some day it will bring them in a sum worth having. For me such a loss would be truly irreparable.

But I plan to get in touch with art-dealers and gallery-directors here. Perhaps I can discover something I can do in order to fulfil your wish after all. I still don't know how, my ideas about it are very vague, but perhaps something can be done.

In any case thank you once more, very much, for your invitation. I should like to know whether I could perhaps send you photographs — reproductions of a fair size. That would at least give some sort of idea.

                                                          ARNOLD SCHOENBERG

241. To THE HESSISCHER RUNDFUNK   *Los Angeles*, 15 *June* 1949

Hessischer Rundfunk [Radio Hessia],
Frankfurt-am-Main

Dear Sirs,

Thank you very much for your telegram asking me to send some words of greeting for the inauguration of the celebrations — the message is garbled at this point — probably it ought to be 'chamber-music concert'. I have just sent a night letter-telegram, which ought to be there tomorrow morning; and I suppose that will be in time. But since I am afraid that it may become garbled, just as your telegram was, I herewith repeat the wording:

> 'The honour of taking part in these festival concerts fills me with pride and grateful joy. For I see it as surpassing the purely personal, testifying that music must be free of all trammels if it is faithfully to obey its own inner laws.
>
> 'For this, and for much besides, my very sincere thanks.
>   Signed
>   ARNOLD SCHOENBERG'

I hope this declaration will be read as being intended in an aesthetic rather than in a political sense, although indeed the second would be entirely justifiable at the moment.

To the Hessischer Rundfunk   JUNE 1949

Once more I wish you all success with your festival concerts and should be very grateful if you would in due course send me a programme of the whole series.

242. TO OSKAR ADLER*   *Los Angeles, 2 July* 1949

My dear, good, old friend,

It's so long since I had any address of yours, and now here at last is the chance to write to you. How are you? I have heard that you still play in quartets a lot, which I'm afraid I haven't done any more for a long time now, and I admire your being so active. We are the same age, aren't we, and you'll be 75 this year, or are you already?

I'm afraid my health, at least at the moment, or for the last five years, hasn't been of a kind to give me much pleasure in living. There are many days when I'm really not up to work and ought to rest instead. All the same, I do still get some work done and have something to show for it: — one book is finished, which is entitled 'Structural Functions of the Harmony' [sic]; and I have got a book on counterpoint to the stage where I could finish it in anything from three to six months. But I have no publisher for all this stuff. Well, we are no longer in Austria or Germany, where there wasn't so much ado about publishing such a work.

Do you manage to go to concerts? And have you heard some of my later works? Do let me know how you feel about them. In any case, do write to me sometimes.

[..........]

With very, very best wishes,

                affectionately, as ever,

                                       ARNOLD SCHOENBERG

243. TO THE DRAMATISTS' AND COMPOSERS' ASSOCIATION, VIENNA
                                        Los Angeles, 4 August 1949

Herr Dr. Fritz Stein:

Your letter informing me that the Dramatists' and Composers' Association in Vienna had elected me as honorary member by acclamation

---

* Dr. Adler was a friend of Schoenberg's youth, his first teacher and quartet partner. Schoenberg wrote of him: 'Oskar Adler ... was to play a great role in my evolution. I am obliged to him for a great many matters he taught me.' It was not until Schoenberg was eighteen that he obtained any other instruction than that given him by Adler, who died in London in 1955. [TRANS.]

AETAT 74 *To Bernard Herrmann*

has given me singular pleasure. I must stress this most warmly, in order to convey to you that I am far from having become so dull and 'detached' as not to feel pleasure in being thus honoured.

It naturally reminds me that old age is the time of harvest, and although, if I have reaped better than I sowed, it is no merit of mine, it is nonetheless in the highest degree gratifying.

Allow me to express my very cordial thanks to you and to the gentlemen who proposed me and to those who carried the motion. I myself dearly wish that my health may permit me to come to Vienna, where I still have — in intensity and perhaps even in number — friends so many as to exceed the number and power of my opponents.

With kind regards,

I am, yours faithfully,

ARNOLD SCHOENBERG

[Written in English]
244. TO BERNARD HERRMANN[1]   *Los Angeles*, 30 *August* 1949
Mr. Bernard Herrmann,
Conductor,
C.B.S., Inc.,
485, Madison Avenue,
New York, 22, N.Y.

Dear Mr. Herrmann:

I want to write you already for so long a time! You have no idea how busy people keep me, by asking me to write articles for my 75th anniversary. Thus I have to celebrate it prematurely by hard labour.

I have with great pleasure received the recordings of your performance of my second chamber symphony.

Let me say at once: this is quite different from what I heard from the broadcast. It was really distorted in an extremely annoying manner. One heard for instance very seldom the basses (could this not also be the fault of the radio station???): there were many sections mixed with other sounds and there was often noise. This was no pleasure.

Let me tell you I find now that your performance was very good, very convincing and expressive, though, in order to show the sincerity of my judgement, I would say that the first movement was too slow. I am sure if you would try to read this movement now in the tempo which my

[1] The conductor of the Columbia Broadcasting System, New York.

To Bernard Herrmann AUGUST 1949

metronome marks indicate, that everything would fit very well to this tempo. Curiously, Stiedry[1] also played it too slow. What might be the reason? I think, I am right.

Now thank you again for helping me to [form] this good impression, and I hope to see you should you once visit California.

I am, with cordial greetings,
                              Sincerely yours,
                                          ARNOLD SCHOENBERG

[*Written in English*]
245. TO THE MAYOR OF LOS ANGELES
                              Los Angeles, 24 *September* 1949

Honorable Fletcher Bowron,
Mayor of Los Angeles,
City Hall, Los Angeles, 12.

My dear Mayor Bowron:

Allow me to express to you my most sincere appreciation of the letter of greeting and congratulation which you tendered me on the occasion of my 75th birthday. I thank you for your expressions of regard, which I treasure as tokens of not only your personal esteem, but of my fellow-citizens of Los Angeles, extended through you, their representative.

Your letter was doubly touching to me, for on that same day I also received a letter which officially notified me that I had been made an honorary burgher of Vienna. Thus it was that the city of my birth and the city in which I and my family have made our home for the past fifteen years both united to extend me their regard and recognition.

In expressing to you my thanks for your felicitations, I feel it is an appropriate time to voice to you my awareness of and belief in the actions of this city in paying official recognition to music through its music program in the public schools, and the emphasis on music as a tool of citizenship, as furthered by the city's Bureau of Music. Though naturally I can hope that this is but a beginning which will eventually lead to municipal support for music in all its aspects, as has been the case in Europe for many decades, it is a pleasure to learn of the interest you have personally taken in the activities of these policies.

Again, with many thanks for your message, I am
                              Yours most cordially,
                                          ARNOLD SCHOENBERG

[1] Fritz Stiedry had conducted the first performance of the work.

AETAT 75   *To Luigi Dallapiccola*

246. To Eduard Steuermann[1]   *Los Angeles, 3 October* 1949

My very dear Steuermann,

I am so glad to hear from you that you have already recorded my piano music. I do not at all share your anxiety lest anyone should hear a wrong note. I am convinced that it has happened only a few times in the history of musical reproduction that some wrong notes did not get in. There is no absolute purity in this world: pure water contains infusoria. But I am convinced that you can play music so convincingly that it evokes the impression of purity, artistic purity, and, after all, that's what matters. Let's leave this quasi-perfection to those who can't perceive anything else.

[..........]

                                                           ARNOLD SCHOENBERG

247. To the Burgomaster of Vienna

                                          Los Angeles, 5 October 1949

Dear Herr Bürgermeister:

It was with pride and joy that I received the news that I had been given the freedom of the city of Vienna. This is a new, or rather, a renewed, bond bringing me closer again to the place, its natural scenery and its essential character, where that music was created which I have always so much loved and which it was always my greatest ambition to continue according to the measure of my talents.

Perhaps I may cherish the hope that this honour bestowed on me by the Burgomaster and Senate of the City of Vienna is due to recognition of that profound desire and of the intensity with which I have striven — however little it may amount to — always to give of my best.

And so I should gladly live to have the opportunity of exercising the right of free entry into the city where I spent so many years. Then I shall not fail to call on you, Herr Bürgermeister, in order personally to express my thanks for this enhancement of my birthday celebrations.

I am, with esteem and regard,

                     Yours faithfully,

                                               ARNOLD SCHOENBERG

248. To Luigi Dallapiccola[2]   *Los Angeles, 10 December* 1949

My dear friend,

I thank you for your letter, which gave me much joy. Of course I accept the dedication of your composition with great pleasure. It gives

---

[1] The pianist, formerly a pupil of Schoenberg's and of Busoni's.
[2] The composer.

To Luigi Dallapiccola DECEMBER 1949

me great pleasure to learn from the dedication of your extremely interesting new work that you are a real friend, and that is why I begin this letter by calling you 'my dear friend'.

The idea of writing variations for a singing voice is highly original and very promising. I envy you for having done it. I am sorry it never occurred to me. Which are the 14 instruments? I am very eager indeed to see this score. I hope Scherchen will have the printing done quickly so that I may soon have it.

With all very best wishes and apologies for not being able to write to you in French or Italian, [..........]

ARNOLD SCHOENBERG

249. TO THOMAS MANN[1] *Los Angeles, 2 January* 1950

Dear Herr Dr. Mann,

I have been ill — for more than two weeks — and therefore could not keep to a pressing deadline. At the time I should have liked — but was unable — to finish the letter I began at once after reading your letter, and so I am afraid much time has passed, which I greatly regret.

Here is what I wrote:

> If the hand that I believe I see held out is the hand of peace, that is, if it signifies an offer of peace, I should be the last not to grasp it at once and shake it in token of confirmation.
>
> In fact: I have often thought of writing to you and saying: Let us bury the hatchet and show that on a certain level there is always a chance of peace.

(*Continued on the 9th January!*)

I had intended making public this declaration of peace. It was pointed out to me, however, (and this is the reason why I did not finish the letter), that by so doing I would, as it were, stab in the back all those who supported me in this fight — friends, acquaintances, and strangers.

So I suggest an intermediate stage of neutrality. Some day one or the other [of us] will be celebrating his 'eightieth' — but it need not even wait till then —: a fitting occasion to forget all pettiness — finally.

[..........]

Let us make do with this peace: you have reconciled me.

I remain, with deep regard, yours faithfully,

ARNOLD SCHOENBERG

[1] This handwritten letter concludes the Schoenberg-Mann controversy. See Letter 224.

AETAT 75

250. To JACQUES MARTET[1]

To Minsa Craig
Los Angeles, 6 January 1950

M. Jacques Martet,
Banque de France,
Villefranche s/Sâone

[..........]

Your letter gave me very great pleasure indeed, above all because you are one of the extremely rare kind of people who are of such importance to our musical culture. I mean: it is not the professional musician, the musician who lives by his art, who is needed to keep musical culture going; it is the amateur, and it always has been the amateur who has really promoted and encouraged art. This is all the more gratifying since your profession is one that claims much of your time; and what is astonishing is the way you have come to know my music — I am thinking of piano pieces and scores that are really very difficult to grasp, difficult to read, difficult to decipher, and which demand a great knowledge of various different aspects of music. I am extremely delighted at having discovered such a musician in you.

It makes me extremely proud to have received such a letter particularly from you, and for me it will remain one of a few letters that have given me the greatest pleasure in my musical career.

I thank you for it most cordially and hope to hear from you again soon. [..........]

ARNOLD SCHOENBERG

[*Written in English*]

251. To MINSA CRAIG   *Los Angeles*, 17 *April* 1950

Mr. Minsa Craig,
850 1/2, South Robertson,
Los Angeles, 35, California

Dear Mr. Craig,

In former times I have never agreed that my pieces should be used for dancing. I said: this is chamber music, and when I compose for the theater, or for scenic performance, I compose differently.

Recently I have changed this viewpoint, because it seemed to me that today's dancers have a different approach to music and a deeper understanding of problems of style. Of course, music which does not contain a certain rhythmic regularity of its accents cannot be combined with dancing-movements.

[1] Evidently a French music-lover, hitherto a stranger, who had come to hold Schoenberg's music in high regard.

To Minsa Craig   APRIL 1950

For this reason I have ceased to object to combining my music with dance. Of course, it must be handled very tactfully. The moods which you suggest in your letter: macabre, mysterious, seeking the Unknown, dream of escape, or fear of our future, might quite well fit some of my music.

Let me hear which of my music you have in mind for your performance.

                                                             ARNOLD SCHOENBERG

252. TO HERMANN SCHERCHEN   *Los Angeles*, *22 May* 1950

My dear Scherchen,

I shall be able to tell you exactly how many players are required for 'Die Jakobsleiter' only when I have gone back to work on it. My plan is to use if possible fewer than quadruple woodwind, and normal brass.[1] The soloists are: Gabriel, bass (singer and speaker), and also A Devotee, An Agitator, One who Wrestles, The Elect One, and The Monk; all these are male voices, and then there is a Dying Woman, a high soprano. The chorus is often divided into two parts, each of six voices: soprano, mezzosoprano, alto, tenor, baritone, one bass, in other words, 12 voices. In other places there are shorter sections, with perhaps not more than 32–40 singers.

(1) Style: it is not a twelve-note composition, but rather more like the style of my 'Erwartung' and 'Die glückliche Hand'.

(2) I assume it will take about $\frac{3}{4}$ hour. But this may be quite wrong. It might just as easily last an hour and a quarter. . . . I can't remember.

(3) Whether I can promise you the score for the 31st August depends, first, on whether my plan to write it out on enlarged paper[2] can be carried out. Secondly, whether I shall be well enough at all and, if so, long enough. It would be rash for me to promise you anything more than that.[3]

I am sorry not to have been able to answer till today, and then so unsatisfactorily. I spent a long time thinking about it. I hope this won't upset your plans. But I should hate to tie you down to anything before I see clearly.

                                                              ARNOLD SCHOENBERG

---

[1] As the music written down in 1917 shows, the original plan was for a much larger orchestra.

[2] Because of Schoenberg's failing sight.

[3] Schoenberg was unable to continue work on *Die Jakobsleiter*. What was under discussion was only the completion of the first part of the work, and it is to this that the specifications — as to number of musicians required and playing time — refer.

AETAT 75   *To Thor Johnson*

[*Written in English*]

253. To THOR JOHNSON   *Los Angeles*, 24 *July* 1950

Mr. Thor Johnson,
Cincinnati Symph. Orch.,
1106, First National Bank Bldg.,
Cincinnati 2, Ohio.

Dear Mr. Johnson:

    I was very much pleased by getting the message that you are going to perform next February 2 and 3 my Gurrelieder. It is furthermore very pleasant to me to realize that you seem to like my music — at least my music of this period — and you like to do this performance. I appreciate this very much.

    I am of course glad to give you any information which can be of advantage to you.

    The first information would be that the Stokowsky records, which you perhaps know (made by RCA Victor) are in some respects very good, but in others a little poor. Stokowsky is generally a little too free with violent changes of tempi, and some of the tempi he takes do not agree with my music. The orchestra plays very fine, but almost all of the soloists are rather poor.

    Let me first speak about the two which are the worst: this is the singer of Klaus Narr, who does not sing but speaks, and if he sings, he usually sings a melody of his own. This is terrible to me. This piece must be, for every second, every fraction of a second, sung at the right pitch, in the right time and right rhythm, because in most cases the melody upon which the whole piece is based appears only in the voice. The second, who is almost as bad as this, is the speaker. This speaker makes the opposite mistake: he sings all the time, and he sings his own melodies, and these melodies are, of course, not shaped so that they fit to the harmony, and I did not want to have melodies. I was able to write melodies myself when I wanted them. I do not need the assistance of a Mr So-and-So. This must be avoided entirely.

    I think you will certainly find a tenor with a light voice who is flexible and who has the necessary compass to sing Klaus Narr without any difficulty. At least, I had always one at the many places where I conducted this piece myself.

    The question of the speaker is a little more difficult. Finally I found out the best thing is to give it to a singer who no longer has the necessary beauty of voice to sing great parts. It should, if possible, be a higher voice, about Tenor range or high Baritone. It should, if possible,

To Thor Johnson   JULY 1950

be a voice which should not be too fat, too thick, too bombastic. It should be a light voice.

I had in Vienna and in Amsterdam a speaker who was an actor, not quite musical enough to make the performance faultless, but he worked very hard and could do it quite fine. As concerns expression and mood and everything, he was the best I ever had. His name is Klitsch and I am told he is still an actor in Vienna. I could try to locate him. I have friends in Vienna who could give me his address. But it might be too costly to bring him over.

For the first performance, which I conducted myself in Leipzig in 1914, I had the part of the speaker carried out by Mrs. Albertine Zehme, who also commissioned Pierrot Lunaire. She was very, very good and it was quite possible to make this piece also with a woman's voice, because it is orchestrated in this manner. Mrs. Zehme is now dead, but I would consider also having Mrs. Erica Stiedry who was the speaker in my Pierrot Lunaire in recent performances, in the last twenty years. She is very good and also musical and I am sure she can make a good performance.

Speaking of a singer who has previously done it, there is Mr. Hans Nachod, who lives in London now and who has always sung with me the part of Waldemar — the main part in other words. He is quite musical and talented. I would not take him any more as a singer because he might be over sixty. Formerly he was a very good actor, and not only did he sing this piece, but he has also sung all the Wagner operas and Verdi and so on in many, many cities. Again there is the question whether you would not find it too expensive to bring him over. But he could study it alone, and he has people who can study this with him; above all, my former pupil Karl Rankl who is director of the Covent Garden Opera in London and who assisted me in many performances.

There is also another plan which might not be impossible. My daughter, Nuria, wants to do it, but I do not know if she will have the time to study it because she is just now in her second year of medicine at the University and has very much work to do. In case she can learn it, I will inform you. It might be good. If not, I will not let her do it. One thing,

ONE THING IS VERY IMPORTANT:
Make the performance in *ENGLISH* not in German. People do not understand German, neither here, nor in Australia, England, Canada and in many other places. There is an excellent translation in the Stokowsky Victor Album. I possess besides a translation into English,

which I myself used in my performance in London and which is also very, very good. There is no reason why it should be given in German.

More about the records. In this performance, the microphone was used by the singers, and by this the singers are so loud that they cover the orchestra. You don't hear the orchestra almost for the whole performance. In a well-balanced performance you will hear both the orchestra and the singers.

According to my experience, the chorus is never sufficient if it is put behind the orchestra. I have never had the possibility of trying the opposite, but I am quite sure it would be the best to have the chorus, women and men, in front of the orchestra, and perhaps some of the instruments in a small alley, so to speak, keeping in contact with the conductor. I will send you a sketch how one could arrange this, and I think it would be worthwhile to try it. But there is also another possibility to get better results, and perhaps it might be wise to manage with a smaller group of singers. If, for instance, you can have 200 or 240 women for the mixed choruses at the end (it is in 8 parts), you should not have more than the same number of men in this part, at the utmost 240. Now, the first chorus of the men demands, because it is in three groups, more than 240 if you place the chorus behind the orchestra, but maybe if you give to every group a microphone, it might be possible to restrict the number of singers. Perhaps you could manage with a smaller number of women and also men. This would also give a better balance, because I always had the trouble that the 500 men, which I sometimes had, wanted to sing also in the mixed chorus, and this was too loud. This was not right and did not produce a good balance.

Another thing is the question of the tempi. I confess that many of the tempo indications in my big score are exaggerated. I would not make all these violent changes today any more, which at the time when the score was published were not so extravagant. But we have today a style of performance which rather avoids too violent changes of tempo, and I would say that this asks for some modification. I would say, don't take the metronome marks too literally.

If I would perhaps tell you the differences, based on the Stokowsky records, it might be helpful, but it might take a little [rather] much time. Is it possible that you could, after a few rehearsals, make a tape or wire recording and send it to me? Then I could tell you quickly how I feel about it.

May I ask something? Is this performance in connection with a plan of recording? Does perhaps one of the companies intend to make new records? Especially in this case I would like to co-operate very much.

To Thor Johnson JULY 1950

I am looking forward to your answers and let me tell you again that I enjoy this really very, very much.

ARNOLD SCHOENBERG

[*Written in English*]
254. TO ROBERT CRAFT   *Los Angeles*, 11 *November* 1950

Mr. Robert Craft,
8624, Holloway Drive,
Hollywood, 46, California

Dear Mr. Craft:

Thank you very much for the good news of the successful performances of the Septet Suite and Pierrot Lunaire. I am very interested in your intention to perform my opus 27 and 28, and it is very flattering to me that through your comparison with the Musikalisches Opfer — though overestimating me — you put me in the neighbourhood of Bach. Where did you get the canon for the Concertgebouw? Was it published? Of course you can perform it in the manner mentioned.* I am sure you did not overlook that A means A major, S [*Es*] means E flat major, C means C major and G (not E) means G major. In other words there are four different tonalities and the task of the cello part is to make them understandable. But it must be checked, whether the cello part is not only to be used when all the four voices are together. Probably I have examined it at the time, but I don't recall it. In case the sound is disturbing with the fifth voice, the cello so near to the bass voice, I recommend to double the cello in the lower octave by the double-bass. Could you make me a record of these performances?

The chorus Dreimal Tausend Jahre is only one of three choruses, the third of which is not yet finished. It would be better to wait until this opus is complete.

I have no transcription of the piano concerto for 12 instruments. Such a transcription would ask for at least 20 to 24 instruments, doubling some of the strings, using enough brass. Ask Schirmer whether he would order such an arrangement. I know people who would be ready to make it.

I hope to hear soon from you,

Most cordially yours,

ARNOLD SCHOENBERG

* Mr. Craft, with Schoenberg's agreement, performed the canon privately in Los Angeles with four solo voices and 'cello (the 'cello's C string tuned down to A). [TRANS.]

AETAT 76   *To Oskar Adler*

255. To Francesco Siciliani   *Los Angeles, 27 November* 1950

Francesco Siciliani,
Direttore Artistico,
Maggio Musicale Fiorentino

It is with the greatest joy that I hear of your intention to give a performance of my opera 'Moses und Aaron'[1] during the Maggio Musicale Fiorentino. However, only the first and second acts have been composed, the third existing only as a libretto. There are therefore the following possibilities:

1. A performance of the first two acts, either
   (*a*) omitting the third, or
   (*b*) having it merely spoken. (It is a dialogue between Moses and Aaron, followed, after Aaron's death, by a long monologue of Moses'.)
2. A performance of only the 'Dance round the Golden Calf' (from the second act) or
3. Of the second act only.

However:

4. It would in principle be of much interest to me if instead of this work you were to give performances of one, two, or all three of my one-act operas.

The monodrama 'Erwartung' and the drama with music, 'Die glückliche Hand', (each lasting ½ hour) are published by Universal Edition, who can, I hope, supply all the parts.

The third opera, 'Von heute auf morgen', is longer, lasting 70 minutes. I published it myself and, before leaving Germany, left 80 scores, 120 piano arrangements and two carefully corrected voice-parts with Universal Edition. [..........]

All this is not meant to convey that I should prefer performances of these small works to that of 'Moses und Aaron'. But I do think it is time to present these works to the public, to give [it] a chance to judge their value.

[..........]   Arnold Schoenberg

256. To Oskar Adler[2]   *Los Angeles, 3 March* 1951

My dear old boy,

I have just received your book 'Das Testament der Astrologie' ['The Testament of Astrology']. I have had some of it read to me and found

---

[1] In this letter Schoenberg spells the name 'Aaron', whereas in earlier letters, as in the manuscript, he uses the normal German spelling, 'Aron'. Nothing came of the proposal to perform the work in Florence.

[2] See Letter 242.

To Oskar Adler MARCH 1951

all that I have heard admirable; both as regards style and as regards ideas. Unfortunately I cannot read for myself — I have a nervous affliction of the eyes. I can read typescript and can even read the newspaper for a very short time without spectacles. I cannot use spectacles, for after a time it just makes my eyes swim. So I have to have things read aloud to me. I'm particularly sorry about this because of your book. But gradually

[*continued by hand*]

today is the 23rd. April and I have given up hope of ever finishing this letter. So I shall send you, perhaps soon, a collection* that I call:

'Psalms, Prayers, and other Conversations with and about God' and I am sure you will understand me. So: with love and all very best wishes —

ARNOLD SCHOENBERG

* I want to do a lot of correcting first. So far there are 12 of them — but I have material for 50 or more: our contemporaries' religious problems. [S.][1]

257. TO FRANK PELLEG *Los Angeles*, *26 April* 1951

For the official attention of
Mr. Frank Pelleg,
In charge of the Department of Music;
and to be conveyed also to
The Director of the Israel Academy of Music,
Jerusalem, Mr. O. Partosh.

While with pride and satisfaction accepting my election as honorary president of the Israel Academy of Music, I nevertheless feel myself under an obligation to explain why it seems to me so important that you should have chosen to bestow this honour on me.

Both to your friends who recently visited me in Los Angeles and to yourself, Herr Direktor Partosh, I have already declared that for more than four decades my dearest wish has been to see the establishment of a separate, independent State of Israel. And indeed more than that: to become a citizen of that State and to reside there.

[..........]

I have no words to express how much I should like to make my contribution by taking charge personally, and by teaching at this Academy. I have always had a passion for teaching. I have always felt the urge to discover what can most help beginners and how they can be made

[1] Schoenberg left 15 texts and a fragmentary sixteenth. Each of the first ten is entitled 'Modern Psalm', the others only 'Psalm'. Only the music for the first psalm was written, and even that was not quite completed.

thoroughly acquainted with the technical, intellectual, and ethical demands of our art; how to teach them that there is a morality of art, and why one must never cease to foster it and always combat to the utmost any attempt to violate it.

I am unfortunately compelled to resign these hopes. But it seems to me that the half-century by which my experience exceeds that of many of my colleagues entitles me to explain what I would have endeavoured to make of this Academy if I had [had] the good fortune and still had the strength to tackle it today.

And here I address myself with my most fervent blessings to the Director, Mr. O. Partosh.

I would have tried to make this Academy one of world-wide significance, so that it would be of a fit kind to serve as a counterblast to this world that is in so many respects giving itself up to amoral, success-ridden materialism: to a materialism in the face of which all the ethical preconditions of our art are steadily disappearing. A universal model must not send forth anyone who is only semi-qualified. It must not produce any instrumentalists whose greatest skill is merely skill, merely the ability to adapt itself completely to the general craving for entertainment.

Those who issue from such an institution must be truly priests of art, approaching art in the same spirit of consecration as the priest approaches God's altar. For just as God chose Israel to be the people whose task it is to maintain the pure, true, Mosaic monotheism despite all persecution, despite all affliction, so too it is the task of Israeli musicians to set the world an example of the old kind that can make our souls function again as they must if mankind is to evolve any higher.

Those are my wishes for you, and if I can to be of service to you by elaborating and expounding any matters of details, I can only hope that you will ask me.

ARNOLD SCHOENBERG

258. To JOSEF RUFER　　　　　　　　　*Los Angeles*, 13 *June* 1951

My very dear Rufer,

For many weeks I have not only been far from up to scratch, I have been very much down with all sorts of things. I haven't been out of my room for months. This is why I can't answer all your questions. But there is one thing I would say.

In Grove's Dictionary of Music there is quite a good article that

To Josef Rufer JUNE 1951

includes a discussion of 'Moses and Aaron'. Partly nonsensical; in that it brings the artist in. That's late-19th-century stuff, but not me.[1] The subject matter and the treatment of it are purely of a religious-philosophical kind.

[..........]

ARNOLD SCHOENBERG

259. TO KARL RANKL[2] 27 *June* 1951

My dear Rankl,

It seems likely that I must face not ever being able to finish composing 'Die Jakobsleiter'. Even should that be so, I still hope to be capable of composing an end to the first part.[3] But there is no chance at all of my still being able to write out the score. Now what I want to ask you is if you would, in principle, be willing to do such a score. In the manuscript there are plenty of often very full indications of my orchestral intentions. It would then be a matter of supplying, with the necessary discretion, such interpretations and elaborations as [would] make it possible to perform this part effectively.

I know Scherchen could also do this, but I assume that you know 'Erwartung', 'Die glückliche Hand' and 'Von heute auf morgen' well and are more familiar with my orchestral style than anyone else.

I should be very glad indeed if you would take this on, since alas I shall have to leave so many of my works unfinished. When am I going to get your opera?

With all very best wishes,

ARNOLD SCHOENBERG

260. TO TIBOR VARGA[4] *Los Angeles*, 27 *June* 1951

Dear Herr Varga,

My illness hitherto prevented my hearing your records of my violin concerto, also the fact that I had no suitable record-player. I once played it through on my very inadequate machine and even then received an amazing impression of your overpowering presentation of my music. But it is only now that I have heard it decently that I can

[1] In the article Schoenberg's contrast between Moses (as the spiritual principle) and Aaron (representing matter, with its limitations) is compared to the artistic conception of a work and its realisation in the given artistic medium.

[2] The composer and conductor, formerly a pupil of Schoenberg's.

[3] Schoenberg did not live to compose the end of the first part of *Die Jakobsleiter*. Winfried Zillig (see note 1 to Letter 100) was eventually entrusted with the preparation of the score. This completion of it was performed in Vienna on June 16th, 1961. [TRANS.]

[4] The violin virtuoso.

fully and completely understand why everyone talks of you and your playing with such enthusiasm. It really sounds as if you had known the piece for 25 years, your rendering is so mature, so expressive, so beautifully shaped. I must say that I have never yet come across such a good performance without having myself helped with every detail. The fact that you discovered all this for yourself is not only evidence of your outstanding talent; it gratifies me, besides, in that it shows me how distinctly my music can speak to a true musician: he can know and understand me without explanations, simply through the medium of the written notes.

I am very grateful to you for this experience, and I wish I were younger in order to be able to provide you with more material of this kind. I shall in any case follow your performances with the closest of attention.

I hope I shall soon hear the performance of my Fantasia for Violin.
With very best wishes,

ARNOLD SCHOENBERG

261. Letter of thanks to those who sent their good wishes on the occasion of Schoenberg's 75th birthday. *Los Angeles*, 16 *September* 1949

To gain recognition only after one's death . . . . . !

In these last few days I have met with much personal recognition, which has given me great pleasure because it testifies to the respect in which I am held by my friends and other well-disposed people.

On the other hand, however, I have for many years been resigned to the fact that I cannot count on living to see full and sympathetic understanding of my work, that is, of what I have to say in music. I do indeed know that more than a few of my friends have come to feel at home with my mode of expression and are familiar with my ideas. It is likely then to be such as they who will fulfil what I prophesied in an aphorism exactly thirty-seven years ago:

'The second half of this century will spoil by overestimation whatever the first half's underestimation left unspoilt.'

I am somewhat embarrassed by all these hymns of praise. But I nevertheless also see something encouraging in them. For: Is it so much to be taken for granted if in the face of the whole world's resistance a man does not give up, but continues to write down what he produces?

I do not know what the great have thought about this. Mozart and Schubert were young enough not to have to come to close terms with this problem. But Beethoven, when Grillparzer called the Ninth a jumble, or Wagner, when the Bayreuth scheme seemed about to fail, or Mahler, when everyone found him trivial—how could they go on writing?

I know only one answer: they had things to say that had to be said. Once, in the army, I was asked if I was really the composer A.S. 'Somebody had to be', I said, 'and nobody else wanted to, so I took it on, myself.'

Perhaps I too had to say things — unpopular things, it seems — that had to be said.

And now I ask you all, all of you who have given me real joy with your congratulations and tokens of esteem, to accept this as an attempt to express my gratitude.

My heartfelt thanks!

ARNOLD SCHOENBERG

Section VI
VIENNA
1909–1910

FOUR LETTERS TO GUSTAV MAHLER

262. To Gustav Mahler [*Vienna*,] 29*th December* 1909
My dear Herr Direktor,

I have really been so busy that I could not find time to write to you immediately after the Seventh.* Besides, there was something rather odd. Earlier, I always felt the urge to rush and say something to you about a performance immediately afterwards, while the *full, warm* impression of the work was still with me. Perhaps I secretly feared that the impression might evaporate, might diminish. And in fact — I must confess this — it did not last very long. But this time (and for me this is the most important point) I knew I could wait as long as I liked, for this impression, that of the Seventh, and previously that of the Third: these are *lasting* impressions. I am now really wholly yours. This is a certainty. For I had less sense than previously of something extraordinarily sensational, something that immensely excites and works one up, something, in short, that moves the listener in such a way as to make him lose his balance without giving him another in exchange. What I felt this time was a perfect repose based on artistic harmony. Something that moves me without just ruthlessly shifting my centre of gravity; something that draws me tranquilly and pleasantly to itself — an attraction such as guides the planets, letting them travel along their own courses, influencing these, yes, but so evenly, so entirely according to plan, that there is no longer any jarring, any violence. Perhaps this may sound rather like a purple patch. However, it seems to me to express very clearly one thing that I principally felt: I reacted to you as to a classic. But one who is still a *model* to me. I mean — and this is surely a difference —: Without any outward excitement at all! In tranquillity and calm, as one does, after all, enjoy a thing of beauty! And previously, you know, it did go differently with me; I know that for a fact, even if I cannot express the difference clearly even now. Perhaps there were some elements of artistic struggle involved; personal elements; outward ones; aesthetic details; questions of instrumentation; this time there was absolutely none of all that!

I did not have much time to look at the score carefully beforehand. I hardly knew it. My requests to the Konzertverein for permission to

* Mahler's seventh symphony. See also Letter 230. [trans.]

To Gustav Mahler DECEMBER 1909

come to the last rehearsal remained unanswered, although critics were present.

So this time it was quite without preparation, almost at the very first hearing, that I had this great, entirely clear impression.

I cannot say whether the performance was a good one. On the whole I think it was not bad in so far as Löwe* was obviously trying very hard to carry out the score's directions exactly. True, he does not seem to have achieved much more than that; I often had the feeling that one thing or another ought to be done differently — but I think even that much is a great deal for Löwe to have achieved, and after all there is no reason why (as I once said) he should be expected to understand precisely this work, considering how many years he has been conducting without ever having understood anything.

As for which movement I liked best: All of them! I cannot prefer any one to the others. Perhaps I was rather indifferent at the beginning of the first movement. But anyway only for a short time. And from then on steadily warming to it. From minute to minute I felt happier and warmer. And it did not let go of me for a single moment. In the mood right to the end. And everything struck me as pellucid. Finally, at the first hearing I perceived so many formal subtleties, while always able to follow a main line. It was an extraordinarily great treat. I simply cannot understand how I was not won over to this before.

I should be very glad to hear how you are and what you are doing there. Of course I did not believe that talk about the opera 'Theseus', at once picturing the joke that started it all. But of course everyone in Vienna took it seriously. Nobody stopped to think. 'What does that mean — Theseus?' I only know him from the Theseus Temple.† He occupies no further place in my mind, since I have by now discarded whatever was acquired in history lessons. And that, of all things, was supposed to be the material by means of which you would express yourself!! It did not occur to anyone that: Weingartner-Orestes; Strauss-Elektra; therefore I, Mahler: Theseus, likewise Greek — was a parodistical joke to fob off an impertinent questioner ('But how is it, Herr Direktor, that you have never yet composed anything for the stage, seeing that you are, after all, . . .'). In my view that is how the rumour must have started. I should be very proud to know I had guessed aright.

My own news amounts to very little. I have made a contract with Universal Edition, a very satisfactory one for *them*.

* Ferdinand Löwe, the Austrian conductor. [TRANS.]
† A building in the Volksgarten, Vienna. [TRANS.]

AETAT 35 *To Gustav Mahler*

On the 14th January there will be a concert of mine in the Ansorge-Verein: Gurre-Lieder, with piano, a song-cycle after Stefan George, three new piano-pieces.* My monodrama is to be performed in Mannheim.†

And my second quartet in Paris. I wonder whether anything will come of it?!?

Perhaps one of these days you will send me a picture-postcard with a little (very little picture) leaving room for a message.

With very cordial regards and deep veneration,
I am, yours sincerely,
ARNOLD SCHÖNBERG

And now to your wife.

Dear lady, you promised to send me news from New York‡ ... ! I have not received any. Perhaps because I do not write? But I *did* write! After the Third! Or because I do not write about myself? But that does not interest you. And: although I talk about *myself* a great deal, since I cannot write equally much about myself, I prefer not to do so at all. Just a little won't meet the case. It isn't the sort of thing to be polished off in brief. — And you really must not be cross with me for not having written to you — to make up for that I have thought of you frequently, and that is at any rate in better taste and better style than if I write it. And more legible too!

And it does not give me writer's cramp, either, or give you cramp in the jaw from yawning with boredom.

And *I* escape feeling offended, I do not need to suspect that I am considered boring.

Well then: I can take my oath on these four points.

But another thing: the last time I was in Döbling with you I gathered you were thinking of staying in Vienna. Is that true? Are you sticking to that? And how far have you got with plans? It would be very nice indeed.

How is your little girl getting on? And how are you? Perhaps you *will* write and tell me all about everything one of these days! And I very much wonder if you and the Herr Direktor have read my essay in the *Merker*. Did you like it?

My wife sends you her very best wishes. And so do I.
Your very devoted
ARNOLD SCHÖNBERG

* The *Three Pieces* for piano, op. 11. [TRANS.]
† A reference to *Erwartung*. See note 2 to Letter 3. [TRANS.]
‡ Mahler was conductor of the New York Philharmonic Society at this time but returned in the summers to Austria, for composing. [TRANS.]

To Gustav Mahler   JULY 1910

263. TO GUSTAV MAHLER   *Hietzinger Hauptstrasse* 113,
Vienna XIII, 5th July 1910

My dear Herr Direktor,

    Your fiftieth birthday affords an occasion for me to tell you what I always want to keep on saying: in what high regard I hold you. And how I cannot help remembering, with much distress, that in earlier days I so often annoyed you by being at variance with you. I feel that I was wrong to try to thrust my opinions on you instead of listening when you talked and letting myself be enriched by what is more important than opinions: the resonance of a great personality. Even if the overtones of my opinions could not, or at least could not always, vibrate in accord with the gist of what you would say — I know that, being younger, I have a right to be different, even if that also means imperfect, since I must learn by my own experience and must not let myself be theoretically convinced — , still, there is *one* thing to which I should have yielded absolutely: the essential quality that emanates from whatever is great, that indefinable thing which I have so strongly sensed in your presence and which is for me the power of genius; something the existence and force of which is fully clear to my feeling.

    And if I have nevertheless been at variance with you — I do not know why. Perhaps it was shortsightedness, perhaps contrariness? Perhaps too it was love, for with all this I have always venerated you awfully. It was flapperish: love that pursues with hatred.

    I have so long been wanting to write you this letter, or if possible one putting all this better, because it has been weighing on my mind for a long time. I do find it relatively shaming that I did not understand you at once; but that I must needs have been a cause of annoyance to you is something I deeply repent of.

    I have only one excuse: I was no longer young enough, I was already too much occupied with my own development. Perhaps you will be disposed to let that serve.

    And perhaps you will also count to my credit the way I now feel about you, about your work. How deeply I now venerate you — in every at all conceivable respect.

    And now what I wish for us on your fiftieth birthday is that you will soon be back again in our loathed and beloved Vienna; permanently. That you may enjoy living here; and that you may have the inclination to conduct here and yet not do so, because the rabble simply does not deserve it; or that you may, though not having the inclination, nevertheless do so, in order to give pleasure to us, who do perhaps deserve it. Anyway: that you may be back here among us again! And that you, who have been given so much cause to feel embittered, may nevertheless accept veneration and lay it as balm on the wounds inflicted by shortsightedness (for it was more that than malice). I know that if you were now, if you were back, in Vienna, you would be enfolded in such warm veneration that you might well forget all former, justified, resentment.

It is my most heartfelt hope and wish that this will soon come to pass, and I should be happy indeed if I could do anything towards bringing it about.

With affectionate veneration and devotion,
I am, yours sincerely,
ARNOLD SCHÖNBERG

264. TO GUSTAV MAHLER [*Vienna,*] *2nd August* 1910
My dear Herr Direktor,

I can scarcely tell you how awful it is for me to have to write this letter to you of all people. But you cannot imagine what impossible things I have tried, but also what possible ones, and it was all no use. I am really in a position of desperate need, otherwise I could never have brought myself to write this. And the fact that last year you offered me this does more to stop me than to encourage me.

The fact is that I have no money and have to pay the rent. It was doubtless very rash of me to take a larger flat when I was earning less. But there are many circumstances tending to excuse me, disappointments of hopes that were so near fulfilment that anyone would have counted on it, and such things. So I must beg you to lend me from 300 to 400 guilders. I shall quite certainly be able to pay it back next year when I am at the Conservatory.

I cannot tell you how unhappy it makes me to have to tarnish my relationship to you by bringing up such a matter. And I must say: I should not have done it on my own behalf; I can get over such a thing all right. But when one has a wife and children one is no longer the only person who counts.

May I ask you to telegraph letting me know whether you can grant my request. And — if it is not asking too much — if you can help me, if possible to telegraph the money or at least send it express.

I earnestly ask you not to be angry. And I have only one wish: that your attitude to me will not be unfavourably influenced by this.

Hoping to have news soon,
I am, as ever, your devoted
ARNOLD SCHÖNBERG

To Gustav Mahler   AUGUST 1910

265. TO GUSTAV MAHLER   *Hietzinger Hauptstrasse* 113,
Vienna XIII, 3rd August 1910

My dear Herr Direktor!

I have today been sent 800 crowns* by Miethke, in your name. This was done as quickly as every good deed, which the really noble-minded man needs make no resolve to perform and for which he does not even need to receive an impulse from outside. It simply gushes forth, a secretion of his essential being.

Can one express thanks for such a thing?

One ought to; and I should like to. But because I would wish that my veneration for you should have no such irrelevant origins, it weighs on my mind. Not that there is any danger; but I should like to keep my veneration independent of gratitude. Nor should it even seem that the two are connected with each other. But neither are they: and when I reflect what an honour it is even to be admitted to your closer acquaintance, so that one may have the opportunity to be grateful to you as well, then I feel easier. And when I reflect that even in a matter of which I cannot be proud the purity of your sentiments guards me from any unjust suspicion of fecklessness; how the proximity of one who harbours these sentiments very nearly makes good what I cannot approve of in itself; and when I contrast this with the way that even the good that emanates from me turns bad whenever it enters into the realm of what is impure, then I am consoled; for I sense a manifestation of that power which it is the whole endeavour of my self-education to approach.

Perhaps this is again a purple patch! but if you knew how these thoughts are always with me and how much this is merely an attempt to say it, you would count to the credit of the extravagant emotion whatever sins it commits against good taste.

For extravagant emotion is the fever that purges the soul of impurity. And it is my ambition to become as pure as yourself, since it is not permitted to me to be so great.

                                      Ever yours,

                                                   ARNOLD SCHÖNBERG

---

* Approximately a year's rent. [TRANS.]

INDEX OF CORRESPONDENTS

(The numbers refer to pages, not letters.)

Academy of Arts in Berlin, The, 126
Adler, Oskar, 274, 285
Amersdorfer, Professor Dr. Alexander, 145, 153
Aram, K. [Kurt?], 249
Asch, Joseph, 163
Austrian Association of Teachers of Music, The, 112

Bandler, Professor Heinrich, 85
Bauer, Professor Julius, 239
Behrens, Bud, 268
Bekker, Paul, 109, 133
Benedict, H. H., 213
Berg, Alban, 70, 137, 142, 151, 157, 166, 184, 193
Birthday Wishes, Thanks for, 191, 289
Bistron, J., 112
Bodanzky, Artur, 24, 42
Boissevain, Mr., 99
Botstiber, Hugo, 63
Boult, Sir Adrian, 184
Bowron, The Honorable Fletcher, 276
Burgomaster of Vienna, The, 239, 277
Busoni, Ferruccio, 33
Butting, Max, 118, 149

Casals, Pau, 155, 171, 182
Catalan Musicians, 154
Coolidge, Elizabeth Sprague, 199, 200
Costa, *see* da Costa
Courier Musical, Paris, 107
Cowell, Henry, 256
Craft, Robert, 284
Craig, Minsa, 279
Czernin, Ferdinand, 223

da Costa, Raffael, 142
Dallapiccola, Luigi, 277
de Filippi, Amadeo, 271
Dehmel, Richard, 35
Dessau, Paul, 210, 212
Deutsch, Max, 265
Deutsche Zeitung, Bohemia, 68
Dieterle, Charlotte, 198
Dodd, Professor Paul A., 254
Downes, Olin, 206, 260, 263

Dramatists' and Composers' Association, Vienna, The, 274
Dutch Patron of the Arts, A, 99

Eidlitz, Walter, 172
Eisler, Hanns, 76, 119, 121

Ferroud, Pierre, 76
Filippi, *see* de Filippi
Flesch, *Intendant*, 134, 136, 141
Fraenkel, Bessie Bartlett, 195
Frank, Serge, 250
Frankenstein, Alfred V., 207
Freund, Marya, 74, 81
Friends, 225
Fromaigeat, E., 66
Fürstenberg, Prince Egon, 108
Furtwängler, Wilhelm, 130, 131, 134

Gerhard, Roberto, 102, 169
German Students' Commonroom, Prague, Chairman and Committee of the, 48
Goldbecker, Fräulein, 75
Graf, Herbert, 129
Greissle, Felix, 204
Grote, Ludwig, 272
Gutheil-Schoder, Marie, 40, 73

Harris, Roy, 233
Hartmann, Karl Amadeus, 252
Hauer, Josef Matthias, 103, 105
Heffernan, Helen, 216
Hendsch, Renée, 99
Herrmann, Bernard, 275
Hertz, Alfred, 203
Hertzka, Emil, 23, 25, 31, 37, 43, 46, 49
Hessischer Rundfunk, 273
Hinnenberg, *see* Stuckenschmidt
Hinrichsen, H., 77, 123
Hoffmann, Richard, Sen., 219
Hutcheson, Ernest, 190, 193, 194
Hutchins, Robert Maynard, 240

Imperial-Royal Academy of Music and the Fine Arts, Vienna, The Board of the, 28

Index of Correspondents

Jalowetz, Heinrich, 24, 133, 147
Jemnitz, Alexander, 148
Jewish Year Book, The Editor of the, 238
Johnson, Thor, 281
Jones, Perry T., 246

K., Dr., 39
Kandinsky, Wassily, 70, 88, 89
Kestenberg, Professor Leo, 117, 132, 158, 160, 162, 208
Klatte, Professor Wilhelm, 87
Klatzkin, Jacob, 181, 205
Klemperer, Otto, 192, 211
Klenau, Paul von, 81
Kokoschka, Oskar, 242
Kolisch, Rudolf, 164, 188, 270
Koons, Walter E., 186
Krasner, Louis, 211
Krenek, Ernst, 210
Kulka, K., 197
Kyogoku, Viscount Takatoshi [?], 248

Landesfinanzamt, Berlin, Das, 189
Legal, *Intendant*, Berlin, Oper am Platz der Republik, 139
Leibowitz, René, 236, 247, 253, 255, 257, 269
Leichtentritt, Hugo, 206
Lehner, Eugen, 268
Lemberger, Dr., 173
Liebermann, Max, 122, 125
List, Kurt, 219, 237
Loos, Adolf, 110, 146

Mahler, Gustav, 293, 296, 297, 298
Mahler-Werfel, Alma, 69, 94, 102, 196
Mann, Thomas, 144, 278
Marschalk, Max, 30
Martet, Jacques, 279
Moe, Henry Allen, 231, 233

National Institute of Arts and Letters, The, 245
Nikisch, Arthur, 45

Partosh, O., 286
Pella, Paul, 94, 95
Pelleg, Frank, 286
Prussian Minister for Science, Art and Education, The, 117

Rankl, Karl, 288
Reclam's Universum, Leipzig, 97
Redlich, Fritz, 56

Reiner, Fritz, 221
Reinhart, Werner, 100, 101
Resnick, Rose, 214
Rosbaud, Hans, 149, 156, 159, 161, 169, 243
Rufer, Josef, 154, 252, 254, 271, 287
Ruvine, Ingeborg, 257

Schalk, Franz, 56
Scheinpflug, Paul, 72
Scherchen, Hermann, 47, 96, 111, 198, 237, 280
Schillings, Professor Max von, 168
Schlamm, William S., 234
Schuster, Bernard, 73
Sessions, Roger, 222
Seventy-fifth Birthday, Thanks for good wishes on, 290
Siciliani, Francesco, 285
Siloti, Alexander, 51
Singer, Professor Gustav, 123
Society for Private Concerts in Prague, The, 82
Soot, Fritz, 40, 42
Speiser, Maurice, 189
Sproul, Robert G., 202
Stefan, Paul, 86
Stegmann, G. F., 266
Stein, Erwin, 84, 124, 126, 214
Stein, Fritz, 274
Steuermann, Eduard, 277
Stransky, Josef, 74, 77
Stuckenschmidt, H. H., and Frau Margot Hinnenberg, 244

Temming, Max, 96
Tiessen, Professor Heinz, 170
Trimble, Lester, 224
Turnau, *Intendant*, 129
Twa, Andrew J., 217

Universal Edition, 64, 65
Unknown Correspondents, 50, 57

Varèse, Edgar, 78
Varga, Tibor, 288

Webern, Anton, 69, 128, 146, 152, 155, 165
Wiener, Karl, 26, 32
Wiesengrund-Adorno, Theodor, 145
Windisch, Fritz, 101

Zehme, Albertine, 53
Zemlinsky, Alexander (von), 52, 54, 68, 79, 83, 119
Zillig, Winfried, 127, 183, 258

INDEX

*Note: S. indicates Schoenberg. In general, chronological order is preferred to alphabetical.
(The numbers refer to pages, not letters.)*

Accompaniment to a Film-Scene (S.), op. 34, 1929–30, 116; Jalowetz conducts, 148, 148 n
Adler, Guido, 207
Adler, Oskar, S.'s early teacher, 274, 274 n
Alco (recording company), 268 n, 269
Allen, Professor Leroy W., 203, 213
Altenberg, Peter, 89
Alter, Georg, 82
Amar Quartet, 111
Amateurs, S. on the role of, 279
America; S.'s years in, 177–8, 184 *seqq.*; some criticisms of, 244, 266, 270; S. on American composers, 266–7, 270; American Relief Fund for German and Austrian Musicians, 86, 87, 87 n; *see* Universities
Amsterdam, S. conducts his works in, 20
Andra, Herr, 130
Ansermet, Ernest, 265, 266
Antisemitism, 20, 88, 89–93, 94, 167, 177, 204, 209, 238
Apostel, H. E., 253
Armitage, Merle, 245
Art and Intellect (Kandinsky), 71
Association of German Composers, 194
'Atmospherics', S. on, 148, 152
Atonal style, 19, 253; S. resents reference to, 217–18
Austria, annexation of, 1938, 178, 203–5
'Austrian Action', 1944, 223–4
Austrian Association of Teachers of Music, S. resigns from, 112

Bach, J. S., S.'s respect for, 284; S. proposes fantasia on a work of, for Casals, 155; S. on the counterpoint of, 146, 147; *see Two Chorale Preludes* (S.) and *Prelude and Fugue in E flat Major* (S.), 74–5, 116
Baden-Baden, S.'s operas produced in, 1930, 139 n
Bandler String Quartet, 85 n
Barcelona, S. living in, 115–16, 153–64
Bartók, Béla, 61, 243; American imitators of, S. on, 267, 270

Beethoven, as 'emotional' composer, 268; *Diabelli Variations* of, 206
Bekker, Paul, 109, 109 n
Bellermann, *Kontrapunkt*, 207
Berg, Alban, pupil of S., 19, 20, 75, 95, 124, 138, 147, 164, 183, 231, 253; S. on promise of, 23; poverty of, 88; Society for Private Concerts performs works of, 61; *Der Wein* (concert aria), 157; *Lulu*, 143, 143 n, 151; *Lyric Suite*, 128; *Reigen* (from Three Orchestral Pieces), 75; *Wozzeck*, 70, 138; as admirer of Mahler, 260; proposes Webern's election to Berlin Academy of Arts, 171; death of, 196, 196 n
Berg, Helene, 70, 166–7
Berlin: S.'s 1901 move to, from Vienna, 19, 31 n; his 1911 move to, 20; S.'s appointments, Academy elections, 62, 112 n, 117 *seqq.*; the Hochschule für Musik, 132, 132 n; S. appeals to Academy, on behalf of Loos and Webern, 145, 170–1; Association of German Composers in, 149 n, 150; 1923 Austrian Music Week in, 94 n; S. leaves, 1933, 116; 1948 blockade of, 255 n
Biblische Weg, Der (S.), 1926–7, drama, 116, 126–7, 181, 184
Bittner, Julius, 95
Blaue Reiter, Der, and Expressionism, 272–3
Blonda, Max (pseudonym of S.'s second wife), 133, 133 n
Bodanzky, Artur, 24 n, 40, 132; and *Erwartung*, 42
Bohnen (baritone), 133
Bomart Music Publications, 265
Boston, S. in, 177
Botstiber, Hugo, of Vienna, 63–4
Boulanger, Nadia, 270
Boult, Sir Adrian, 209
Brahms, S. on, 147, 170, 233 n; Hugo Wolf criticizes, 265; *Brahms's Piano Quartet in G minor, arranged for orchestra* (S.), op. 25, 179, 207–8, 215

Index

Breslau, *Die glückliche Hand* performed in, 1928, 115, 129–30
Bruch, Max, *see Kol Nidre*
Bruckner, Anton, 265
Brunner (agent), 63
Buch der hängenden Gärten (Stefan George), 19, 21, 111 n, 295
Büchse der Pandora (Wedekind), 143, 143 n
Busoni, Ferruccio, 33–5; as teacher of Steuermann, 277 n

Canon for Bernard Shaw (S.), 272
Casals, P., 169–70, 182; welcomes S. to Barcelona, 154; asks S. to write work for 'cello, 155; S. offers 'Monn' concerto (*see Concerto for Harpsichord*, etc.) to, 171–2, 182–3
Casella, Alfredo, 86, 86 n, 103, 127
Cassirer, Fritz, *Beethoven und die Gestalt*, 207
Chamber Symphony (S.), op. 9, 1906, 21, 215; proposed 1915 performance of, 1939, 52; proposed 1923 performance of, 95; at Frankfurt, 111 n; proposal to record, 215
Chamber Symphony, Second (S.), op. 38, 1939, completed, 178; a performance of, 275–6
Chatauqua, S. convalesces in, 177, 188–90
Chicago, S.'s contacts with, 177, 188; S. lectures at University of, 1946, 229
Chop, Professor, 98
Clark, Edward, pupil of S., 33, 33 n, 34
Claudel, Paul, S. criticizes, 67
Cologne, Jalowetz in, 147
'Composing with Twelve Notes', lecture by S., 177, 218
Concerto for Harpsichord (G. M. Monn), arranged for 'cello and orchestra (S.), 1932, 116, 169, 171, 181–2, 185, 215
Concerto Grosso (G. F. Handel), op. 6, no. 7, arranged (S.) as concerto for string quartet and orchestra, 116, 185, 215; London performance of, cancelled, 185 n
Contrapuntal style, S. on, 253, 255
Coolidge, Mrs. E. S., commissions S.'s fourth String Quartet 199–200; sponsors Pasadena concerts, 200 n; and the University of South California concerts, 200–1
Copland, Aaron, 192, 234
Copyright law, S. on, 235
Cortolezzi, 130
Cosmic Trilogy (Strindberg), and *Moses und Aron*, 143 n
Courier Musical, Paris, 107
Cowell, Henry, 234

Craft, Robert, performs works of S., 284

Dallapiccola, L., dedicates work to S., 277–8
Damrosch, Walter J., 78
Dance combined with music, S. on, 279–80
Debussy, C., 86 n; Society for Private Concerts performs works of, 61
Dehmel, Richard, 21; on S.'s *Verklärte Nacht* (sextet), 35, 35 n; reluctant to collaborate in *Die Jakobsleiter*, 36 n
Denver, Colorado, 1937 music festival at, 178, 209
De Profundis, for mixed chorus (S.), op. 50 B, 1950, 230
Deutsch, Max, pupil of S., 265–6
Deutsche Allgemeine Zeitung, 142
Diamond, David, 234
Dieterle, Wilhelm, 198 n
Dissonances, S. defines, 218; 'emancipation' of, 253; use and misuse of, S. explains, 248, 267, 260
Donaueschingen Music Festival, 62, 108–109, 110
Downes, Olin, 256; S. defends Mahler against, 260–2
Dreililien Verlag, Berlin, 19, 30 n
Dreimal Tausend Jahre for mixed chorus (S.), op. 50 A, 1949, 230, 284
Duhan (baritone), 133

Eidlitz, Walter, *Der Berg in der Wüste*, 172 n
Eight Songs (S.), op. 6, 1904, 21
Einem, Gottfried von, 253
Einstein, A., 91, 93
Eisler, Hanns, 75, 75 n, 76, 231; as teacher in New York, 240; S. on 'reforms' of, 252
Engel, Carl (of G. Schirmer publishing house, New York), 177, 194 n, 204–5, 223
Erdgeist (Wedekind), Berg's use of, for *Lulu*, 143, 143 n
Erpf, Hermann, *Studien zur Harmonie*, 207
Erwartung (S.), op. 17, 1909, 21, 131, 280 285; first performance of, in Prague, 24 n, 40 n, 84, 84 n; in Mannheim, 1909, 295; S. conducts for B.B.C. 1931, 115, 147; Wiesbaden, 109, 129; S. describes production problems of, 139; in Baden-Baden, 1930, 139 n; proposed 1947 performance of, 257–8; Milhaud and, 69

Fantasia (S.), op. 47, 1949, 230, 270–1; S.'s hopes for Varga recording of, 289
Feuermann, Emmanuel, 183 n, 185
First String Quartet (and others) (S.), *see* String quartets

302

Five Pieces for Orchestra (S.), op. 16, 1909, 21, 77 n, 265; performed in Prague, 1923, 84, 84 n; S. proposes recording of, 215; Mitropoulos conducts in New York, 1948, 256; in Frankfurt, 1948, 259; in New York, 256, 261
Five Pieces for Piano (S.) op. 23, 1920–3, 61, 62, 83, 83 n
Flesch, Dr., Intendant of Radio Berlin, 115
Four Pieces for mixed chorus (S.) op. 27, 1926, 116
Four Songs (S.) op. 2, 21
Four Songs for voice and orchestra (S.) op. 22, 1913–16, 21
France, S. in, 1933, 177
Frank, Serge, translator of S., 250–2
Frankfurt-am-Main: Festival of New Music, 100; Scherchen's and Hindemith's plans in, for S.'s 50th birthday, 111; first performance of *Von Heute auf Morgen*, 1930, 115, 134 n; projected lecture by S. in, 156, 159–60, 161–2
Frankfurter Allgemeine Zeitung, 109 n
Frederick, 257
Freund, Marya, 111, 128; S. criticizes interpretation by, in *Pierrot Lunaire*, 149
Friede auf Erden (S.) op. 13, 1907, 21; Scherchen conducts, 1923, 96, 96 n; S. mentions, 100
Fuleihan, Anis, 233, 234
Fundamentals of Musical Composition (S.), 232
Fürstenberg, Prince Egon, 108, 108 n
Furtwängler, Wilhelm, 1928 performance of *Variations for Orchestra* (S.) op. 31, in 1928, 115, 131; S. on, 238

Ganz, Rudolph, 188 n; Ganz's College, Chicago, 188
Gargula, Herr, 130
George, Stefan, *Buch der hängenden Gärten*, 19, 21, 111 n, 295
Gerhard, Roberto, 102, 102 n
German Musical Society, 1923 Music Festival of, 96, 96 n
Gershwin, George, 192
Giraud, Albert, 21
Glückliche Hand, Die (S.) op. 18, 1910–13, 21, 280; completed, 41, 42, 43; possibility of filming, 43–5; first performance of, in Vienna, 1924, 62; and Milhaud, 69; performed in Breslau, 1928, 115, 129–30; performed in Baden-Baden, 1930, 139 n; S. describes production difficulties of, 140–1; S. on theatre proposal for, 258
Goehr, Walter, 215

Goldbecker, Fräulein, 75, 76, 76 n
Goldschmidt, Adalbert von, 203
Graener, Paul, 183
Graf, Herbert, 130
Greissle, Felix, S.'s son-in-law, 204, 204 n
Greller, Lotte K., *Grundlagen der neuen Musik*, 207
Grove's *Dictionary of Music and Musicians*, S. quotes, 287–8
Gruenberg, Louis, 234
Guggenheim Foundation, S.'s 1945 appeal to rejected, 229
Gurrelieder (S.) no op. no., 1900–1, 19, 20, 21, 63, 65, 66, 130, 201; special music paper for, 26, 26 n; score sent to lithographers, April 1914, 49; in Vienna, 20, 26, 37, 37 n, 52, 61, 64, 66 n; Munich performance frustrated, 40 n; S. conducts in Leipzig, 20, 46 n; in Amsterdam, 1921, 61; in Berlin, 95, 115, 125; in London, 1928, 115, 128; reduced score of, 125; Scheinpflug conducts in Duisberg, 1922, 72; S. advises on 1951 performance, 281–4; comments on 1909 performance, 295
Gutheil-Schoder, Marie, 40, 40 n, 73 n, 133, 138, 258

Hába, Alois, *Neue Harmonielehre*, 207
Hamburg, 97; S. visits Dehmel in, 35; Philharmonic Orchestra, 85 n
Handel, G. F., *see Concerto Grosso* op. 6, no. 7; S. on 'Handelian style', 171
Hanging Gardens, 111 n, *see* George, Stefan
Hansen, Wilhelm, publishing house (Copenhagen), 61, 83 n
Harmonielehre (S.), 1910–11, revised version 1921–2, 21, 71, 165, 167, 168, 218, 236
Harris, Roy, 233 n, 234
Harrison, Lou, 234
Hartmann, Karl Amadeus, 252 n
Hauer, J. M., 86, 88, 103–7, 165; collaboration proposal, 103–7
Heldenleben, Ein (R. Strauss), 51
Herrmann, Bernard, records S.'s *Second Chamber Symphony*, 275–6
Hertz, Alfred, in San Francisco, 203 n
Hertzka, Emil, publisher of S.'s early works, 30, 50, 77, 83, 95, 123
Herzgewächse (S.) op. 20, 1911, 21
Hindemith, Paul, organizes festival for S.'s 50th birthday, 111; S. comments on status of, 243; and on American imitators of, 267, 270
Hinnenberg, Margot, rescues S.'s music from Prague, 244, 244 n

Index

Hitler, Adolf, 89, 116, 204
Hoffmann, 'Uncle Richard', 219–20
Hoffmann, Richard, son of above-named, 219, 219 n, 270–1
Hofmannsthal, Hugo von, 127
Holland, opponents of S. in, 184
Hollywood, S. living in, 177, 178
Howard, Walter, 146; *Auf dem Wege zur Musik*, 207
Hutcheson, Ernest, of Juilliard School, New York, 190, 190 n, 193

'Intellectual constructivism', S. condemns term, 150
Internationale of 'Things of the Mind', Paris, 1919, 66
International Society for Modern Music, The, 118 n 3

Jacob Wrestling (Strindberg), 35, 36
Jacobsen, J. P., poet of *Gurrelieder*, 21
Jakobsleiter, Die (S.) no op. no., beginnings of, 1917, 20, 21, 36 n; text for oratorio, 1915–17, 21; interruptions to progress of, 53 n, 70, 71, 83, 280, 280 n; S. mentions to Kandinsky, 71; S. resumes work on score of, 1944, 223; state of, in 1945, 232; in 1948, 256; S. despairs of finishing, 288; asks Rankl to work on score of, 288; Zillig completes score of, 288 n
Jalowetz, Heinrich, pupil of S., 19, 24, 24 n; organizes Austrian Music Week, 1923, 94 n, 95; S.'s attitude towards, 147–8; conducts S.'s *Accompaniment to a Film-Scene*, in 1930, 148, 148 n; in later years, 237–8
Jemnitz, Alexander, conducts S.'s *Verklärte Nacht*, 1931, 148
Jewish attitude to Jewish musicians, S. comments on, 238; Jewish music, future of, *see* letter to O. Partosh, 286–287
Juilliard School of Music, New York, 177, 190–1, 194

Kahn, Herr, of Radio Frankfurt, 161
Kandinsky, Wassily, 44; in First World War years, 70–1; S. condemns anti-semitism of, 88; S. comments on, 243; *Das Geistige in der Kunst*, 71
Kaudela, Herr, of Vienna Konzertverein, 64
Keller, Fraülein, 70
Kestenberg, Leo, 133 n; as director of Palestine Orchestra, Tel Aviv, 208 n
Kleiber, Erich, 132
Klemperer, Otto, 127, 132; S.'s attitude toward, 199, 211, 269; in Los Angeles, 192, 192 n, 207 n; and S.'s *Violin Concerto* op. 36, 201; and S.'s arrangement of Brahms quartet op. 25, 207
Klitsch, as 'Klaus Narr' (*Gurrelieder*), 282
Kokoschka, Oskar, 44, 190
Kol Nidre (S.) op. 39, 1938, 178, 212, 212 n, 213, 215; Max Bruch's, 213 n
Kolisch, Henriette, 220
Kolisch String Quartet, 164 n, 185, 200 n, 201, 268 n
Koussevitzky, Sergei A., S. on, 221, 238, 269
Krasner, Louis, 211–12
Krenek, Ernst, at Vassar, 210 n

Lachner, Franz, 150
Lalo, Edouard, 67
Lehner, Eugen, on recording of S.'s string quartets, 268
Leibowitz, René, 210–11, 236, 245, 247, 251, 254, 257
Leipzig, S. conducts *Gurrelieder* in, 20
Lenin, 92
Liebermann, Max, Prussian Academy of Arts, 115, 122, 125, 125 n
Liebermann, Rolf, 259
List, Kurt, magazine editor, 253
Listen (Guide to Good Music), 219
London, S. in, 115, 116, 169; conducts *Five Pieces for Orchestra* in, before First World War, 20
Loos, Adolf, S.'s regard for, 144, 145, 146, 197, 259; *Ins Leere gesprochen*, 144–5; S. writes to, for 60th birthday, 146; birthday book for, 150
Los Angeles, S. living in, 177, 229 *seqq.*; Klemperer in, 192, 192 n, 207 n
Löwe, Ferdinand, 294, 294 n
Lulu (Berg), 143, 143 n, 151

Maeterlinck, Maurice: post-War I attitude of, towards German music, 66–7; and *Pelleas und Melisande*, 21
Mahler, Gustav, 89, 93, 121, 147; four letters to, 293–8; *Second Symphony* of, 265, 293; *Eighth Symphony* of, 56; S. defends, 259, 260–2, 263–5; and admits to earlier criticism of, 264, 296; in New York, 295 n; Guido Adler's biography of, 207; Paul Stefan's works on, 207; death of, 50 n; Mahler Memorial Fund, 50, 51; S. awarded Mahler Memorial Prize, May 1918, 56–7; *see also* Mitropoulos
Mann, Thomas: and the twelve-note method, 255, 257; letters of, 257, *and see* Index of Correspondents; on Adolf Loos, 145 n; *Dr. Faustus*, 255, 255 n; S. makes peace with, 278

304

Index

Marianoff, Dr., 184
Marx, Bernhard, 95; *Kompositionslehre*, 207
Massine, Leonid, 67, 69 n
Mayrhofen, *Der Kunstklang*, 207
Mengelberg, Willem, 209
Mersmann, Hans, 146
Milhaud, Darius, 69; S. on, 80
Minnich, Dr., 159
Mitropoulos, Dmitri, 237, 256, 260, 263; performs Mahler's *Seventh Symphony*, 260-2
Models for Beginners in Composition (S., textbook, 1942), 179, 215
'Modern Psalms', S. writes words for, 230, 286 n; *Modern Psalm*, op. 50 c, 1950 (1st of these, with music), 230, 286 n
Mödling German Relief Fund, 107-8
Monn, G. M., *see Concerto for Harpsichord*
Monotonality, S. on, 219
Moses und Aron, 139, 143, 184, 202; Berg receives libretto of, 157 n; comments on, at various stages, 115-16, 151-2, 163, 172, 232, 256; proposed Florence performance, S. discusses possibilities, 285
Mozart, in 'logical development towards 12-note composition' (S.), 146
Musical education, S.'s ideas on, 240-2 *and see under* Schoenberg, Arnold; music defined by S., 186
Musik (Berlin musical periodical), 73, 73 n, 183 n
Musikblätter des Anbruch, Vienna, 86 n

Nachod, Hans, as singer and 'speaker', 282
National Institute of Arts and Letters, S. elected a member of, 245-6
Naval (tenor), 133
Neues Wiener Journal, 112
Newlin, Dika, 234, 245
'New Magazine', 234
New York, S. moves to, 177; New School of Social Research of, 240
New York Times, music criticism in, 206; *see* Downes, Olin, *and* 263 n
New Zealand, S. envisages living in, 219-220
Nikisch, Arthur, 41, 45-6
Nohl, music historian, 97-8

Ode to Napoleon Buonaparte (after Byron), for reciter, piano and string quartet, op. 41a, 1942, 178, 215, 248, 249; same *Ode* with string orchestra, op. 41b, 1942, 178
Offenbach, J., S. on, 249
Ormandy, Eugèen, S. on, 238

Paris, 1949 projected visit to, 269
Partisan Review, 253
Partosh, O., director of Israel Academy of Music, 286-7
Pasadena, S. in, 200, 200 n
Pella, Paul, originator of Austrian Music Week, 1923, 94, 94 n, 95
Pelleas und Melisande (S.); first performance, 1904, 19; mentions, 21, 30, 201, 214, 215; agreement to publish, 30; proposed St. Petersburg performance of, 1914, 51 n; S. on Viennese reception of, 52; Zemlinsky proposes cuts in, 54-6; 1918 Prague production of, 54 n; proposed publication of reduced score of, 125; S. conducts in Boston, 1934, 177; in Tel Aviv, 208-9; S. proposes recording of, 215 n
Peters, C. F. (Edition Peters), 77 n
Pfitzner, Hans, 31
Piano Concerto (S.), op. 42, 1942, 178
Piano Piece (S.), op. 33a, 1928-9, 116
Piano Piece (S.), op. 33b, 1931, 116
Pierrot lunaire (S.), op. 21, 1912, 20, 21; origin of, 53 n; S. mentions, 128, 131, 249; possibility of cheap score, 46; proposed 1914 St. Petersburg performance of, 52; Prague performance of, 52, 68; performed at Frankfurt-am-Main for S.'s 50th birthday festival, 111 n; in 1921, in Vienna and elsewhere, 61; A. Zehme in, 282; proposal to 'dance' 69, 69 n; M. Gutheil-Schoder's connection with, 73, 73 n; Varèse and, 78-9; S. on Paris performance of, 81-2; Bandler's proposal for, 85-6; S.'s stipulations concerning, to Jemnitz, 148-9
Piston, Walter, 234
Prague, German Theatre in, 84 n; *Pierrot lunaire* in, 52, 68; first performance of *Erwartung* in, 1924, 62; Society for Private Concerts in, 68, 79, 80, 82, 83
Preliminary Exercises in Counterpoint (S.), 232, 232 n
Prelude and Fugue in E flat Major (J. S. Bach) arranged for large orchestra, 1928, 74-5, 116; S. gives Furtwängler first performance rights, 134
Prelude for Chorus and Orchestra (S.), op. 44, 1945, 230
Princeton honours S., 1946, 229
Privatdozent appointment, Vienna, 26-8, 28-30; granted to S., 20, 30 n
Prohaska, Carl, 95
Psalms, *see* 'Modern Psalms'
Pult und Taktstock (periodical), 124 n, 126 n

u   305

Index

Quartets, 111 n, 128; *see* String quartets
Quintet for Wind Instruments (S.), op. 26, 1923–4, 62; at Frankfurt-am-Main festival for S.'s 50th birthday, 111 n

Radio, S.'s comments on, 148, 152
Raff, Joseph J., 150
Rankl, Karl, 75, 75 n, 76; in England, 209, 209 n, 282, 288, 288 n
Ravel, Maurice, 61
Reclam-Verlag, S. criticizes, 97–8
Reger, Max, 31, 80
Reichold, Mr., possible American patron, 249–50
Reinecke, Karl, 150
Reiner, Karel, 237
Reinhardt, Max, 181
Reissiger, Karl, 150
Roller, Alfred (painter), 44
Rosbaud, Hans, 152, 169, 244; in Munich, in 1940s, 243, 243 n
Rosé Quartet, 19, 40 n
Rufer, Josef, 96, 96 n, 97, 158, 178, 244, 257; *Composition with Twelve Notes*, 154 n; *The Works of Arnold Schoenberg*, 154 n

St. Petersburg, S. conducts *Pelleas und Melisande* in, 20
Saint-Saëns, Camille, S. on, 67
Salzburg, antisemitism in, 89, 89 n
Saminski, Lazare, 213, 213 n
Schaffende Musiker, Der, S. quotes, 150
Schalk, Franz, director of Vienna Opera, 56; conductor of Gesellschaftskonzerte, 64 n; contract with, 64–6
Schenker, Heinrich, 146, 154, 207
Scherchen, Hermann, 47–8, 278, 288; in Tel Aviv, 208
Scheyer, Galka, 243
Schillings, Max von, President of Academy (Berlin), 116
Schirmer, publisher, New York, 177, 194 n, 204, 205, 205 n, 215, 221 n
Schmidt, Franz, 95; as admirer of Mahler, 260
Schmitt, Florent, 77
Schnabel, Artur, 118, 118 n, 133 n
Schoenberg, Arnold: early works listed, 20–1; 1920–2 works listed, 62; 1926–7 works listed, 116; 1934–42 works listed, 178–9; 1945–50 works listed, 230; early years in Vienna and Berlin, 19–57; in Mödling, 1919–25, 63–112 (at Traunkirchen, 69–78, 95–101); again in Berlin, 1926–31, 115–49; in Switzerland, 1931, 149–53; in Spain, 153–70; in Berlin, early 1933, 170–3; in France, later the U.S.A., 1933–44, 177–290; *landmarks, outstanding events*: refuses Vienna professorship, 1912, 32–3; founds (with Zemlinsky) Society for Private Concerts, 1918, 61; lectures and conducts in Holland, 1921, 61; twelve-note composition matures, 1923, 61; first wife dies, 1923, 62; at Donaueschingen, 1924, 62; 50th birthday celebrations, 62, 111; Berlin appointment, 1925, 62, 117 *seqq.*; remarriage, 1926, 123; conducts in several capital cities, 1927, 115; lectures at Sorbonne, 1927, 151; daughter born, 1932, 162, 163; loses Berlin Academy appointment under National Socialism, 116, 177, 182, 183; returns to Jewish religion, 177, 184; accepts Boston engagement, 177; son born, 1936; becomes an American citizen, 1941, 178; health becomes precarious, 178; in Chatauqua, 188–91; seeks aid for Kokoschka, 190; is refused membership of Austrian Association of Composers, etc., 194 n; has 60th birthday in Hollywood, 191–8; moves to Los Angeles, 191 n; proposes Webern for post in U.S.A., 195; University appointments of, 197 n, 200; proposes Beethoven film, 198–9; in Los Angeles, 1945–51, 229–89; applies for a Guggenheim award, 231; 1946 illness of, 229; elected member of American Academy of Arts and Letters, 229; elected to Vienna Dramatists' and Composers' Association, 245; 70th birthday letter from, 290; is made burgher of Vienna, 276, 277; makes peace with Thomas Mann, 278; made honorary president of Israel Academy of Music, 286; four letters to Mahler, 293–8; death of, aged 76, 230; *views and opinions*: academic intrigues, 132; American composers, 250, 266–7; American life, 192, 242; American musical education, 210, 267, 270; antisemitism, 88–93; definition of beauty, 97; beauty of musical form, 154, 235; choice of pupils, 102; composer's presence at rehearsals, 129; compulsion, in educational establishments, German style, 126; critics and criticism, 109, 222, 256, 263; radio criticism at its best, 141–2; 'cuts' in published works, 54–5; education, 135–6, 202–3, 240–2, *and see* American musical education; the 'emancipation of the dissonance', 253; filming of *Glückliche Hand*, 43–5; *Gurrelieder*, performance details, 281–4; Han-

Index

delian style, 171; Hauer's divergences from, in 12-note composing, 165; 'heroism' in composers, 219; inadequate rehearsing, 63–5, 79, 81, 101; Israel Academy of Music, 287; Jewish attitudes, 205, 208–9, 238; 'love of music', 249; *Moses und Aron*, background to, 143–4, 172, 285; 'movements' generally, 71; definition of music, 186; music, books dealing with, German, 207; his painting ('Blaue Reiter', etc.), 25–6, 272–3; radio, 141–2, 148, 152; religion, 82, 177, 184; dislike of business dealings, 77; 'Sprechmelodie', 149; Stefan's proposed biography of, 86–7; 'taste', 264; teaching, 27–9, *see* Education; translations, 168, 250–2; versification and musical prose, 218
Schoenberg, Mathilde, Arnold Schoenberg's first wife, 19; death of, 1923, 62, 102–3
Schoenberg, Nuria, 162, 247, 282
Schoenberg, Ronny, 216, 247
Schoenberg Society, 1914, proposed form of, 50
Schöne, Lotte, 133
Schreker, Franz, 20, 132, 132 n; in Berlin and Vienna, 25 n; as first conductor of *Gurrelieder*, 26 n, 37, 37 n, 38, 39; and Berg, 138
Schubert, Franz, 268
Schuman, William, 234
Schumann, Robert, 23, 268
Schünemann, 133
Searle, Humphrey, 267
Serenade (S.), op. 24, 1923, 62, 83, 83 n, 209; Hansen publishes, 61; S. conducts at Donaueschingen, 1924, 62, 108; at the 50th birthday festival, Frankfurt-am-Main, 111 n
Sessions, Roger, 192, 234, 249
Shaw, G. B., 272, 272 n
Shostakovich, Dmitri, S. on, 219
Sibelius, Jean, 192
Siloti, Alexandre, 51–2, 187
Six Little Piano Pieces (S.), op. 19, 1911, 21, 111 n
Six Pieces for Male Chorus (S.), op. 35, 1929–30, 116
Six Songs (S.), op. 3, 1899–1903, 21
Six Songs for Voice and Orchestra (S.), op. 8, 1903–5, 21, 52, 94
Society of the Friends of Music, 64 n, 66 n
Society for Private Concerts, Vienna, 61, 67, 67 n, 68, 79 n; of Prague, 68, 79, 80, 82, 83; S. leaves, 82–3
Sonderling, Rabbi Dr. Jacob, 212
Soot, Fritz, 40, 40 n, 41, 42

Stefan, Paul, proposes biography of S., 86, 86 n, 87
Stein, Erwin, 19, 73, 80, 82, 84–5; performs *Pierrot lunaire*, 215; as pupil of S., 19; S. on, 24, 146; *Andante*, 24; *Rondo*, 24; *see* Index of Correspondents
Stein, Leonard, 232, 271, 271 n
Stein, Marion [Lady Harewood], 216
Steuermann, Eduard, 95, 111 n, 128, 215; records S.'s piano music, 277
Stiedry, Erika, in *Pierrot lunaire*, 282
Stiedry, Fritz, conducts first performance of S.'s *Second Chamber Symphony*, 276, 276 n
Stock, Frederick, 78
Stöhr, Moritz, 31
Stokowski, L., 78; S. records by, 281, 282–283
Strang, Gerald, 202–3, 234
Stransky, Josef, S. rebuffs, 77, 77 n; S. mentions, 78
Strauss, Johann, S. on, 249
Strauss, Richard, 31, 84, 249; as critic of S., 50–1
Stravinsky, Igor, 61, 86 n, 192; American imitators of, 267, 270; S. comments on, 243
Strindberg, August, *Jacob Wrestling*, 35, 36; in translation, S. on, 143, 168
String quartets (S.): *First*, in D minor, op. 7, 1905, 21, 134–5, 268–9; first performance of, 1907, 19; *Second*, in F sharp major, op. 10, 1907–8, 21; first performance of, 19, 63 n, 124; at 50th birthday festival for S. at Frankfurt-am-Main, 111 n; published by Universal Edition, arranged for string orchestra, 124, 124 n; *Third*, op. 30, 1927, 116, 164, 200; *Fourth*, op. 37, 1936, in U.S.A., 178, 199–200, 215
String sextet, *see Verklärte Nacht*
String Trio (S.), op. 45, 1946, 230
Structural Functions of Harmony (S.), 229, 230, 232, 233 n, 274
Stuckenschmidt, H. H., biographer of S., 97, 97 n, 244, 244 n
Style and Idea (S.), 170 n, 223, 229, 230; S. objects to translation of, 250–1
Suite for Piano (S.), op. 25, 1921–3, 62, 83, 83 n
Suite for Piano, Three Clarinets and Strings (S.), op. 29, 62
Succession states, post-1918, 148
Suite in G major (S.), 178
Survivor from Warsaw, A (S.), op. 46, 1947, 229, 230; S. completes, 244, 257; to be broadcast, 265
Swedlund, Fräulein, 130

Index

Tansman, Alexandre, 192
'Taste', S. defines, 264
Tauber, Richard, 133
Tchaikovsky, 243
Territet, Switzerland, S. moves to, 115
Testament der Astrologie (Oskar Adler), 285–6
Theme and Variations for Wind Band, in G minor, (S.), op. 43a, 1944, 179, 221, 221 n, 259
Theme and Variations for Large Orchestra (S.), op. 43b, 179; Munich 1948 performance of, 259
Theory of Harmony (S.), *see Harmonielehre*
Theory of Musical Unity, S. proposes to write, 71
Thomson, Virgil, 256
Three Folksongs for Mixed Chorus (S.), 1948, 230
Three Pieces for Piano (S.), op. 11, 1909, 21, 209, 295, 295 n
Three Satires for mixed chorus (S.), op. 28, 1926, 116; S. comments on, 271–2; described, 272 n
Three Songs for low voice (S.), op. 48, 1933, 116
Toscanini, Arturo, S. on, 238
Trotsky, L., 92
Twelve-note composition: method matures, 1923, 61; letters to Hauer, 103–5; S. on, 146–7, 164, 165, 236, 247, 248; works of S. according to, 83 n; lecture on, 1934, 177; and controversy with Thomas Mann, 255, 255 n; S. on success of, 255, 255 n; Eisler and, 119–21
Two Ballads (S.), op. 12, 1907, 21
Two chorale preludes, J. S. Bach, arranged (S.) for large orchestra, 1922, 62, 74, 77
Two Songs (S.), op. 14, 1907–8, 21
Two Songs (S.) for male voice, op. 1, before 1900, 21

Universal Edition (publishers), Vienna, 19, 123, 124, 189, 285, 295; *see* Hertzka, Emil, *and same name in Index of Correspondents*
Universities: of California, 197 n, 213–14, 231; of South California, 178, 197 n, 200, 202–3; of Chicago, 229; Princeton, honours S., 229

Varèse, Edgar, S.'s differences and friendship with, 78–9, 79 n
Varga, Tibor, records S.'s violin concerto, 288
Variations for Orchestra (S.), op. 31, 1926–8, 115, 116, 131, 134, 206; 1931 Frankfurt broadcast of, 149

Variations for Wind Band (S.), op. 43a, *see Theme and Variations for Wind Band*
Variations on an Original Theme (S.), *see Variations for Orchestra*; S. on his failure to complete, 130
Variations on a Recitative for organ in D minor (S.), op. 40, 1940, 178, 215, 248, 248 n
Venice, 1925 Festival of International Society for Modern Music, 118 n, 156 n
Verklärte Nacht (S.), op. 4, 1899, string sextet, 19, 21, 63 n, 124, 130, 142, 221; Jemnitz conducts, 1931, 148; S. proposes recording, 215; recorded without S.'s permission, 189
'Victor' album (S. recorded by Stokowski), 281–3
Vienna: S. born in, 1874, 19; S. as Privatdozent in, 20; S. refuses professorship in, 20, 32, 33; S.'s standing in, 19, 32–33, 38–9, 194 n; 1903 return to, 19; 1915 return to, 20; 1946 invitation to S. to return to, 239; honours S. in 1949 and after, 274–5, 276, 277; Academy of Music of, 20, 152; Association of Authors, Composers, etc., in, 193, 193 n, 194 n; Exhibition Orchestra of, 20–1; first performance of *Gurrelieder* in, 20; Philharmonic Choir, 130, 131, *see* Schreker, esp. 37 n; and 'Sezession', 125, 125 n; Universal Edition (publishers), *see that entry*
Violin, Moriz, 203–4
Violin Concerto (S.), op. 36, 1936, 178, 201, 215; played by Krasner, 211–12
Von Heute auf Morgen (S.), op. 32, 1928, 115; first performance of, in Frankfurt-am-Main, 1930, 115, 133, 134 n; broadcast by Radio Berlin, 1930, 136, 136 n; Sir Adrian Boult conducts, 185; mentioned, 285
Von Schuch, Ernst, 42, 42 n

Wagner, Erika, 73 n, 111 n, 215
Wagner, Richard, critics of, 67, 265
Wallenstein, Alfred, 256
Walter, Bruno, 40, 40 n, 41, 42
Wassermann, Heinrich J., 127
Webern, Anton (von), pupil of S., 19, 20, 61; mentions of, 64, 75, 80, 95, 124, 152, 164, 231, 253; in poor circumstances, 88, 99, 100, 101; S. pleads for help for, 99–101, 198; S. proposes for Juilliard School post, 195; conducts for Concerts Society, 69, 69 n, 70; contributes to A. Loos book, 151; as chairman of International Society for Contem-

Index

porary Music (Austrian branch), 155, 156 n; health of, in 1932, 165–6; in Barcelona, 166; death of, 237 n; his *Passacaglia*, 75; *Songs*, 148
Wedekind, Franz, and Berg's *Lulu*, 143 n
Weigl, Joseph, 31
Weimar project (S. and Kandinsky), 88 n
Wein, Der (concert aria by Berg), 157
Weiss, Adolphe, 205, 234
Weker, Wilhelm, *Über den Bau der Fugen*, 207
Wellesz, Egon, 127, 146
Werfel, Franz, 138
Wiesbaden, 133
Wiesengrund-Adorno, T., 146, 161, 164
Wildermann, Professor, 130
Winckelmann, Hans, 46
Windisch, Fritz, plans 1923 performances of S.'s works in Berlin, 101–2
Wolf, Hugo, as critic of Brahms, 265

Wood, Sir Henry, 78
Wozzeck (Berg), 70, 138

Zehme, A., 52, 53–4; in *Pierrot lunaire* originally, 53 n; S. praises, 282
Zemlinsky, Alexander (von), 75, 78; and Eisler, 119–21; and *Wozzeck*, 70; founds, with S. (1904) the Society of Contemporary Musicians, 19; as musical director of the German Theatre, Prague, 46 n, 52–3; S. praises, 46; proposes cuts in *Pelleas und Melisande*, 54–6; *Florentine Tragedy*, 53
Zemlinsky, Mathilde, *see* Schoenberg, Mathilde
Zillig, Winfried, 253; *Overture for Large Orchestra*, 127, 127 n; in Frankfurt, 258; completes score of *Die Jakobsleiter*, 288 n
Zukunftsmusik, 150 n